Public Sector Revenue

T0289870

In this time of acute financial pressure on public budgets, there is an increasing interest worldwide in alternative ways for governments to raise money and how public authorities can develop the capacity to administer revenues efficiently and effectively. Taxation, the primary source of public revenue, is exposed to various threats, while alternative sources of public revenues have much potential but are rarely carefully designed and harnessed.

Public Sector Revenue: Principles, Policies and Management sets itself apart from other textbooks through its exclusive focus on the revenue side of public financial management. It provides the reader with the theoretical foundations and practical tools to understand the generation and management of revenues in the public sector, and it weaves a wide range of international examples throughout the text. Students will also benefit from a companion website with supplements including test questions and answers to the end-of-chapter discussion questions inside the book.

This textbook will be essential reading for students, managers and policymakers within the areas of public financial management, public sector accounting and public administration.

Alberto Asquer is Director of the Centre for Financial and Management Studies of SOAS University of London.

Public Sector Revenue

Principles, Policies and Management

Alberto Asquer

LONDON AND NEW YORK

First published 2018
by Routledge
2 Park Square, Milton Park, Abingdon, Oxon, OX14 4RN

andb y Routledge
711 Third Avenue, New York, NY 10017

Routledge is an imprint of the Taylor & Francis Group, an Informa business

©2018 Alberto Asquer

The right of Alberto Asquer to be identified as author of this work has
been asserted by him in accordance with sections 77 and 78 of the
Copyright, Designs and Patents Act 1988.

All rights reserved. No part of this book may be reprinted or reproduced or
utilised in any form or by any electronic, mechanical, or other means, now
known or hereafter invented, including photocopying and recording, or in
any information storage or retrieval system, without permission in writing
from the publishers.

Trademark notice: Product or corporate names may be trademarks or
registered trademarks, and are used only for identification and explanation
without intent to infringe.

British Library Cataloguing in Publication Data
A catalogue record for this book is available from the British Library

Library of Congress Cataloging-in-Publication Data
A catalog record for this book has been requested.

ISBN: 978-1-138-21727-0 (hbk)
ISBN: 978-1-138-21728-7 (pbk)
ISBN: 978-1-315-44100-9 (ebk)

Typeset in Times New Roman
by Sunrise Setting Ltd., Brixham, UK

Printed and bound by CPI Group (UK) Ltd, Croydon, CR0 4YY

Visit the companion website: www.routledge.com\cw\asquer

Contents

Figures

Tables

Preface

Since the earliest recorded history, various forms of government – generally understood as a form of authority over a population, country or state – faced the issue of acquiring resources for the exercise of power in its many forms. With the development of monetary economies, where material value could be appraised, stored and transferred through monetary claims, the acquisition of financial resources became a convenient and practical way for governments to purchase goods and services, hire staff and soldiers, construct assets and subsidise activities that were regarded as instrumental to the attainment of policy goals. Raising public sector revenue – or 'treasury' – became a central function of government, which would largely affect the fortunes and fate of countries over the centuries.

Raising public sector revenue consists of the systems, institutions and mechanisms that result in the increase of financial resources at the disposal of a government. As a function of government, revenue performs the specialised task of providing cash inflows within the public financial management process. The function can be performed in many ways, however. Deciding how a government is to get the money they need for the implementation of public policies and programmes is a policy issue in itself. As such, raising public sector revenue poses various issues in terms of what are the most advantageous, practical, efficient and socially acceptable ways for letting the government acquire financial resources.

Only partially is the revenue function related to providing the government with the money that is needed for the implementation of public policies and programmes. Revenue also serves as a tool for the pursuit of various policy goals, from the reduction of poverty and inequality in society to the stimulation of the economy, from the discouragement of unwelcome behaviour to the protection of domestic industries. Forms of public sector revenue-generating activities, like the progressive personal income tax, the privatisation of state-owned enterprises, the taxation of tobacco, alcohol and sugar-sweetened beverages and the levy of custom duties, also enable the government to reallocate resources in society and to orient the conduct of individuals and businesses towards desired ends.

This books aims to provide an overview of the principles, policies and management of public sector revenue. The book offers a discussion and the basis for a critical appraisal of various approaches that governments have to raise revenue. Some of these approaches build on the exercise of the authoritative powers of the government, such as the levy of taxes, the provision of inter-governmental grants and the extraction of value through the control of money issuance. Other approaches make use of market-based means for raising revenue, such as the commercialisation of public services (like healthcare and education), the privatisation and sale of public assets, the issuing of concessions, franchises and licences, the exploitation of natural resources and the borrowing of funds. Governments generally rely on a mix of approaches to acquire the financial resources that they need for their operation.

The book devotes a large amount of attention to taxation, which is generally considered to be the main source of revenue in many countries – especially industrialised ones. The book includes a review of the literature on public economics and optimal taxation theory, which provides theoretically and empirically based arguments for the design of taxation. The book also pays attention to various issues about taxation that are relevant in the contemporary public policy discourse, including, for example, those related to international cooperation to tackle tax evasion, fiscal federalism and decentralisation, and the behavioural effects of taxation.

The book also dedicates adequate room to the many other non-taxation methods by which governments raise revenue, which have rarely been considered as a whole set of tools at the governments' disposal. Topics that are discussed in the book include, for example, the receipt of revenue from foreign aid, the setting of user charges and fees, the finance through public–private partnerships, the design of franchise and concession contracts, the resource curse, the cost of public borrowing and seignorage. On the whole, the discussion should provide the reader with a better appreciation of the various issues that are encountered in administering systems of public sector revenue.

Raising public sector revenue can be tackled from different angles – economic, financial, legal and political, to mention but a few. An overarching message of this book, however, is that any approach to raising public sector revenue should be considered as a policy issue. As such, deciding how the governments should finance public policies and programmes calls for the careful consideration of the implications that revenue policy design choices have.

As raising public sector revenue is a function performed by any government, this book is not focused on particular countries or regions in the world. The discussion of the various approaches and tools for public sector revenue is supported by selected evidence and examples from various countries – for instance, from the US to the UK, from Russia to Saudi Arabia, from Botswana to Pakistan. The book does not pay focused attention to the details of the specific legal, regulatory and administrative systems of public sector revenue across countries in the world. Rather, the discussion of the institutional and financial schemes for public sector revenue is kept at a level of abstraction that aims to facilitate a dialogue on public sector revenue policy irrespective of any specific country context.

1 Financing the public sector

Public sector spending

Public sector spending grew in many countries in the world during the last two centuries. From about 1870 until the First World War, a general inclination towards principles of laissez-faire favoured 'minimal' government intervention in the economy, with the effect that public spending was limited to the most essential functions like defence, police and administration. Around 1870, unweighted average public expenditures amounted to about 10% of gross domestic product (GDP) in the world (Tanzi and Schuknecht, 2000). Only gradually did ideas about greater involvement of the government in economic and social affairs gain traction, and paved the way towards innovative forms of social protection and intervention of the government in economic activities.

By the late 1920s, many countries had introduced some form of social security. It was during the next couple of decades, however, that many governments started spending at levels that had never been experienced in the past. During the 1930s, increased public spending originated from expansionary policies that aimed to counteract the negative effects of the Great Depression. Then in the first part of the 1940s, public budgets soared because of military spending. In relative terms to the GDP, the size of public spending was also magnified because of the drop of business activity since 1929 and during the Second World War.

The post-war period witnessed the persistence of expansionary policies that had been recast as a desirable public venture rather than a temporary measure to offset the collapse of financial and economic activity. Keynesian ideas about the role of public spending to compensate for a shortfall of private sector demand intersected with socio-democratic (or, in the US, liberal) ideas about the merits of public spending for the redistribution of wealth (Musgrave, 1959) and the protection of citizens from risks (Galbraith, 1998). As Tanzi and Schuknecht (2000: 16) put it, the period 1960–1980 can be described as the 'golden age' of public sector intervention.

Since the 1980s, the role of the government in society and the economy has come under attack. Arguments against the capacity of public policies to allocate resources efficiently and the benevolence of policymakers to make decisions in the public interest fuelled preferences for a smaller government role. Epitomised by such political figures as Margaret Thatcher in the UK and Ronald Reagan in the US, neoliberal ideas gained traction in many countries and resulted in the partial dismantling of welfare state institutions and programmes. Privatisation and regulatory reforms also contributed to shrinking the size of the public sector in many areas such as the provision of infrastructure and utilities services.

The influence of neoliberal ideas on the reduction of public spending faded away after the turn of the last century. In many countries, public spending with respect to GDP increased in the early 2000s. It was the coming of the great financial crisis in 2007–2008, however, that triggered a dramatic surge of public spending, which was primarily related to exceptional measures to bail out financial firms and stimulate economies. Exceptional spending efforts, together with relatively modest public sector revenues, resulted in an increase of public debts that called, in the following years (and until the present day), for 'consolidation' (or 'austerity') programmes to bring the state of public finances back into healthier shape (OECD, 2011a; Riley and Chote, 2014).

The reasons for public spending

What accounts for the secular growth trend and for the fluctuations of public spending over time? Various explanations for the dynamics of public spending have been put forward. They include a role for changed demographics and lifestyles, such as, for example, increased public spending that is required to fulfil the expectations of populations that relocate to live in urban areas, expect to live longer and demand more protection from risks of unemployment, sickness and other unwelcome events (Tarschys, 1975). They also include a role for an increased level of economic development, according to which, progress in technology, division of labour in society and diversification of industrial activity are accompanied by greater efforts of governments to retain control of society (Bird, 1971). An additional role is played by ideas and partisan influence on public policies, especially in the form of a tendency for 'leftist' parties to spend more than right-oriented ones (Blais et al., 1993; Cusack, 1997).

While these explanations help to account for historical tendencies and variations, many scholars have argued that public spending rests on more fundamental rationales about the nature of public sector production (Cornes and Sandler, 1996; Samuelson, 1954, 1995). According to this view, the public sector is primarily oriented to obtaining so-called *public goods*, which are defined as those goods that exhibit properties of non-excludability and non-rivalry. A good is defined as *excludable* when it is possible to prevent an individual from consuming it. A good is defined as *rivalrous* if its consumption by an individual diminishes the consumption of another individual. The combination of excludable and rivalrous features of goods results in the four categories that are illustrated in Table 1.1.

Goods that are excludable and rivalrous fall into the category of *private goods*. Private goods (such as, for example, a pair of shoes) are typically produced by the private, or business, sector: because they are excludable goods, access to private goods can be granted upon payment of a price; because they are rivalrous goods, access to private goods can be allocated on the basis of individuals' willingness to pay for privileged access. At the opposite side of the table, goods that are non-excludable and non-rivalrous are characterised as *public goods*. No business would be interested to produce public goods (such as, for example, national defence), because they would not be able to charge individuals for access to the goods and to differentiate prices to cream-skim the market. Rather, the government has been typically regarded as the producer of public goods *par excellence*. The government, in fact, provides public goods regardless of the possibility to exclude individuals from consumption (which

Table 1.1 Types of goods depending on excludability and rivalry of consumption

	Rivalrous consumption	*Non-rivalrous consumption*
Excludable consumption	Private goods	Toll or club goods
Non-excludable consumption	Common goods	Public goods

may not be desirable anyway) and to discriminate depending on their willingness to pay (which may not be relevant to granting them access to the goods anyway).

According to this model, public spending originates from the production of public goods, whose definition depends on excludability and rivalry features. Public goods include various types of services, however, and the actual production of public goods depends on what is (was) demanded in particular historical and local circumstances. Lighthouses, for example, have been provided by public authorities since long ago, while street lights and official statistics have been supplied in relatively recent times. The volume of spending on public goods, therefore, is dependent on technological change and social expectations.

Table 1.1 also shows that the combination of features of excludability and rivalry results in two additional categories, namely those of *common goods* and *toll or club goods*. Common goods consist of goods that are non-excludable but rivalrous (such as, for example, clean air and water). The lack of the possibility to block access to common goods makes them unattractive to private production. Open access to common goods, however, results in the deterioration or erosion of the same common goods (e.g. through the pollution of air and water). The provision of common goods, therefore, calls for some forms of coordination and rationing, which may be obtained through public authorities (although also systems of community self-regulation may result in the preservation of common pool resources; Ostrom et al., 1994).

Finally, toll or club goods consist of goods that are non-rivalrous but excludable (such as, for example, transit on highways and listening to concerts). In principle, the possibility to block access to consumption makes it possible for business to profit from the production of toll or club goods. Non-rivalry also entails that, once production costs have been incurred, an indefinite number of individuals can jointly consume the toll or club goods. Consumption of toll or club goods may result, therefore, in widespread social benefits that may justify a public interest to produce them (e.g. improving connectivity between regions of a country). Because of such social and economic considerations, toll or club goods may be provided by public authorities, although on various occasions they are supplied by private entities or by some form of mixed public–private arrangement (e.g. highways that have been built with public funds but which are operated in a regime of franchise concession). In addition, sometimes the non-rivalry feature of toll or club goods holds up to a certain volume of consumption only (e.g. a highway may become congested), and some forms of discriminatory pricing may apply to contain demand in peak time.

The four categories of public goods, private goods, common goods and toll goods suggest that the size of public spending depends on the selection of which goods a government decides to produce and in which kind of institutional arrangement. In the heyday of government intervention, public spending included the production of public goods, of services for the preservation of common pool resources and of toll or club goods, although they could be supplied, in principle, by business entities. Public provision may extend up to goods – called *merit goods* – which are supplied by public authorities purely because they are considered worthy of social consideration, such as, for example, concerts (which can be provided by business but which can also be produced by the government because of a general interest to diffuse consumption of cultural artefacts in the society). A similar argument is made for those goods that result in massive positive externalities (that is, benefits to individuals other than those who consume the goods), such, as for example, vaccinations.

There are additional reasons for public spending that especially refer to the stabilisation of the economy and to the redistribution of income. The stabilisation of the economy is a public policy objective that includes such goals as curbing unemployment, containing inflation, limiting the negative effects of business cycles and improving the growth prospects of the economy. In part, these goals are often pursued through monetary policies, which in many countries have been put under the competencies of central monetary authorities (central banks). In part, they are pursued by governments through fiscal means, which include public spending for implementing public policies and programmes (e.g. unemployment benefits) as well as other measures that are intended to stimulate economic activity (e.g. privatisation and liberalisation of sectors of the economy). Nowadays many countries have stipulated mechanisms for economic stabilisation in legislation, especially in the form of 'automatic stabilisers' (e.g. entitlements to welfare benefits) that result in forms of public spending that are somehow isolated from the contingent political climate.

Redistribution of income is another public policy objective that is typically pursued through public spending. Even in countries whose economic regime is based on liberal market principles, there is often a concern with unwelcome allocation of opportunities and rewards. Inequality in the distribution of income can be measured through the Gini coefficient (Gini, 1909). Public spending may partially tackle income redistribution issues in various ways by providing unemployment and welfare benefits (e.g. food and school vouchers) to low-income individuals and families. For example, the Bolsa Familia programme in Brazil contributed to improving the material conditions of many families by transferring cash under conditions that families comply with social policy requirements, such as vaccinations and school attendance for their children.

Funding public spending

Public spending consists, essentially, of the use of money and other financial means of the government ('treasury') for the delivery of public policies and programmes. Public spending includes, for example, expenditures for purchasing durable goods, consumables, salaries, services, and the giving away of money whenever a public policy or programme so provides (e.g. the provision of unemployment benefits). It is generally argued that, in order to spend public monies, the governments need to acquire money and financial resources in the first place. Revenue is the function that precisely consists of the systems and processes through which a government can acquire public monies.

Put in such abstract terms, public sector revenue originates from a variety of sources. Taxation is probably the most common form of public sector revenue, or at least the first that comes to mind to many. As a way to raise money for public authorities, taxation has been present in most sophisticated human societies since the earliest recorded history. Sumerian tablets, for example, exhibit records of payments of 'burden' taxes about 2,500 BC. In Ancient Egypt, taxes were levied on the basis of a 'cattle count' that was carried out originally every two years and later more frequently. In the Roman Republic and later Empire, public authorities employed private tax collectors, called *publicani*. At present, some forms of taxation are present in practically every country with a working government (although, as we shall see, some countries may not have income tax and the total tax burden is minimal).

While taxation – as a form of imposition on taxpayers – is exemplary of the authoritative power of a state, alternative forms of public sector revenue are illustrative of the commercial (or transactional) capacity of governments. Instances of revenue from non-taxation sources include the provision of services for a user charge or a fee, the sale of assets, the extraction and commercialisation of natural resources and the undertaking of business ventures by state-owned enterprises. While these forms of revenue may play a relatively minor role – in terms of magnitude – with respect to taxation, they should not be discounted as irrelevant or marginal in today's economies. In many countries, and especially for sub-national governments, revenue from non-taxation sources plays an important role in public financing.

General principles of prudent fiscal administration might suggest that revenue from taxation and non-taxation sources that are raised in a given period of time suffice to pay for the expenditures that the government incurs in the same period. It is financially advantageous, however, to relax this criterion in at least two respects. First, in the short term a government may incur expenditures that exceed the revenue collected in the same period. Rather than curbing spending (with detrimental effects to the implementation of public policies and programmes) or raising taxes or other forms of revenue (which may be unpopular and unpractical at short notice), the government may borrow to meet temporary needs. Financial resources collected through short-term borrowing should be repaid in periods when revenue exceeds expenditures, however.

A second way to relax the aforementioned criterion is to distinguish between expenditures that arise from the delivery of present public policies and programmes and those that aim to carry out investments such as public works. Public works (such as those in roads, harbours, airports, railways and telecommunication networks) generally result in the development of infrastructure that provide the fundamental backbone of contemporary economies. Expenditures in public works often stimulate increased economic activity, which could result in additional public sector revenue in taxation or non-taxation forms at a later time. Governments may fund public works from long-term borrowing, and expect to pay back interest and principal over time out of the flow of increased future revenue streams.

An additional, albeit a less explicit, approach to funding public spending consists of just issuing money. If a government controls the monetary policy of the domestic currency, they can create (mint) money for paying for any purchase of goods, service and labour. Although the effects of money creation on the economy have been discussed from different perspectives (Reich, 2011), the exogenous expansion of the monetary base may result in inflation, which takes a toll on the purchasing power of every money holder (Fischer, 1982). The government also reaps additional advantages, in the form of savings from alternative means of financing (e.g. if expenditures are financed through money creation, then the government does not need to pay interest for financing through debt) and possibly of additional tax revenue because of fiscal drag (i.e. the increase of real tax revenue in a progressive tax system as nominal income increases).

The use of money creation for funding public spending was an important tool for governments since long ago, when it became known as *seignorage*. In commodity money systems (i.e. where currency takes the form of a tangible good, such as gold in a coin), seignorage was often practiced as a percentage fee upon the value of the commodity that was mint into coins. In contemporary *fiat* money systems (i.e. where the currency takes the form of whatever the public authority sanctions to be money and the citizens consistently believe to hold value), seignorage originates from the difference between the interest earned on securities that central banks purchase when issuing new money and the cost of issuing, distributing and replacing the amount of physical money in circulation. While some amount of seignorage typically takes place in the economy, as a means to raise public revenue, it lacks transparency for taxpayers and, therefore, it is often regarded as an undesirable approach to public financing.

Forms of public sector revenue: an overall framework

The various forms of funding public spending that have been discussed in the previous section can be conveniently arranged in an overall framework. A distinction can be drawn, first,

Table 1.2 Kinds of public sector revenue

	Based on authoritative powers	Based on market exchanges
Effects on the present	Taxation, inter-governmental transfers	Commercial activity
Effects on the present and the future	Seignorage	Borrowing

between means of public sector revenue that rely on the authoritative powers of the state and those that are carried out through voluntary market exchanges. The first kind of financing includes the capacity to impose payments on taxpayers, while the second kind relates to market transactions such as selling public services, public assets and commodities like natural resources. Another distinction can be drawn between means of public sector revenue that primarily affect public finances at present and those whose repercussions extend into the future. The first kind of financing includes revenue from taxation, inter-governmental transfers and commercial activities, while the second kind includes borrowing (which requires taxpayers to pay back public debt in the future) and seignorage (which may result in inflation and increased taxation because of fiscal drag in the future). The resulting combination of kinds of public sector revenue are illustrated in Table 1.2.

Each form of public sector revenue has peculiar features, which should be taken into consideration when deciding the funding of public spending. Forms of public sector revenue differ, first, in terms of the controllability of funding flows. Revenue from taxation is controlled through various features of the tax policy design, from the setting of the tax rates to the mechanisms for enforcement. Tax revenue, however, depends on the size of the tax base (i.e. the measure upon which taxes are calculated), which especially relates to the volume of taxable economic activity (e.g. income, wealth or trade). Governments may estimate the size of the tax base but they may have relatively little leeway to affect the volume of taxable economic activity.

Another form of revenue that is based on the authoritative powers of the state and which has effects mainly on the present is the inter-governmental transfer, which may take place within a country (e.g. grants from the central government to sub-national governments), between countries or between a country and a super-national or international institution (e.g. foreign aid). By and large, however, inter-governmental transfers originate from some forms of tax revenue from the donor entity.

Revenue from commercial activities depends on what the government decides to produce and sell, but also on the market conditions under which transactions are carried out. For example, revenue from the sale of natural resources is affected by commodity prices, over which governments may have relatively modest influence, if any. Revenue from commercial activities, moreover, also depends on the availability of assets and resources (e.g. public assets can be privatised only once, at least before they are re-nationalised again) and on a favourable political climate (e.g. privatisation may be opposed by citizens and political parties). Also, raising funds through borrowing depends on what kind of securities (bonds or gilts) the governments decide to issue, but also on market conditions that are beyond governments' control (e.g. the risk spread premium on the particular government bonds). As a last tool of public sector revenue, finally, the amount of revenue raised through seignorage is related to the rate of money growth, and seignorage revenue grows only up to a maximum money growth rate (after which, seignorage revenue decreases) (Cagan, 1956).

Forms of public sector revenue also differ in terms of their repercussions into the future. As we shall discuss in more detail in subsequent chapters, taxation typically results in more distortionary effects on the economy, especially in terms of less production, trade and consumption, than without the tax burden (McGrattan, 1994; Jaimovich and Rebelo, 2012). Present gains from tax revenue, therefore, may have repercussions resulting in lower tax revenue in the future if relatively high taxation hampers economic growth. Also, raising revenues through commercial activities bears some implications on future options. Once public assets are sold or natural resources have been exploited, for example, they are obviously not available for raising further revenue in the future. Governments should consider, therefore, the relative advantages of the commercialisation of asset-based services, without losing control of asset resources (e.g. temporary concessions or rent) to those of investments to preserve asset resources (e.g. reforestation).

Borrowing entails that governments should take into account future consequences in terms of payments for interest and principal, which bear a burden on the next generations of taxpayers (Buchanan, 1958; Bowen et al., 1960; Alesina and Passalacqua, 2015; Otaki, 2015). Additional issues arise from the shape of the distribution of holders of government bonds (whether it is dispersed or concentrated in the hands of a few, and whether it is mainly in the hands of domestic or foreign investors) and on the consequences of the features of rentiers on economic growth (Hager, 2016). Increased public debt may also limit fiscal options for future governments (Alesina and Tabellini, 1990). Finally, seignorage calls for the careful pondering of future consequences of money printing, especially when repercussions include the spiralling of inflation and possibly the loss of confidence towards the value of fiat currencies.

An additional source of discrimination between the forms of public sector revenue relates to their degree of transparency. In principle, those who bear the cost of funding public spending should be informed of their contribution to the implementation of public policies and programmes. In practice, the various forms of public sector revenue differ in the extent to which individuals are aware of their transfers to the governments (or 'fiscal illusion'). As we shall discuss in more detail in the next chapters, direct taxation (i.e. those taxes that are paid directly from taxpayers to imposing entities) provides a more transparent way of levying taxes than indirect taxation (i.e. those taxes that are paid indirectly from the bearer of the ultimate tax burden to imposing entities through an intermediary). Commercial activities of the government generally make it explicit who pays (the user) for what (the public service provided for a user charge or fee). The disposal of public assets and natural resources, however, may not adequately take into consideration the interests of future generations if revenue is used to fund current expenditures. Also, borrowing does not make it so clear who bears the cost of paying back debts (e.g. whether present taxpayers adjust their saving decisions in anticipation of future tax increases, or whether future governments will reformulate tax policies to tackle debt repayment) (Barro, 1989; Buchanan, 1976; Calvo, 1988; Seater, 1993). Finally, seignorage obfuscates who bears the cost of funding public spending because its effects are spread across money holders. In the extent to which seignorage stimulates inflation, an additional effect is the one of reducing the real cost of debt holders, including both the government and any other debtor whose obligations are not inflation-indexed.

Table 1.3 summarises the main arguments that have been made above. Each form of public sector revenue exhibits peculiar features that make one form or another more or less desirable depending on alternative criteria. No form of revenue is clearly preferable to others, because their score with respect to criteria of controllability, repercussions into the future and transparency depends on various conditions of the economy, or commodity and securities markets, and of taxpayers' expectations. However, some forms of revenue pose the threat of more disadvantageous effects than others; for example, seignorage may undermine money holders' confidence towards the value of fiat currencies, which could potentially destabilise entire economic systems. In this respect, alternative forms of revenue like taxation and

Table 1.3 Summary of the features of different forms of public sector revenues

	Taxation (inter-governmental transfers)	Commercial activity	Borrowing	Seignorage
Controllability of revenue	Depends on the tax base	Depends on market conditions	Depends on market conditions	Depends on money rate of growth
Repercussions into the future	Depends on effects of taxes on economic growth	Depends on the kind of commercial activity	Depends on burden on future taxpayers, features of rentiers and limits on future governments	Depends on spiralling inflation and effects on confidence toward the value of fiat currencies
Transparency of cost burden	Depends on whether taxation is direct or indirect	Depends on consideration for future generations	Depends on taxpayers' expectations and future tax policies	Depends on distribution of money and debt holders

borrowing are more tolerable for risk-adverse governments, which can also resort to commercial activities whenever political, technological and market conditions are supportive.

Public sector revenue and fiscal stability

Public sector revenue is primarily collected for providing the financial means to implement public policies and programmes. As we discussed, revenue may originate from various sources such as taxation, commercial activity, borrowings and seignorage. From a financial management perspective, however, these sources of revenue possess quite different qualities. Revenue from taxation and commercial activity results in an increase of the wealth of the government, while borrowing consists of increased financial means at the government's disposal because of increased debt. Revenue for seignorage may be calculated in different ways, but the Bank of England, for example, accounts for seignorage as income from assets that back the notes in circulation (net of the costs of note production and supply), which is paid to HM Treasury via the National Loans Fund.

Financial statistics of governments around the world typically exhibit revenue from taxation as the main or only revenue source, possibly in combination with some commercial activities (such as, for example, revenue from the sale of goods and services and from the sale of assets). The difference between revenue and expenditures is called *budget surplus* if positive and *budget deficit* if negative. In any given financial year, revenue and expenditure depend on the state of the economy (e.g. revenue may boom when the economy grows and more taxes are collected, and expenditures may mushroom when the economy slows down and the government spends more on social benefits). The terms *structural surplus* or *structural deficit* are used to indicate the (estimated, positive or negative) difference between revenue and expenditures when an economy is at full employment rather than experiencing a contingent boom or bust. The terms *cyclical surplus* or *cyclical deficit* are used to indicate the (estimated, positive or negative) difference between the surplus (or deficit) and the structural surplus (or deficit). A cyclical deficit, therefore, signals a contingent state of public finances where expenditures exceed revenue in a particular condition of the business cycle.

A structural deficit, instead, signals a more worrisome state of public finances where expenditures exceed revenue even if the economy is in a steady state of full employment.

Another fiscal indicator that is relevant to appreciate the financial state of a government is the *primary budget surplus* or *deficit*. The indicator refers to the difference between revenue and expenditures but without counting interest payments. It is possible for a government to attain a primary budget surplus but to achieve a deficit, if interest payments are large enough. Such state of public finances shows that revenue exceeds the expenditures that are required to carry out government policies and programmes, but more than the surplus is claimed to service public debt.

Time series of public sector revenue, budget surplus or deficit, and public debt exhibit some remarkable variation, both within particular countries and across countries. Figures 1.1 and 1.2 show, for example, the time series of deficit (surplus) of the US Federal Government in the period 1998–2016, respectively in nominal value and in percentage of GDP. A relatively large budget deficit in the year 2009 resulted when the US Federal Government revenue decreased considerably with respect to past trends, as illustrated in Figures 1.3 and 1.4 (which show US federal revenue in 1998–2016, respectively in nominal value and in percentage of GDP). Relatively large budget deficits in the period 2009–2012 resulted in an increase of government debt, which is shown in Figures 1.5 and 1.6 (which show US federal debt in nominal value and in percentage of GDP, respectively, in 1998–2016).

A comparison between the top five world country economies (by nominal GDP) shows that they all experienced relatively large budget deficits in the period 2008–2009, which was followed by a slow recovery towards smaller deficits (in the UK and Japan) or some surplus (in China and Germany) (Figure 1.7). Apart from China (for which no data were available from OECD), these countries have experienced a remarkable increase in public debt since 2008, which, in the case of Japan, mushroomed above 240% of GDP (Figure 1.8). Many other countries in the world present, to a greater or lesser extent, a similar pattern of deterioration of public finances after the great financial crisis of 2007–2008.

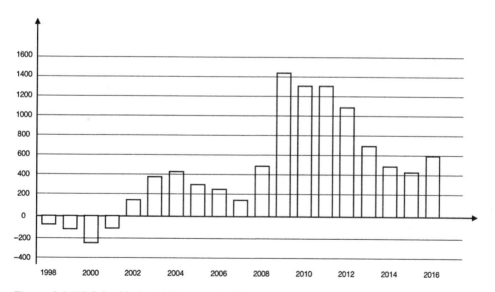

Figure 1.1 US federal budget deficit, nominal $bn.

Source: www.usgovernmentdebt.us

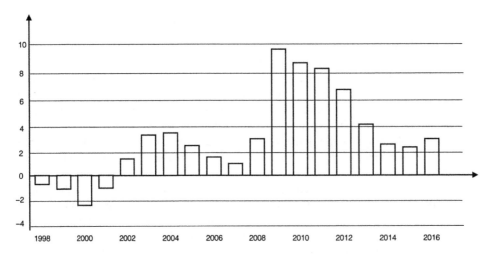

Figure 1.2 US federal budget deficit, %GDP.

Source: www.usgovernmentdebt.us

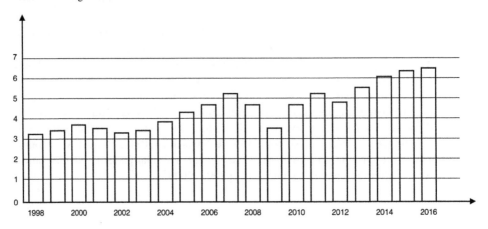

Figure 1.3 US federal revenue, nominal $tn.

Source: www.usgovernmentdebt.us

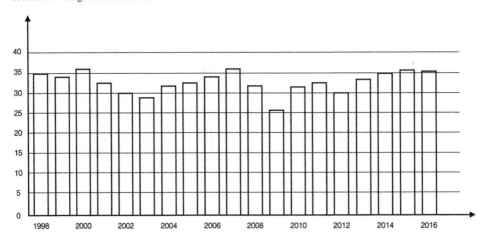

Figure 1.4 US federal revenue, %GDP.

Source: www.usgovernmentdebt.us

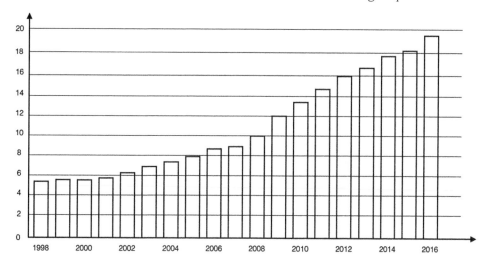

Figure 1.5 US federal debt, nominal $tn.

Source: www.usgovernmentdebt.us

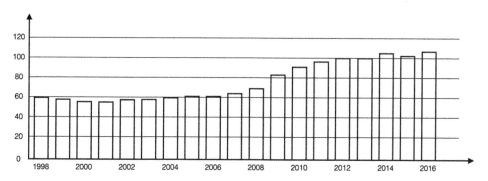

Figure 1.6 US federal debt, %GDP.

Source: www.usgovernmentdebt.us

The contemporary state of public finance shown in the figures of this section suggests that public sector revenue plays an important role in fiscal stability. Fiscal stability refers to the general principle that public sector finances should be managed in a sustainable way; that is, by sustaining current spending on public policies and programmes while avoiding conditions of insolvency or default. Fiscal stability depends on specific financial and economic conditions. Explicit requirements – often set in legislation – may specify how fiscal stability should be attained. For example, the so-called Fiscal Compact (part of the Treaty on Stability, Coordination and Governance in the Economic and Monetary Union in 2012) of the European Union provides the conditions that ratifying countries should satisfy in order attain a balanced budget: the budget deficit should not exceed 3% of GDP and the structural budget deficit should not exceed a country-specific medium-term budgetary objective (which is set at most 1% of GDP or 0.5% of GDP, depending on whether the country debt-to-GDP ratio is within or above the threshold of 60%). In addition, the Fiscal Compact includes a restatement of the provision (already included in the Stability and Growth Pact in force since 1998) that countries whose debt-to-GDP ratio is above 60% should commit to reduce debt levels at specific rates.

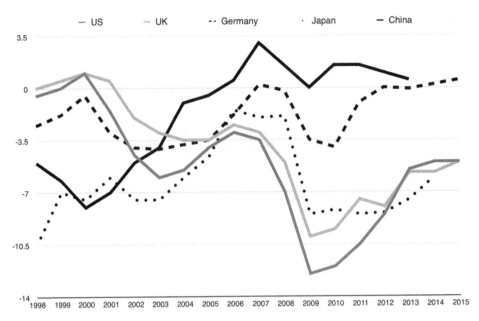

Figure 1.7 Government deficit of top five world country economies, %GDP.

Source: https://data.oecd.org

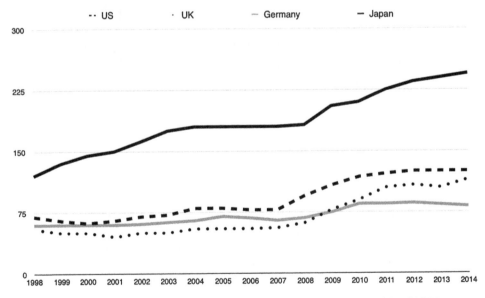

Figure 1.8 Government debt of top five world country economies excluding China, %GDP.

Source: https://data.oecd.org

Management of public sector revenue is pivotal to attain fiscal stability. Revenue from current operations, like taxation and commercial activity, should be used to implement public policies and programmes and for the repayment of debt. Revenue from borrowing should be used to fund investment, which should aim to improve the capacity of the government to operate in the medium–long term and of the economy to flourish (e.g. investment in infra-structure). If current revenue is not sufficient to meet expected public spending, then govern-ments need to borrow more, with detrimental effects on debt-to-GDP ratio and potentially on their capacity to pay back public debt over time.

Managing public sector revenue is especially challenging when governments experience an unexpected drop of revenue, such as, for example, when tax revenue plunges because of a sudden economic downturn. In such a scenario, governments face a dilemma about which policy intervention is more advantageous. For example, raising tax rates in an effort to collect more tax revenue may harm the economy, with the result that tax revenue declines; but also, decreasing tax rates in an effort to stimulate business activity and consumption may result in a further decline of tax revenue, at least in the short term until the stimulus of lower taxation results in improved business activity and consumption. As we shall discuss in the following chapters, principles of good fiscal management suggest that governments could set aside revenue funds in periods of budget surplus in order to compensate for an unexpected drop of revenue that might occur in the future.

The view that governments should be concerned with maintaining fiscal stability, espe-cially through rigid budget rules, has been challenged from many perspectives. Arguments that build on John M. Keynes' theory claim that governments should pursue deficit spending in order to stimulate the economy, especially in downturns. Some views from Neo-Keynesian economics – and especially in the Chartalist approach known as Modern Monetary Theory – hold that deficit spending is required for the very creation of fiat money. In this approach, a government budget is qualitatively different from the budget of a private entity, which can-not issue its own money to settle debts and provide monetary support to a growing economy. These views are generally rejected from more conservative approaches to fiscal stability, how-ever, which argue about the risks of inflation from excess budget deficits and money creation (apart from controversies about the theoretical foundations of Modern Monetary Theory).

Budgeting public sector revenue

The fiscal administration of the public sector builds on institutional and procedural require-ments that are peculiar to the government. In contrast to private sector entities, the govern-ment typically plans in advance the forms and amount of revenue and public spending that accompany the execution of public policies and programmes. In part, the practice to budget public sector revenue and spending originates from pressures for increased accountability and transparency in the use of public monies. For example, in 1733 the UK Chancellor of the Exchequer, Sir Robert Walpole, was urged to disclose plans for the introduction of excises on various goods, such as wine and tobacco, in an effort to lift the burden of taxation on the landed gentry. Later in the eighteenth century, presenting the budget to the House of Com-mons of Great Britain became common practice, which still persists to the present day.

In part, the formulation of budgets for the fiscal management of governments also orig-inates from international pressures. The International Monetary Fund (IMF), for example, introduced the 'Fiscal Transparency Code' in 1998 (revised in 2007 and 2014) in order to provide countries with a framework for fiscal administration. Both the IMF and the World Bank have played an important role to promote the adoption of more transparent institu-tions and procedures for the management of financial resources in the public sector, also as a conditionality attached to foreign aid. Concerns with the poor financial management of funds for development assistance (Easterly and Pfutze, 2008) also led to an increased focus on strengthening planning and budgeting practices, as well as financial reporting and auditing functions.

The budgeting process of public sector fiscal administration does vary considerably across countries. In the US, for example, the President submits a budget proposal to the Congress, where the Budget Committees of the House and the Senate, after meeting with Administration officers, develop budget resolutions that are passed to the legislative body for approval. The Congress, however, can amend the budget resolution by a majority vote before approval. The use of the discretionary part of the budget, then, is drafted in twelve Appropriations Committees before approval by the House and Senate. In the UK, instead, the budget is presented by the Chancellor of the Exchequer to Parliament, who is required to provide a 'Vote on Account' to allow existing services to continue during the early months of the coming financial year. The HM Treasury then provides Parliament with Main Supply Estimates, which enable the monitoring of department spending. Other countries present further variations, which generally range across a spectrum between systems where the government is more in control of the budgetary process (and any parliament or consultative body has limited powers to approve, amend or scrutinise revenue and spending) and systems where the parliament (or any other elected body) limits the discretion of the government.

It should be highlighted that, in principle, the budgeting process should provide a comprehensive view of public sector revenue and spending. In practice, the budget of a government is partially fragmented when the financial management of agencies and entities of the state and of the parastatal sector is kept separated from central government administration. In addition, when the institutional structure of a country consists of multiple layers of government, each sub-national government has distinctive planning and budgetary processes. The fiscal conditions of any sub-national government, however, may have repercussions on the finances of the central government and of other sub-national governments. For example, in case of the default of a sub-national government administration, the central government may carry the burden of the financial loss. For these reasons, many countries have undertaken measures to provide a comprehensive view of public sector revenue and spending through the consolidation of public sector accounts. In the UK, for example, whole-of-government accounting consolidates the audited accounts of over 5,500 public sector entities in order to produce an overall financial position of the country's public sector.

The formation of public budgets is, of course, an arena for confrontation over alternative policies. The budgeting of public sector revenue, in particular, combines the formulation of estimates about future revenue streams from existing sources with those about new revenue-generating measures. On the one hand, Treasury departments calculate expected revenue on the basis of present tax and commercial policies while taking into account estimates of the future state of the economy. On the other hand, government officers struggle over alternative revenue-generating measures and their impact on citizens, taxpayers and electoral constituencies. For example, the introduction of new forms of taxation, or the increase of rates on existing taxes, results in a worsening of the economic conditions of some taxpayers who may engage in various forms of opposition to protect their interests. Also, the undertaking of commercial activity may trigger resistance from various stakeholders, such as, for example, citizens who disagree with the charging of fees for services which have been provided for free or at subsidised prices in the past. In principle, next generations should also be considered when making fiscal decisions that affect public finances and policies in the medium–long term (e.g. the privatisation of public assets or the increase of long-term debt), although they typically lack an adequate representation in political arenas.

Conclusions

This chapter has outlined the general features of managing public sector revenue. We discussed that revenue provides an essential tool for the implementation of public policies and programmes. Without public monies, governments would not be able to provide the means that are needed to operate the systems of public service delivery. If financial resources are not available, governments would have little scope to carry out any operations other than by commandeering the use of individuals' time and property (a form of slavery) or by exhorting communities to provide public services by themselves (a form of self-production of public goods). Neither slavery nor community self-care, however, seem compatible with the scale and complexity of operations of governments in the contemporary age. The capacity to raise revenue for funding public policies and programmes, therefore, is a fundamental function of any government.

Questions for discussion

- Does public spending inevitably grow over time?
- Should public sector spending be restricted to the production of public goods only?
- Could a government rely on authority-based sources of revenue only? Why should a government worry about raising revenue through market exchanges?
- Could a government entirely fund public spending by only printing money?
- What happens if a government does not meet the criteria for fiscal stability?
- How could the interest of future generations be taken into account in the public budgeting process?

2 Taxation

Principles, types and effects

Principles of taxation

Taxes constitute a main source of public sector revenue in many countries nowadays. While there are many definitions of taxes, especially across different countries, a general understanding of the term is the one provided by the Organisation for Economic Co-operation and Development (OECD, 1996), which defined it as 'compulsory, unrequited payments to general government'. The meaning of the term 'unrequited' is that taxes are paid without any proportionate benefit provided by government to taxpayers. Taxes also include social security contributions, if they are not paid on voluntary basis. Taxes can also include licence fees, although the borderline between taxes and fees (or charges) is not sometimes too straightforward.

A distinguishing feature of taxes is that tax obligations arise from the power of the government to impose them on taxpayers. In this sense, taxes are a quintessential manifestation of the sovereignty of states. Governments can require particular categories of citizens (or, in some case, residents irrespective of their citizenship) and private entities (such as companies and charities) to pay taxes to contribute to the running of the government and the implementation of public policies and programmes.

Taxes, however, are not arbitrarily decided. As has been long debated within scholarly and political circles, taxes should comply with the fundamental principles of 'good taxation'. One of the earliest formulations of these principles is found in the writings of Adam Smith (1776), who identified the principles of fairness, certainty, convenience and efficiency.

- Fairness. As Smith (1776) put it, 'The subjects of every state ought to contribute towards the support of the government, as nearly as possible, in proportion to their respective abilities . . .'. This principle states that the cost of taxes for every taxpayer should be commensurate with the capacity of taxpayers to contribute to the public budget. In practice, this principle is enacted in various forms, which generally appraise the economic condition of a taxpayer – especially in terms of income and/or wealth – for determining the amount of taxes due.
- Certainty. As Smith (1776) wrote, 'The tax which the individual is bound to pay ought to be certain and not arbitrary . . .'. This principle refers to the formulation of explicit rules and regulations for determining what is taxed (the tax base), how much is taxed (the rates or sometimes the fixed amount) and who must pay (the taxpayer). If these rules and regulations are not stipulated, either the public authorities can extract taxes at will or the administration of taxation would be subjected to endless controversies.
- Convenience. As Smith (1776) argued, 'Every tax ought to be levied at the time, or in the manner, in which it is most likely to be convenient for the contributor to pay it.'

This principle affirms that compliance costs should be kept to a minimum. As a matter of fact, sometimes taxpayers are required to incur additional costs on the top of the taxes, in such forms as, for example, money paid to accountants to comply with tax rules and regulations and time spent to carry out tasks to fulfil the tax levy.

- Efficiency. As Smith (1776) maintained, 'Every tax ought to be so contrived as to take out of the pockets as little as possible, over and above that which it brings into the public treasury of the state.' This principle relates to the trade-off between the benefit that taxation brings to fiscal administration – and, relatedly, to the possibility to implement public policies and programmes – on the one hand, and the cost that taxation puts on taxpayers on the other one. As we shall discuss below, taxation results in a net cost to the economy, the so-called 'deadweight loss'. Tax systems should minimise the overall deadweight loss to the economy.

The application of these principles results in various practical challenges. The principle of fairness, for example, calls into play the distinction between *horizontal* and *vertical equity*. Horizontal equity means that taxpayers under similar economic conditions should pay the same amount of taxes (Musgrave, 1990). Vertical equity means that taxpayers under better economic conditions should pay more taxes than those in worse economic conditions (Pigou, 1912). In practice, these criteria are not always implemented. In many tax systems, income may be taxed differently depending on the source; for example, a certain amount of income from salary may be taxed at a different (typically higher) rate than the same amount of income that originates as a return on financial assets. In most tax systems, a large part of tax revenue arises from taxes on the production (excises) and transaction (sales tax and value added tax or VAT) of goods, which are levied irrespective of the economic condition of the taxpayers.

Also, the other principles of good taxation of Adam Smith are sometimes not fully implemented. The principle of certainty is sometimes hampered by Byzantine tax codes. The principle of convenience is often contradicted by relatively large sums that taxpayers are required to pay and by payments that taxpayers may be required to make in advance with respect to the economic event that forms the tax base (e.g. tax payments in advance with respect to the receipt of an income). The principle of efficiency is typically hard to apply, when the various forms of taxation result in deadweight losses. In addition, part of the benefits of taxation to fiscal administration may vanish if tax administration is poorly managed and too costly.

Another important contribution in the scholarly literature on the principles of taxation is that of Knut Wicksell, who argued that a unanimity-voting rule for determining taxation would guarantee that all individuals receive benefits from public goods that are higher than the tax cost (Johnson, 2006; Wicksell, 1958). The theoretical work of Wicksell, as well as of others like Lindahl (1958), builds on the principle of 'benefit taxation', according to which taxpayers should contribute to public finance according to the benefits that they receive from public expenditures. The principle of benefit taxation has some theoretical and practical limitations, however, which arise from the possibility that taxpayers free ride on tax obligations and the difficulty to reveal taxpayers' preferences for alternative public goods.

Principles of taxation have also been formulated, in the contemporary age, within accounting professional circles. The American Institute of Certified Public Accountants (AICPA), for example, outlined ten guiding principles of taxation as follows (Nellen, 2002):

1 Equity and fairness: similarly situated taxpayers should be taxed similarly, both in the sense of vertical and of horizontal equity.
2 Certainty: tax rules should specify when and how a tax is to be paid and how the amount is determined.

3   Convenience of payment: a tax should be due at a time and in a manner that is convenient to the taxpayer. If payment of taxes is convenient then it is more likely that taxpayers will comply with their tax obligations.
4   Economy of collection: the cost of collection of taxes should be kept to a minimum for both the government and the taxpayers.
5   Simplicity: the tax code should be simple so that taxpayers can understand the rules and regulations and comply with them correctly and cost-efficiently.
6   Neutrality: the effects of taxes on the decisions of taxpayers as to whether to carry out a particular transaction should be kept to a minimum. The purpose of taxes is to raise revenue, not to change behaviour.
7   Economic growth and efficiency: the tax system should not impede or reduce the economy's productive capacity or favour one industry more than another.
8   Transparency and visibility: taxpayers should know that a tax exists and when and how it is imposed.
9   Minimum tax gap: taxes should be designed to minimise non-compliance or the 'tax gap', which is the difference between the amount of taxes owed and the amount of taxes collected.
10 Appropriate government revenue: a tax system should enable the government to anticipate how much taxes will be collected and when.

It should be noted that also these principles are not entirely followed. As we shall discuss in the next chapters, sometimes governments make use of taxes to deliberately induce changes of behaviour, for example when increasing taxes on the production or sale of goods, like tobacco, alcohol and sugar beverages, with the aim to discourage consumption that may have negative side effects on individuals' health and on the wellness of communities at large.

Direct and indirect taxation

Contemporary tax systems are populated by a variety of taxes, which include, for example, personal income tax, corporate income tax, sales tax, VAT, excises, custom duties, stamp tax and so on. Some taxes have been levied for many years, like, for example, the personal income tax in the UK, which was first established by William Pitt the Younger in 1798 to pay for preparation for the Napoleonic Wars and that, after a number of periods when it was repealed, became a stable component of the British tax system during the nineteenth century. Other taxes have been introduced relatively recently, like, for example, VAT which was first established in France in 1954 and then spread throughout most countries in the world. Sometimes, however, taxes are short-lived: for example, in 2015 the Punjab government of Pakistan introduced a 19.5% tax on Internet connections, which was repealed after some months following popular protest.

A broad distinction is commonly made between two types of taxes, namely *direct* and *indirect* ones (Atkinson, 1977). Direct taxes are paid directly from taxpayers to imposing entities. They consist of levies that are based on the economic conditions related to an entity (an individual or a legal entity), such as their income or property. Examples of direct taxes include personal income tax, corporate income tax, property tax, inheritance tax and social security (e.g. National Insurance contributions in the UK). Indirect taxes, instead, are paid indirectly from the bearer of the ultimate tax burden to imposing entities through an intermediary. They consist of levies that are based on economic events, such as acts of production and transaction of goods. Indirect taxes are typically collected and paid by an entity (such as the producer of a good or a merchant) although the actual cost of the tax is charged to another entity (typically the final consumer of the good). Examples of indirect taxes include sales tax, VAT, excises and custom duties.

Nowadays most countries in the world employ a mix of direct and indirect forms of taxation. But which one of the two forms of taxation is preferable? Before addressing this question, which has attracted considerable attention in the scholarly literature (Atkinson and Stiglitz, 1976; Auerbach, 1985; Cremer and Gahvari, 1995; Cremer et al., 2001; Martinez-Vazquez et al., 2011), a distinction should be drawn between *progressive* and *regressive* taxation. Progressive taxation refers to a tax design where tax rates increase as the taxable amount increases. A typical instance of progressive taxation is the structure of incremental tax rates that are applied to tranches of income above certain thresholds (tax brackets). Regressive taxation, instead, consists of a tax design where the incidence of taxes decreases as the taxable amount increases. An instance of regressive taxation is the poll tax (also called head tax or lump-sum tax or capitation), where a fixed amount of tax is levied irrespective of the economic event that is subjected to taxation (e.g. if a poll tax is paid on property, the amount of tax is lower the higher the value of the property). Generally, progressive taxation is advocated because of its redistributive effects, provided that taxpayers with higher income and wealth are required to contribute more to public finances than those with lower income and wealth.

The distinction between progressive and regressive effects of taxes is important because indirect taxes typically have regressive effects, while direct taxes that implement increasing tax rates have progressive effects. To some extent, it is possible to design indirect taxes to also have a progressive effect, especially if we take income, wealth and spending capacity as the economic condition that redistributive policies aim to correct. For example, different VAT rates (or sales tax rates or excises or custom duties) may apply to different categories of goods, where luxury goods (that are presumably consumed by affluent individuals) are taxed at higher tax rates than ordinary or basic goods. On the other hand, direct taxes may not have progressive effects if, for example, the income tax rate is flat (as it is, at the time of writing, in countries like Russia, Hungary, Bulgaria, Romania and the Baltic countries).

Direct and indirect taxes also differ in other dimensions. In terms of transparency, for example, direct taxes provide a more intelligible way for taxpayers to know how much they pay than indirect forms of taxation. For final consumers at least, the surcharge from VAT, sales tax, excises and custom duties may not be explicitly disclosed on the price tags of goods. For example, in Italy more than half of the price of petrol (gasoline) consists of various taxes, from VAT (22% at the time of writing) to excises that were charged, among others, for the 1935–1936 Ethiopia war, the 1956 Suez crisis, the 1966 flooding of Florence and the 2009 earthquake in Aquila (and that have never been repealed).

Direct and indirect taxes also differ in terms of the incentives that they provide to individuals and firms when they make economic choices. For example, relatively high marginal tax rates on income may discourage incremental efforts on work and induce individuals to enjoy spare time, although they may also stimulate individuals to work more to compensate for the money paid for taxation. When tax rates are extremely high (like, for example, the top income tax rates at or above 90% in the UK in the 1950s–1960s), they also pose issues about whether they are fair – no matter how high the income is – and advantageous for public finances – as they can encourage tax avoidance, tax evasion or tax exile. Similarly, taxes on income and on the return on investment affect the choices individuals make on consumption and saving. In general, we may expect that the higher the taxes on income are, the less the after-tax income that individuals allocate to consumption and saving; and the higher the taxes on the return on investment are, the less individuals are willing to save and invest the money that they put aside. When high tax rates are applied to indirect taxes, instead, individuals are not discouraged to work more and to save; individuals may consume less because of the higher price (including indirect taxes) of goods.

Another dimension along which direct and indirect taxes differ is the extent to which they can be easily evaded. Indirect taxes are typically levied on the economic events of production and transaction. Many such events can be conveniently detected by tax authorities, either because of the physical acts of manufacturing and trading or because of the visibility of business activity. In contrast, direct taxes are more difficult to detect. Most economic conditions that are subjected to direct taxation, like the formation of personal or corporate income, require extensive documentation in order to determine the tax base (e.g. annual tax reports and financial reports). Because of the abstract notion of income and of the possibility to exchange cash without records, direct taxes on income may be more likely to be evaded than those on production and transaction.

General trends in taxation

Nowadays the governments of most countries in the world raise revenue through a combination of forms of direct and indirect taxation. In the UK, for example, tax revenue in 2015 comprised personal income tax (about 31%), corporate income tax (about 9%), National Insurance contributions (about 21%), VAT (about 22%), various capital taxes (which include taxes like capital gains, inheritance and stamp duty land tax, totalling about 5%) and other indirect taxes (which include all excises, transport and environmental taxes and customs duties, totalling about 12%) (Figure 2.1). In the US, Federal Government tax revenue in 2015 comprised personal income tax (about 46%), corporate income tax (about 11%), social insurance and retirement (SIR) contributions (about 34%), excises (about 3%) and other taxes (including sales tax and totalling about 6%) (Figure 2.2). In OECD countries, average tax revenue in 2014 comprised personal income tax (about 23%), corporate income tax (about 9%), social security contributions (about 27%), taxes on property (about 6%), general taxes on

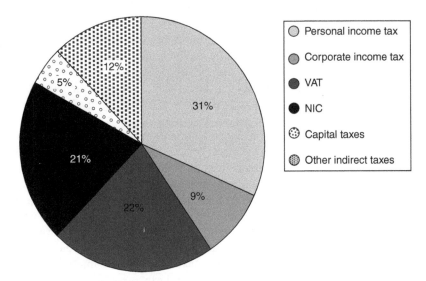

Figure 2.1 Composition of central government tax revenue in the UK, 2014–2015.

Source: HM Revenue & Customs, 2016.

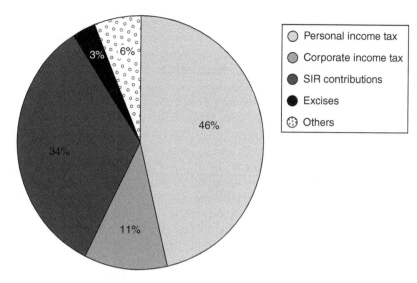

Figure 2.2 Composition of federal tax revenue in the US, 2015.
Source: US GPO, 2015.

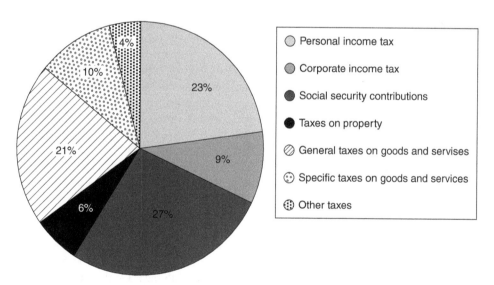

Figure 2.3 Average composition of tax revenue in OECD countries, 2014.
Source: OECD, 2016a.

goods and services (i.e. VAT and sales taxes; about 21%), specific taxes on goods and ser-vices (i.e. excises; about 10%) and other taxes (about 4%) (Figure 2.3).

The data on the composition of tax revenue in the main world economies show that per-sonal income tax provides the main source of revenue for governments. Personal income tax is often implemented in a progressive fashion, with increasing tax rates levied at higher income thresholds. In the UK, for example, at the time of writing there are three personal income tax rates: 20% (for income above £11,000), 40% (for income above £43,000) and 45% (for income above £150,000). In the US, there are seven personal income tax rates (from 10% up to 39.6%) that are levied on various thresholds of income, which also depend on whether the taxpayer is single, married and jointly filling the tax return or head of household. In many countries, the calculation of personal income tax includes various deductions, personal exemptions and tax credits (which, for example, may depend on the number of children or dependents). Generally, personal income tax on salaried income is partially or entirely withheld at source, with the employer acting as tax collector for the government. Personal income taxes differ considerably around the world, with (at the time of writing) some countries having the top tax bracket rate above 50% (e.g. Sweden, Canada and Austria) and some countries not levying any personal income tax at all (e.g. the Gulf Cooperation Countries, although Saudi Arabia levies a personal tax on wealth of natives, *zakat*, at 2.5%).

Corporate income tax plays a relatively minor role in the funding of the public sector. Corporate income taxes differ considerably around the world. In the US, corporate income tax is progressive, with (at the time of writing) eight tax rates starting from 15% up to 35%. Many countries in the world, instead, implement a flat tax rate (e.g. about 33% in France, 32% in Japan, 31% in Italy). Some countries have adopted relatively low tax rates, such as, for example, the UK (20%), Russia (20%), Singapore (17%) and Ireland (12.5%). A few countries (which fall into the category of so-called 'tax havens', which will be discussed in a subsequent chapter) do not levy any corporate tax, such as, for example, in the Bahamas, Bahrain and the Cayman Islands.

The actual burden of corporate income tax may not be fully appraised on the basis of the tax rate alone. In many countries, the tax code can include provisions for special deduction and exemption schemes or for additional surcharges. The Netherlands, for example, may be considered a tax haven because of special exemptions (e.g. on capital gains and dividends from qualifying subsidiaries and foreign branches). In most countries, moreover, the total amount of taxes that business entities pay also includes other forms of taxation, such as contributions to social security for employees and property taxes on real estate. The World Bank 'total tax rate' index provides a clue to the total burden of taxation on corporations. According to this index, countries like France, Italy and Spain have relatively high levels of total corporate taxes, at aggregated rates of 62.8%, 62.0% and 49.0%, respectively. Other countries, like Kuwait, Saudi Arabia and Singapore, have relatively low total corporate taxes, at aggregated rates of 13.0%, 15.7% and 19.1%, respectively.

Also, another main source of public sector revenue, the indirect taxes on transactions, differ considerably across the world. Indirect taxes on transactions take different forms. About 160 countries in the world have adopted VAT (OECD, 2014). Some main economies, instead, implement a goods and service tax (GST) like in Australia, Canada and the US. Although VAT and GST differ in many respects (especially with regard to the administration of VAT credits for business entities), they both result in the taxation of purchases of goods and services, whose burden tends to be transferred to the final consumers. The tax rates of VAT or GST differ across the world, with the highest VAT rates (at the time of writing) in Hungary (27%), Denmark (25%) and Sweden (25%). Relatively low VAT or GST rates are adopted in Malaysia (6%), Japan (which applies a consumption tax of 8%) and Australia (10%). In the US, there is no federal-level VAT or GST, but most US states levy a GST.

Looking at some time series data provides an indication of how the composition of public sector revenue has changed over time. In the UK, the incidence of central government revenue from (personal and corporate) income tax slowly decreased over time during the twentieth century, while – since the Second World War – there has been an increase in the share of total revenue from indirect taxes and social security contributions (Figure 2.4). Data on the US show that the share of federal revenue from personal income taxes has remained relatively constant since the Second World War, while the share of tax revenue from corporate income taxes has declined. During the course of the second half of the twentieth century, there was also a sharp increase in the share of social security contributions and a decrease in the role of excises (Figure 2.5).

Additional insights into the changes of tax policies over time arise from time series data on tax rates. The time series of highest and lowest personal and corporate tax rates in the UK

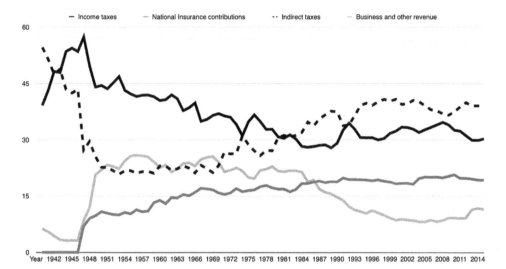

Figure 2.4 Composition of central government tax revenue in the UK, 1942–2014.

Sources: Mitchell, 2011; UK Office for Budget Responsibility, www.budgetresponsibility.org.uk/data; www.ukpublicrevenue.co.uk

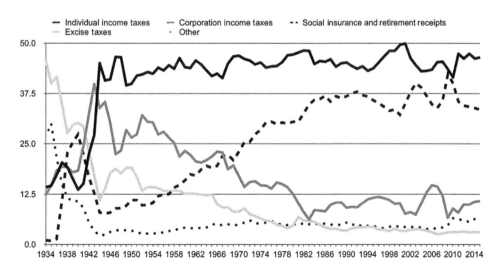

Figure 2.5 Composition of federal tax revenue in the US, 1934–2014.

Source: US GPO, 2015.

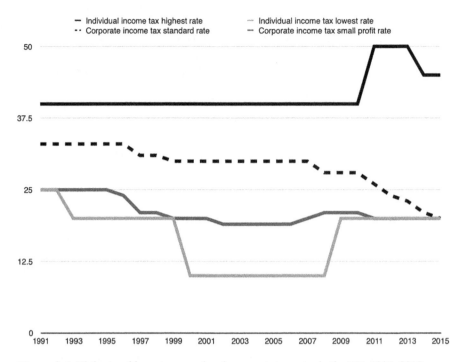

Figure 2.6 Highest and lowest personal and corporate tax rates in the UK, 1991–2015.

Sources: HM Revenue & Customs, 2014; Institute for Fiscal Studies, www.ifs.org.uk/tools_and_resources/
fiscal_facts. Individual income tax excludes the zero rate.

in the period 1991–2015 shows that tax policies tend to consistently discriminate between personal high-income and low-income earners. Differences in corporate tax rates declined over time, instead, and remained consistently lower than the personal income tax rates for top income earners. From 2015 onwards, the UK has applied a flat corporate income tax irrespective of the turnover of business taxpayers (Figure 2.6). A longer time series from the US data shows that during the 1930s–1970s the difference between high-income and low-income earners was much wider than today, when it is relatively aligned to the nominal tax rates for corporate income (Figure 2.7).

Tax incidence and other effects of taxation

When taxes are levied on taxpayers, they produce various effects on individual behaviour and the aggregated working of the economy. At the individual level, the scholarly literature on taxation has long highlighted the effects of *tax incidence* on the behaviour of producers, consumers and savers. In general, the presence of a tax reduces disposable income (direct taxation) or makes goods and services more expensive (indirect taxation). The effects of taxes on individual choices are multiple. Individuals may be stimulated to work more to compensate for the money paid for taxation, although relatively high marginal rates may discourage extra efforts and, rather, induce individuals to enjoy spare time. Individuals may reduce the overall level of consumption because of less disposable income, but they may also just shift their consumption from those goods and services that become too expensive because of taxation

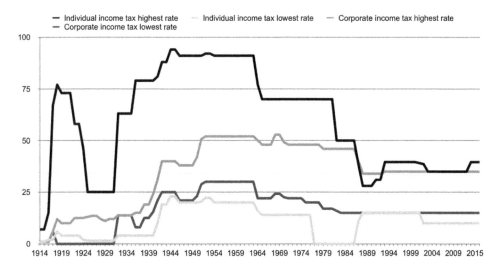

Figure 2.7 Highest and lowest personal and corporate federal tax rates in the US, 1914–2015.

Sources: Tax Foundation, 2013; US Internal Revenue Service Historical Data Tables, www.irs.gov/uac/
soi-tax-stats-historical-data-tables. Individual tax rates refer to head of household from 1952 onwards.

towards those that are taxed less. Taxation can also affect the inter-temporal choices of individuals. For example, a reduction of disposable income because of taxation may reduce the amount of income that an individual might have set aside as savings. Taxation on capital assets (e.g. taxes on real estate) or on the return on investment (e.g. dividends and capital gains) may discourage saving and stimulate consumption.

Economic theory provides a framework for arguing about the effects of taxation on individual choices. In the basic formulation, the argument is presented as the effects of an excise tax on the market for a good or service (Krugman and Wells, 2009). The excise is levied on the producer, which is tempted to pass on the burden of the tax to the consumers. The analysis shows, however, that the producer can pass the burden of the tax to the consumer to a limited extent only; it depends on the price elasticity of demand and supply. In practical terms, the excise drives a wedge between two prices – the price that consumers pay for the good or service and the price that the producer receives from the sale of the good or service. The government gains revenue that depends on the excise times the volume of sales of the good or service in the market.

A more detailed argument is based on the analysis shown in Figure 2.8. The diagram on the left illustrates a market equilibrium for a good or service without the excise. Market equilibrium (E) is the intersection between the demand and supply curves. The diagram on the right, instead, presents a market equilibrium for a good or service with the excise tax. The effect of the excise is to induce the producer to increase the price in order to pass on the excise to consumers. A side effect of increased price is a reduction of demand of the good or service sold, with the effect that a new market equilibrium is found at a lower volume of sales than the market equilibrium without the excise.

The analysis of the tax incidence of the excise shows that both the producer and the consumers are left in a worse condition than before the excise was introduced. The producer sells less goods or services at a higher price, but the actual price that the producer gets is lower than they obtained from market equilibrium without the excise (i.e. the producer's price is the

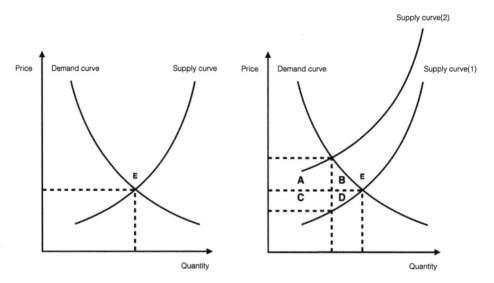

Figure 2.8 Economic analysis of the incidence of an excise tax.

price that consumers pay, less the excise). The consumers purchase less goods or services at a higher price. Both the producer and the consumer would have enjoyed more sales, higher profit and cheaper goods or services without the excise. In analytic terms, the producer loses producer surplus and the consumers lose a consumer surplus, whose amount is indicated by the areas A+B and C+D in the diagram on the right, respectively. Another effect of the excise is that the government can collect tax revenue, which equals the area A+C in the diagram on the right. On the whole, however, the effect of the excise is to reduce welfare, because the net gain for the government (area A+C) is lower than the total loss of the producer's and consumers' surplus (the total of areas A+B and C+D).

The amount of reduced welfare because of the excise (i.e. the area B+D) is called *deadweight loss* (Harberger, 1964). Deadweight losses arise because taxes introduce a 'distortion' in the working of the market price mechanism as the tax wedge results in higher prices for the consumers (purchasers) and lower profits for the producers (sellers). Similar results are obtained when analysing the effects of taxation on income, which affects the choice to allocate time between work and leisure, and on capital assets and return on investment, which affect the choice to allocate income between consumption and saving.

The analysis of the incidence of an excise also shows that the allocation of the burden of taxation depends on the price elasticity of the demand and supply curves. A detailed argument is based on the analysis shown in Figure 2.9. In the diagram on the left, the demand curve has a relatively low price elasticity (i.e. a relatively high variation of price results in a modest variation of quantity demanded) with respect to the supply curve. The excise results in a relatively higher price paid by consumers with respect to the market equilibrium without the excise. In other words, the producer can pass most of the burden of the tax onto the consumers. In the diagram on the right, instead, the demand curve has a relatively high price elasticity with respect to the supply curve. The excise results in a relatively modest price increase for the consumers, while the producer carries the burden of most of the excise tax. More generally, price elasticity has an important effect on the allocation of the burdens of taxation.

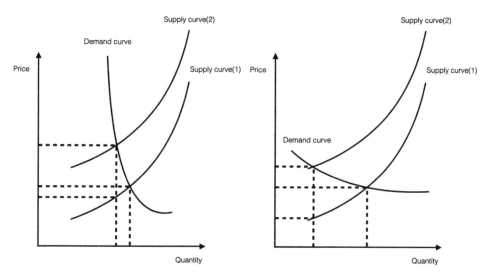

Figure 2.9 Economic analysis of the incidence of an excise tax with low price elasticity (left) and high
price elasticity (right) of the demand curve.

In principle, luxury goods have relatively low price elasticity; that is, individuals who can
afford them tend to be relatively insensitive to price. Indirect taxation of luxury goods, then,
is passed on to consumers more than taxation of ordinary or basic goods.

Not all forms of taxation, however, impact on the working of the market system with
distortionary effects. Poll taxes, for example, are levied without any relationship to an economic condition or event. Individuals, therefore, would not alter their choices between work,
leisure, consumption and saving because of poll taxes (although the reduction of disposable
income might affect saving and kinds of consumption). Poll taxes, however, are very unpopular because they do not take into account the economic conditions of individuals; that is,
whether they are affluent or not. When the UK government introduced a poll tax at the local
level called the Community Charge in 1989 (in Scotland) and 1990 (in England and Wales),
popular protest and riots in central London on 31st March 1990 led to the repeal of the poll
tax and its substitution with the Council Tax in 1992.

Another form of taxation that does not generate distortions is the tax on economic rents,
such as on land and on natural resources. A tax on the rental value of land would be based on
the economic value of land (a scarce resource) where social and economic activity takes
place (Brueckner, 1986; Netzer, 1998). Land is considered as a given to the economy, that is,
not obtained from any capital investment or labour effort. A tax on the rental value of land is
what taxpayers should pay to the government for the use of a resource that belongs to the
entire community (this argument is associated to Henry George, 1879). It is expected that if
the rental value of land is taxed rather than the results of capital investments and labour, then
entrepreneurial activity and jobs would be stimulated.

Additional studies also focused on the macroeconomic effects of taxation. Koester and
Kormendi (1989) showed that increases in marginal tax rates have negative effects on the
level of economic activity, if controlling for average tax rates. King and Rebelo (1990) argued
that taxation has important long-run economic effects, where – for a small open economy
with capital mobility – taxation can lead to either stagnation and regression or rapid growth.

McGrattan (1994) examined the distortionary effects of taxation on the cyclical features of the economy. She showed that government expenditures and tax rate shocks have a significant effect on the variance of most variables in her model. Engen and Skinner (1996) examined the effects of marginal tax cuts on the economy and found relatively modest effects on growth rates, although the cumulative effects of the stimulus to the economy could be significant. Johansson et al. (2008) argued that some taxes are more harmful to growth than others, with the most detrimental being corporate income taxes, followed by personal income taxes and then consumption taxes. Recurrent taxes on immobile property seemed the least harmful. Arnold (2008) suggested that income taxes are generally associated with lower economic growth than taxes on consumption and property.

The political economy of taxation

Theoretical and empirical studies of taxation are helpful to outline the consequences of alternative tax structures. Only partially do evidence and views of tax scholars and experts, however, contribute to explaining tax policies. The political economy of taxation includes multiple stakeholders – especially the various kinds of taxpayers, but also other actors like, for example, super-national organisations – that contribute to shaping the design and administration of taxation in various ways. Tax stakeholders may protect their interests in vociferous ways; as it is well known, an increase in the taxation of British colonies in America in 1764–1773 led to the protest of the Boston Tea Party, which marked an important step in the escalation of events that led to the American Revolutionary War. Tax stakeholders, however, may also resist tax reforms that could potentially unlock the growth potential of an economy, if the tax reforms pose a threat to their privileged positions.

Various interests are at stake in the making of tax policy. A rough distinction, for example, can be made between taxpayers who earn most of their income from rents, business activity and salaried work. Some forms of taxation target some kinds of income more than others. Taxation on property (such as land and real estate) and return on investment (such as capital gains and interest) especially harms the rentiers. Taxation on corporate income tax, consumption taxes, excises and custom duties are particularly adversarial to the interests of business. Taxation on personal income tax and many consumption taxes, excises and custom duties are disadvantageous for those who are salaried. Choices made on the structure of taxation, therefore, are likely to meet opposition from some groups of taxpayers more than others. Some groups of taxpayers, moreover, are more able to organise protests than others, and exert effort to lobby the government to pass advantageous tax provisions or drop unwelcome ones. Business interests, for example, can often concentrate lobbying efforts with beneficial effects on their tax bill (Richter et al., 2009). Individual taxpayers, however, can occasionally orchestrate effective protests, like, for example, in the case of the outrage against the proposal of an Internet tax in Hungary in 2014.

The government itself and public administration are, of course, influential stakeholders in the tax policy domain. Although government officers may have different orientations towards the size of public sector intervention (which may approximately correspond to different political inclinations from the most market-oriented to the most social-democratic-oriented beliefs about the preferred organisation of society), economic theory has often made the case that public sector bureaucracies tend to inflate their budget in order to win the consensus of the electorate and to increase the material interests of public officers (Buchanan and Tullock, 1962; Niskanen, 1968, 1975). In this respect, public sector bureaucracies may be inclined to resist any form of reduction of public spending, and rather advocate for expanding existing public programmes or introducing new ones.

The formation of taxation policies, however, also needs to take into consideration changing features of the context where governments operate. During the last decades, part of these features included an increased role for globalisation, which has come to affect the society and the economy of many countries in various ways. Pressures to open up national borders to international trade, especially through international organisations like the World Trade Organization (WTO) and regional free-trade areas like the European Union (EU), the North Atlantic Free Trade Agreement (NAFTA) and the Association of Southeast Asian Nations (ASEAN), resulted in tendencies to lower custom duties and partially harmonise regulations and taxation. The reduction of barriers to the circulation of capital and labour (e.g. within the EU) brought about greater mobility of financial resources and individuals. Tax regimes have become an important factor in the (re)location decisions of businesses and individuals alike. Although economic actors typically make long-term irreversible investments in the respective local communities, an argument originally put forward by Tiebout (1956) holds that individuals may relocate from one jurisdiction to another depending on the relative advantages that include fiscal administration and the provision of public services.

In the contemporary global context, many fiscal administrations in the world experience an increased tendency towards diverse forms of tax avoidance and tax evasion. Tax *avoidance* refers to mechanisms through which taxpayers can legally bypass tax obligations (e.g. when the tax code provides the deduction of charitable donations from taxable income). Tax *evasion* consists of the outright concealing of economic conditions or events from tax authorities (e.g. undeclared income or unregistered transactions). In an effort to attract corporate income (especially of multinational corporations, MNCs) and personal wealth (especially of the most affluent individuals), some countries (popularly known as 'tax havens') provide generous tax legislation that essentially 'erode' the tax base of other countries where the economic activity is carried out. Various efforts are under way to coordinate actions to contrast the 'base erosion and profit shifting' (BEPS) tendencies (Crivelli et al., 2015).

Another feature of the contemporary context of many governments is the ageing population, which poses issues of the sustainability of existing social security systems. In many countries of the world, the system of social security was long administered according to *defined benefit* plans, according to which employees receive retirement benefits (pensions) that are commensurate with the economic conditions when they give up work (e.g. salary, seniority, etc.). The financial sustainability of such schemes depends on the next generations of workers to contribute to fulfil pension obligations towards previous generations of workers (in a kind of 'pyramid scheme' where additional workers are needed to fund an ever-expanding pension system, especially as life expectancy increases). In part, the fiscal sustainability of social security systems is attained through an increase in workers' contributions. In part, many of the existing social security systems in the world have been partially corrected with the introduction of *defined contribution* plans, according to which employees receive retirement benefits that arise from the return on investment of the contributions made during their working life (Orenstein, 2013). In part, it has been argued that inflows of immigrants are beneficial to countries with ageing populations in order to help to pay the pension bill (Sand and Razin, 2006).

Special kinds of issues arise in the fiscal management of developing countries. Developing countries often lack the administrative capacity to carry out the revenue function of the government. Administering tax revenue, in particular, requires installing various institutional and organisational arrangements, which include, *inter alia*, a tax culture, separation of functions between revenue and spending, robust auditing, a skilled tax workforce, enforcement tools and adequate IT systems. The characteristics of 'weak states', where institutions fail to support the production of public goods (Jackson and Rosberg, 1982; Migdal, 1988), include a lack of capacity to determine the tax base, to collect tax revenue and to shield public finances from corruption and misappropriation of public monies. Developing countries may also exhibit a skewed distribution of income and wealth to the advantage of a small elite, which can often resist any substantive reform of the finances of the state.

Some developing countries as well as more advanced economies, moreover, face the issue of rebalancing the structure of public sector revenue sources, especially if at present they are over-reliant on natural resources. Countries such as Saudi Arabia, Oman, Libya and Kuwait raise more than 80% of public sector revenue from oil resources (Crivelli and Gupta, 2014). Because of various tendencies and conditions, which include the pressure to adopt 'greener' technologies and the presumed attainment of 'peak oil' (Bardi, 2009), these countries are expected to reorient their revenue sources away from the exploitation of natural resources in the next decades. Saudi Arabia, for example, has taken some steps to diversify the national economy away from oil extraction and refinery (Al-Darwish et al., 2015). Efforts to reconfigure public sector revenue sources, however, may harm the interests of those parts of the society that have secured privileged or safe positions within the economy of 'rentier states' (Beblawi and Luciani, 2015; Chaudhry, 1994).

Conclusions

This chapter discussed the principles, types and effects of taxation. The formulation of tax policy is oriented by the identification of criteria of 'good taxation', which especially pay attention to issues of fairness, transparency and efficiency. In addition, the formulation of tax policy should take into account that different types of taxes exist (the fundamental distinction being between direct and indirect forms of taxation), and that they have different repercussions in terms of allocation of the burden of taxation, ease of collection and behavioural effects. Over time, there has been in major economies a tendency towards an increased role for some taxes – especially personal income tax and VAT – rather than others – like excises and custom duties. Most practical forms of taxation, however, have a distortionary effect, at the individual, industrial and macroeconomic levels.

Questions for discussion

- Which types of taxes fare better with respect to the criteria of horizontal and vertical equity?
- Which kind of tax mechanism could help to implement the principle of benefit taxation?
- What are the advantages and disadvantages of direct and indirect taxation for the tax authorities?
- How has the structure of tax revenue sources changed over time in a country of your choice?
- Why are poll taxes unpopular?
- Why should countries implement taxes on the rental value of land?

3   The design of tax systems

Optimal tax theory

Optimal tax theory is an area of inquiry within the field of economics that is concerned with the design of tax systems that maximise a social welfare function. The issue is posed in terms of a social planner that takes the wellness of individuals under consideration (in the analytic form of utility functions) when choosing which taxes should be levied and at what rates. The analysis can be posed in different terms, for example depending on whether individuals are assumed to hold homogeneous conditions and preferences and whether the social planner considers some allocations of economic benefits (e.g. a more equitable distribution of income and wealth) more desirable than others. In general, optimal tax theory aims to find solutions to the issue of designing a tax system that fulfils Pareto efficiency criteria (that is, equilibria where no one's utility can be improved without decreasing the utility of someone else) (Sandmo, 1976).

One of the early efforts to solve the optimal tax problem originated from the work of Ramsey (1927), who focused on the taxation of commodities. Drawing on the analysis of the role of price elasticity of demand in the loss of consumer surplus (the incidence of taxation that was discussed in the previous chapter), Ramsey (1927) argued that commodities should be taxed at an inverse proportion to their price elasticity of demand; that is, commodities with more inelastic demand should be taxed more than those with less elastic demand. The result, however, is of limited practical implementation because it does not address the variety of economic conditions and events that can be subjected to taxation and it does not take into account heterogeneity across taxpayers. Moreover, Diamond and Mirrlees (1971) argued that intermediate goods should not be taxed, and Atkinson and Stiglitz (1976) held that optimal taxes are equal across all final consumption goods (that is, all goods that are sold to consumers as final products).

A more recent contribution to the design of tax systems originated from the work of Mirrlees (1971), who suggested that the social planner can observe certain features of taxpayers (e.g. their income) as a proxy of their capacity to contribute to the production of public goods. Mirrlees (1971) also introduced the role of diminishing marginal utility of consumption and of incentive effects of taxation. Diminishing marginal utility of consumption is important because the benefit loss for taxes for an individual with a high level of income is less than the benefit gain for consumption of public goods for an individual with a low level of income. The incentive effects of taxation refers to how taxes stimulate a change of choices by individuals about the allocation of their time and income. High-income individuals may be discouraged to earn more income, if the marginal tax rate is excessive; it would be better for the social planner to let entrepreneurial and work efforts flourish and to enlarge the tax base rather than to squeeze high tax rates from fewer sources.

One of the controversial aspects of optimal tax theory is the determination of the marginal tax rate for the highest income individuals (i.e. the tax rate that is applied to the very top income bracket). The work of Diamond and Mirrlees (1971) delivered the counterintuitive result that the top marginal income tax rate for the highest earning individual should be equal to zero. This result seems to contradict the general principles of fairness and redistributive concerns. Successive works by Tuomala (1990) found that, indeed, relatively low marginal rates on high-income earners result in incentive effects that compensate for the redistributive consequences of levying high taxes on the top income earners. Other scholars, however, came to different conclusions. Saez (2001), for example, argued that marginal rates should increase for mid- and high-income earners. Differences in results originate from different assumptions about the distribution of abilities to earn income and on the use of proxies (e.g. income or wages) for measuring such abilities (Mankiw et al., 2009). The results of the analysis also depend on heterogeneity of taxpayers, shape of their utility functions and their elasticities of tax income with respect to tax rates.

Another controversial result of optimal tax theory is that individuals should be taxed differently according to personal characteristics that signal their ability to earn. The argument goes that the earning of income, as an economic condition of being a taxpayer, provides a partial approximation only of how much individuals could be taxed with minimal distortionary effect on the economy. Mirrlees (1971) noticed that intellectual quotient, degrees, address, age and colour of skin could be used as indicators of individuals' abilities. Akerlof (1978) argued that individuals could be 'tagged' in relation to various social and physical characteristics. Along this line of reasoning, Mankiw and Weinzierl (2010) showed that individuals who are taller than others should pay more taxes on the same level of income. Although tax systems may actually 'tag' individuals and families for providing deductions and exemptions (e.g. child allowances or tax deductions based on age), tailoring taxation on the basis of innate features such as skin colour or height seems incompatible with the general principles of fairness.

Progressive and flat income tax

Most countries adopt a progressive income tax scheme, where increased tax rates are levied for amounts of income that exceed certain thresholds (tax brackets). For example, in the UK income is taxed (at the time of writing) at 20% (for income above £11,000), 40% (for income above £43,000) and 45% (for income above £150,000). In the US there are seven different tax rates (from 10% up to 39.6%). In Germany income is taxed at 14% (for income above €8,652), 42% (for income above €53,666) and 45% (for income above €254,447). In France income is taxed at 14% (for income above €9,701), 30% (for income above €26,792), 41% (for income above €71,827) and 45% (for income above €151,108). In Italy, income is taxed at 23% (for income up to €15,000), 27% (for income above €15,000), 38% (for income above €28,000), 41% (for income above €55,000) and 43% (for income above €75,000).

Figure 3.1 shows the profile of income tax rates (up to €100,000 only) in the main European economies, namely Germany, the UK, France and Italy. Nominal tax rates provide an approximation only of the actual tax burden because the calculation of income tax may be affected by various deductions and exemptions (e.g. child allowances, health expenditures, and a 'no tax area' for low-income earners in Italy, which provides deductions to nominal income tax). In Germany, a solidarity surcharge (of 5.5% at the time of writing) has been added to taxes since 1991. In addition, country legislation may provide special arrangements for married couples. Nominal tax rates, however, are illustrative of the tendency to increase marginal

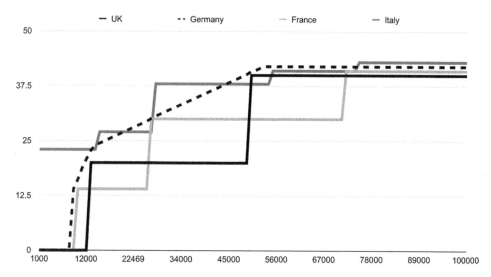

Figure 3.1 Income tax nominal rates structure in the UK, Germany, France and Italy, up to €100,000 taxable income.

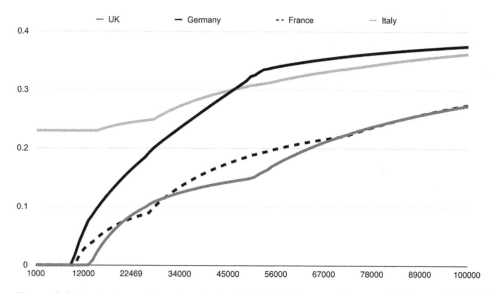

Figure 3.2 Average income tax rates structure in the UK, Germany, France and Italy, up to €100,000 taxable income.

taxation as income increases. The four countries also differ in terms of tax policies, which is evident in Figure 3.2 that shows the average income tax rates structures.

Some countries in the world, instead, have pursued the policy of a flat (constant) personal income tax rate. Flat income tax consists of a design scheme where income is taxed at the same rate irrespective of the amount of income that taxpayers earn (Hall and Rabushka, 1983). Flat income taxes are not very common in the world. Early movers in this direction in the modern age were the Baltic countries, which still have (at the time of writing) flat income taxes of 23% (Latvia), 20% (Estonia) and 15% (Lithuania). Since 2001, a flat income tax of 13% has been applied in Russia. Other Eastern European countries have also followed the flat income tax policy, for example in Romania (16%) and Bulgaria (10%). A flat income tax policy is also implemented in many small and island nations, for reasons that include ease of tax administration, the aim to stimulate the private sector of the economy and the relatively modest size of public services supply.

Although the decision to levy a flat income tax may originate from particular historical and political circumstances, flat taxation of income also builds on theoretical arguments. Mirrlees (1971: 206), for example, noticed that 'Perhaps the most striking feature of the results is the closeness to linearity of the tax schedules.' The argument for a flat income tax is supported by the lack of knowledge of the actual features of the distribution of abilities among taxpayers (Mankiw et al., 2009). The optimality of flat income taxes, however, has been challenged by various scholarly works. For example, Tsujiyama and Heathcote (2014) argued that replacing the present progressive US income tax system with a flat tax would reduce welfare.

The optimal taxation of capital

Optimal tax theory also holds that capital should not be taxed. One reason for this argument, as described in Diamond and Mirrlees (1971), is that capital in the form of physical assets is an intermediary good and, as such, should not be taxed; only final goods should be. Another reason is that capital goods serve future production and, therefore, taxes will be charged on future goods (their production, trade and consumption). If present capital goods are taxed, this would be in addition to taxation charged in the future (Atkinson and Stiglitz, 1976). Similar conclusions about the optimality of long-run zero tax rate on capital are provided in Chamley (1986) and Judd (1985).

The argument that the optimal taxation of capital should be at zero rate has been challenged by various works. Piketty and Saez (2012), for example, observe that such a policy would result in repealing all forms of taxation on inheritance, property, corporate profit and individual capital income (which should compensate for maintaining the present state of public finances, with higher taxes on labour and consumption), and that such a radical tax policy would hardly be conceivable in any country. They notice that international tax competition (the tendency for country governments to attract capital through advantageous taxation) may stimulate the progressive reduction of capital tax rates. However, they argue that the zero rate argument for capital taxation constitutes a manifest divergence between theoretical modelling in economics and actual policy practices. In their model, they show that the optimal tax rate on inheritance should instead be as high as 50–60% or more and that capital market imperfections result in a mix between inheritance tax and lifetime capital taxation. Relatively high inheritance tax rates are not common in the world, however, with the highest rates (at the time of writing) in Japan (55%), South Korea (50%), France (45%), UK (40%) and US (40%) (Cole, 2015).

The case for a positive taxation of capital was also made in other studies. Acemoglu et al. (2011), for example, showed that long-run capital taxation is preferred by citizens when the politician in power is less patient than they are (which may be the case when politicians are interested in winning short-term elections). Straub and Werning (2014) also argued that the same assumptions from the models of Chamley (1986) and Judd (1985) could lead to conclusions where there is positive capital taxation (which arises from the anticipatory savings effect of future tax rates). The case for positive capital taxation was also made, among others, in Golosov et al. (2003) and Conesa et al. (2009). The issue, however, remains controversial. Atkeson et al. (1999) and Chari and Kehoe (1999) argued that the zero capital taxation results of Chamley (1986) hold under various conditions.

In a more recent stream of literature known as dynamic optimal tax theory, studies have paid attention to the design of tax systems as the conditions of taxpayers change over time. A condition of taxpayers that has been especially investigated is the skills that they possess, understood as the capacity to convert effort into income. Skills are observable only by the taxpayer themself (and not by the government, otherwise taxes could be set in accordance with skills) and they can change over time because of random shocks (e.g. illnesses or improved job opportunities). Within this stream, works like Kocherlakota (2005) showed that wealth taxes should not be zero for every person – although the results also deliver the argument that individuals whose skills unexpectedly decrease (for example, because of a sudden illness) should pay a wealth tax, while people whose skills unexpectedly increase (for example, because of discovering a talent for some valuable activity) should receive a wealth subsidy!

Another way of subjecting capital to taxation consists of a tax on financial transactions (financial transaction tax or FTT). The tax was advocated by some eminent economists, including John M. Keynes and James Tobin (1996). A FTT was implemented as early as 1914 in the US, when a transaction tax was levied on sales or transfers of stocks (it was then eliminated in 1966). In the contemporary age, a FTT has been under consideration in the EU and actually implemented in countries like France, Italy, Switzerland and the UK (stamp duty or stamp duty reserve tax).

Corporate taxation

The design of corporate taxation poses special issues because of the difficulty to determine the tax base, the possibility that companies make decisions to avoid taxes and the relationship between the taxation of corporate income and individual income. Auerbach et al. (2008) showed that the taxation of corporations differs according to two main dimensions, namely the location of the tax base and the type of income subjected to tax. Depending on the location of income, taxes can target where income is produced (source-based taxation), where the company or the shareholders are resident (residence-based taxation) or where income is finally consumed (destination-based taxation). Depending on the type of income, taxation can target the full return to corporate equity, the full return to capital invested and economic rents.

Auerbach et al. (2008) argued that it would be desirable to tax economic rent because otherwise there would be distortionary effects to the return to capital (marginal investments may not be undertaken depending on taxation prospects). In some countries the tax code includes a so-called allowance for corporate equity (ACE) scheme, where corporate returns within a 'normal' rate are exempt from taxation through a deduction (Devereux and Freeman, 1991). As a matter of fact, corporate tax systems in the world typically tax the return on capital, which affects the cost of capital and investment choices. How precisely corporate income is taxed, however, does vary considerably across countries. Differences include tax rates, deductible expenses including interest and rules for depreciation of assets, tax incentives and special tax regimes, for example, for foreign direct investments (FDI), start-ups and firms that operate in particular industries. Over time, many tax codes in the world have come to include a plethora of provisions for deductions, exemptions and special regimes, which have resulted in corporate tax systems that lack transparency, burden companies with red tape and induce distortions in investment and financial decisions.

Some works on economics argued that the preferred approach to corporate taxation would be a tax on cash flow (or 'flow of funds'). Such a tax system would remove the need to estimate income, would provide incentives to invest (King, 1987) and would be easier to administer because of the many simplifications (e.g. the rules for depreciation of assets) (Boadway et al., 1983). The proposal for a corporate cash flow tax never really gained the attention of policymakers – apart from a few instances of approximate implementation in Mexico and Macedonia (for a number of years) and Estonia, and partial cash flow taxation in extractive industries (e.g. in Australia) and for small–medium enterprises (SMEs; e.g. in Brazil) (Ernst & Young, 2015). The foundations and prospects for the implementation of such a form of taxation have also been subjected to criticism, for example from a legal perspective (Cui, 2015).

Cash flow taxation can be implemented in different forms, which include taxation on operational (or 'real') business activity, on real and financial activities, and on stocks and the distribution of dividends. The main instance of the implementation of a cash-flow-based system of corporate taxation can be found, at present, in Estonia, where a corporate income tax established in 2000 is levied on the distribution of dividends. The system, which originated from the need for a simpler tax system that would reduce compliance costs, resulted in a favourable environment for business. Indeed, the Estonian corporate tax system has been criticised by other countries, because the policy not to tax retained profits stimulated the establishment of conglomerates that transferred untaxed profits abroad (as loans with no or low interest). The Estonian tax system also includes relatively high payroll taxes, which discourage job creation. The Estonian tax system has been regarded as the most competitive in the world (as a whole and for corporate taxation) according to the 2015 International Tax Competitiveness Index (Pomerleau and Cole, 2015). Issues arise, however, about whether features of the Estonian tax system (a country of 1.3 million people) could be replicated in other countries with a larger system of public services.

The design of corporate taxation is also affected by considerations for the role that business activity plays in the economy. It is generally understood that a too high level of corporate taxation results in detrimental effects on income generation and growth. This argument has been popularised through the so-called 'Laffer curve' (Wanniski, 1978), which posits an inverse-U-shaped relationship between tax rates and tax revenue. The argument for the Laffer curve (Figure 3.3) builds on the acknowledgement that tax revenue would be nil if tax rates

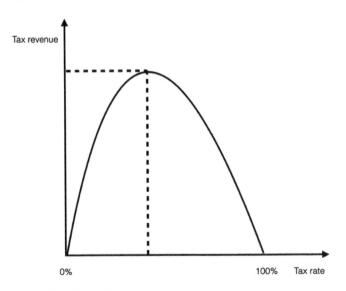

Figure 3.3 The Laffer curve.

equal zero (because no tax would be levied) and if tax rates equal 100% (because no income would be left for business and consumers). Relatively low non-zero tax rates would stimulate business activity and work but the government would collect a relatively modest tax revenue. Relatively high non-100% tax rates would discourage business activity and work and, therefore, the government would collect a relatively modest tax revenue. Finding which level of tax rates results in the highest tax revenue for the government is obscure, but the Laffer curve has been often used as evidence from supply-side economists to argue in favour of a reduction of tax rates, which could stimulate economic activity that would result in increased tax revenue – if the original tax rate before the tax cut is excessive. According to Laffer (2004), the most significant income tax cuts that took place in the history of the US (the Harding–Coolidge cuts in the mid-1920s, the Kennedy cuts in the mid-1960s and the Reagan cuts in the mid-1980s) support the argument that tax cuts result in stimuli to the growth of the economy.

Externalities and Pigouvian taxes

Tax systems can be designed in order to serve the purpose of correcting the working of market mechanisms when some goods and services have externalities effects. Externalities arise when acts of production or consumption cause an impact (costs or benefits) on others (Cornes and Sandler, 1996). Negative externalities arise, for example, from carrying out polluting production activities, because the production activity also triggers the emission of polluting substances that negatively affect other people in the economy. Positive externalities arise, for instance, from keeping bees for producing honey, because the production activity also results in having the bees pollinate crops in the surrounding area. Externalities are obtained as side effects of production or consumption activities and, as such, they are not typically considered in the choice of individuals and firms.

On many occasions, it is desirable that individuals take the externality effects of their production and consumption choices into account. The large use of antibiotics, for example, results in the negative externalities effects of making bacteria even more resistant to drugs. Extensive vaccination, instead, results in the positive externalities effects of making less people likely to carry and spread infections. Individuals, however, would not typically consider the side effects of the choices they make. Public authorities may help to coordinate individual conduct by stimulating the choices that are most advantageous for society at large (e.g. by making vaccination compulsory) or by penalising those that are disadvantageous (e.g. by charging fines if illicit pollution is detected).

Apart from systems of regulation and enforcement, taxation provides an alternative means to encourage individuals to take externalities into account. This approach, which originates from the work of Arthur Pigou (1920), consists of the introduction of taxes in order to correct market failures. With externalities, prices do not fully convey information about how much a good or service is socially desirable. Pollution, for example, is over-produced because entities that carry out polluting productions do not pay for the loss of benefit to those who suffer from pollution. If producers had to pay for the use of a clean environment, then they would 'interiorise' the externality into their production and pricing choices. Their marginal private cost of pollution would correspond to the marginal social cost of pollution.

Pigou (1920) proposed that a tax on the activity that produces negative externalities could mimic the effect of making individuals 'interiorise' the cost of externality. A tax on the production of goods that emit pollution, for example, would work as a 'wedge' that makes the good more costly for the consumers and less profitable for the producers (the extent to which the burden of the tax is split between the consumers and the producers would depend on the price elasticity of the demand and supply curves). The effect would be to induce the polluting industry to reduce output and, therefore, pollution – which is a desirable outcome for society at large.

It has been argued that Pigouvian taxes provide an additional advantage, commonly known as the '*double dividend*'. Double dividend refers to the double advantage that Pigouvian taxes enable, on the one hand, to reduce negative externalities and, on the other one, to provide a source of tax revenue that could be used, in principle, to reduce taxation in other areas of the economy. Bovenberg and van der Ploeg (1996) posit a *triple dividend* that also originates from a better environment that can induce more economic growth. In a sense, Pigouvian taxes enable the trade-off an unwelcome distortion of the economy with another one that impacts on a market where it is desirable to adjust the equilibrium that does not take the negative effects of externalities into account. The argument concerning the double dividend has been criticised from many angles, however (Fullerton and Metcalf, 1997; Goodstein, 2003; Pezzey and Park, 1998), for reasons that especially relate to distortions that Pigouvian taxes bring about to the input market, especially labour supply.

Reforming tax systems

In principle, reforms of tax systems could build on the stock of knowledge gained from theoretical works and from evidence of performance of tax systems in other countries and in the past. Reforming tax systems in practice, instead, is a complex process that is likely encumbered by multiple sources of resistance, veto points and ideological vetoes. Debates over desirable features of the tax system often centre around marginal adjustments which may just add complications to Byzantine tax codes. A critical view, in this sense, was formulated by Johnson (2014) towards UK tax policy changes during the last decade, which he considered lacking any wider coherent strategy, resulting in more complex tax rules and frequently punctuated by policy reversals.

A review of the UK tax system conducted in 2010 (Mirrlees and Adam, 2010, 2011) concluded that reforms of tax systems should look at the whole tax system, seek neutrality and implement progressive tax design principles. Attention to the whole tax system means to avoid earmarked tax revenue (i.e. tax revenue from particular sources that is spent on specific programmes or projects). Neutrality means that similar economic conditions and events should be taxed in a similar way, although it is acceptable to target specific taxation to attain desired policy goals (e.g. taxes on consumption of alcohol and tobacco). Finally, progressive taxation is desirable for redistributive purposes, although higher taxes for higher income levels inevitably distort individual decisions and discourage additional business activity and work efforts.

The Mirrlees review found that the UK tax system performed relatively poorly. The Mirrlees review called for a redesign of the overall British tax system, which would affect taxes on earnings, indirect taxes, environmental taxes, taxation of saving and wealth and business taxes. Table 3.1 shows the summary recommendations of Mirrlees and Adam (2011). The main issues with the present UK tax system are disincentives to work (because of income taxes and features of the system of benefits), lack of integration between parts of the tax system (e.g. between income tax and National Insurance contributions), savings are discouraged and various forms of savings are taxed differently, lack of a consistent system of environmental taxes (i.e. forms of taxation to discourage pollution), disincentives to invest in business and advantages to debt financing rather than equity, inefficient and inequitable taxation of land and property, and distributional goals are not clearly

Table 3.1 A comparison between the present UK tax system and a 'good' tax system according to Mirrlees and Adam (2011: 7)

Current UK tax system	Features of a 'good' tax system
Taxes on earnings	
An opaque jumble of different effective rates as a result of tapered allowances and a separate National Insurance system	A progressive income tax with a transparent and coherent rate structure
A highly complex array of benefits	A single integrated benefit for those with low income and/or high needs
A rate structure that reduces employment and earnings more than necessary	A schedule of effective tax rates that reflects evidence on behavioural responses
Indirect taxes	
A VAT with extensive zero rating, reduced rating and exemption	A largely uniform VAT
– financial services exempt; housing generally not subject to VAT but subject to a council tax not proportional to current property values	– with a small number of targeted exceptions on economic efficiency grounds – and with equivalent taxes on financial services and housing
Stamp duties on transactions of property and on securities	No transactions taxes
Additional taxes on alcohol and tobacco	Additional taxes on alcohol and tobacco
Environmental taxes	
Arbitrary and inconsistent prices on emissions from different sources, set at zero for some	Consistent price on carbon emissions
Ill-targeted tax on fuel consumption	Well-targeted tax on road congestion
Taxation of savings and wealth	
Normal return taxed on many, but not all, forms of savings	No tax on the normal return to savings
– additional but poorly designed incentives for retirement saving	– with some additional incentive for retirement saving
Income tax, National Insurance contributions and capital gains tax together imply different rates of tax on different types of income	Standard income tax schedule applied to income from all sources after an allowance for the normal rate of return on savings
– wages, profits, capital gains, etc. – some recognition of corporation tax in dividend taxation but not in capital gains tax	– with lower personal tax rates on income from company shares to reflect corporation tax already paid
An ineffective inheritance tax capturing only some assets transferred at or near death	A lifetime wealth transfer tax
Business taxes	
Corporation tax differentiated by company profits and with no allowance for equity financing costs	Single rate of corporation tax with no tax on the normal return on investment
Preferential treatment of self-employment and distributed profits	Equal treatment of income derived from employment, self-employment and running a small company
An input tax on buildings (business rates) – no land value taxes	No tax on intermediate inputs – but land value tax at least for business and agricultural land

pursued (e.g. zero and reduced VAT rates only favour individuals with particular tastes and council tax is regressive).

A call for the reform of the tax system has been also made recently by Stiglitz (2014) for the US. He commented that political barriers hamper the search and implementation of a solution to problems of extreme inequality, high unemployment and modest GDP growth, which he considered more pressing problems than the reduction of public deficit. His work called for the reform of the tax system by introducing FTTs, increasing corporate taxes (while also incentivising investments), increasing taxes on rent-seeking, reforming estate and inheritance taxes and making personal income tax more progressive.

Conclusions

This chapter discussed the design of tax systems. Economic theory – precisely in the literature on the optimal tax theory – provides a general framework for the design of taxation that takes into account the characteristics of the taxpayers and social objectives. The findings of optimal tax theory, however, are controversial as sometimes they do not really correspond to actual country experiences or they seem to contradict intuition. As a matter of fact, the design of tax systems is a contentious area where contrasting arguments are made about the advantages and disadvantages of changes to existing tax rules and regulations.

Questions for discussion

• Which prescriptions of optimal tax theory look surprising to you?
• Would it be fair to tax individuals according to characteristics that signal their ability to earn income; like, for example, skin colour and height?
• Why don't more countries adopt a flat income tax?
• How does taxation of capital (capital wealth, in both real and financial assets, and capital transactions) affect saving and investment decisions?
• How could taxes help to stimulate positive externalities; for example, regards vaccinations or education?
• Should the tax system of a country of your choice be reformed? If so, why and how?

4 Taxation and policy objectives

Taxation as a policy tool

The scholarly literature on the 'tools of government' (Salamon and Elliott, 2002; Hood, 2007) has long acknowledged the use of public monies ('treasury') as one of the main instruments at the disposal of governments to attain public policies and programmes. The availability of financial resources certainly provides an important means to carry out government operations by paying staff, purchasing supplies and making transfers (subsidies and incentives) to individuals and firms to make them perform desired actions. The varying process of acquiring financial resources, however, can be used as a policy tool in itself. Provided that most taxes introduce some distortions in the choices of individuals and in the working of the market mechanism – so the argument goes – then public authorities may deliberately seek to induce advantageous changes of behaviour while also raising public sector revenue.

The use of taxation for pursuing policy objectives can be traced back in history. Backhaus (2002) observed that efforts to enlarge the tax base and stimulate the economy were already present in Europe after the Thirty Years' War of 1618–1648. During the last centuries, taxation has been used by governments for pursuing various policy objectives. For example, custom duties (import tariffs) were employed as a protectionist measure to support domestic industries during part of the history of most developed nations like the US, Germany and Japan. Nowadays, the use of taxation especially serves policy aims such as redistributing income, stimulating economic growth and stability, promoting economic development and correcting behaviour.

Redistributing income

To only a partial extent are tax systems designed in order to raise public revenue while keeping the distortion of taxation on the economy at a minimum. Often, tax systems are also designed to serve the purpose of correcting the distribution of income (and, sometimes, wealth) in a population. The aim to redistribute resources in a population is especially sensitive for many political views (in Western countries, they typically inform part of the policy orientation of socialist, social-democratic and Christian-democratic parties). Evidence of skewed distribution of income and wealth across populations, however, resonates as an unwelcome outcome of the working of the society and the economy to many ears.

A way to assess the inequality of distribution is provided by the Gini (1909) coefficient or index. Figure 4.1 shows the estimates of the Gini index for income distribution in OECD countries (OECD, 2016b). The Gini index shows that some countries like Chile, Mexico, the US and Turkey have relatively wide differences across income earners. In other countries,

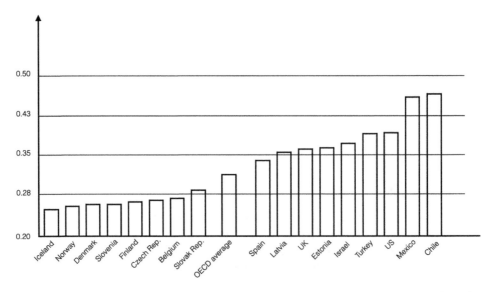

Figure 4.1 Gini index for the distribution of income across OECD countries; lowest Gini index values, highest Gini index value and OECD average.

Source: OECD, 2016b.

like Iceland, Norway, Denmark and Slovenia, income is more equally distributed. Various explanations have been offered for such a pattern, as well as for the increased inequality that has been observed in many countries over the last decades. In part, globalisation enhanced the prospects for the highly skilled workforce to earn income rather than low-skilled individuals, for reasons especially related to increased financial flows and technological change, reduced product market regulation, employment protection, tax wedge and union density, together with other reasons related to the allocation of hours of work and changed household structure (OECD, 2011b).

Some theoretical arguments hold that the appropriate design of tax systems can tackle the redistribution issue if taxation is progressive (Mirrlees, 1971). Higher income earners would pay a larger share of their income to contribute to the production of public goods. Lower income earners would pay less of a share of their income or would make no contribution at all, while they would enjoy benefits from the consumption of public goods. Low-income earners might even receive cash transfers to improve their spending capacity, although the effectiveness of cash transfer programmes has been largely questioned and debated (Farrington and Slater, 2006; Fiszbein et al., 2009; Rawlings and Rubio, 2005).

Other theoretical works, however, have cast some doubt as to whether taxes can help governments redistribute income. Feldstein and Vaillant (1994), for example, argued that individuals avoid unfavourable taxes by migrating to jurisdictions that offer more favourable tax conditions, and that market mechanisms would push gross salaries to adjust until net salaries are comparable to those found elsewhere. Progressive tax systems, in this respect, result in higher labour costs for firms or in the hiring of less skilled people. Bird and Zolt (2004) also argue that income tax does not help redistribute income in developing countries, for reasons that include the size of the shadow economy, the modest role of revenue from income taxes, corruption, poor governance and the cost of tax administration itself.

Stimulating economic growth and stabilisation

The use of taxation for stimulating economic growth and stabilisation has been subjected to various research. A plain direct effect of taxation on the economy is to subtract financial resources from the private sector with negative effects on output. If the same amount of financial resources is spent by the government in the implementation of public policies and programmes (i.e. without any budget surplus or deficit), however, public spending stimulates aggregated demand with positive effects on the economy. Taxation, however, may impact on the economy in different ways depending on what is taxed and how taxpayers adjust their choices because of taxes. Different kinds of taxes impact on the choices between work and leisure, consumption and savings, and investments in various ways. Ill-informed tax systems discourage work and entrepreneurship, with negative effects both on production and productivity. Well-designed tax systems, instead, may stimulate consumption and investment, with beneficial effects on growth prospects. In addition, counter-cyclical forms of taxation – like, for example, progressive income tax – may provide 'automatic stabilisers' that help to correct fluctuations in the business cycle.

The economic theory of endogenous growth provides analytical foundations to the role of taxation in stimulating growth (Myles, 2009). Endogenous growth theory holds that growth results from the choices that rational economic actors make. These choices include the investments that firms make in research and development (R&D) to improve productivity and to innovate. They also include the investments that individuals make in education to develop human capital and increase earnings prospects. Also, governments can contribute to growth through investments in public capital goods (e.g. infrastructure), by encouraging FDIs and by stimulating more opportunities for individuals and business. Taxes can affect these choices, for example, by making it more or less advantageous for firms to invest in R&D and for individuals to invest in education.

Additional studies argued that some kinds of taxes are more likely to stimulate growth than others. Arnold et al. (2011), for example, suggested a ranking order of taxation for growth, starting from recurrent taxes on immovable property, followed by consumption taxes and other property taxes, personal income taxes and corporate income taxes. Taxing immovable property like houses, for example, would encourage individuals to allocate their savings to more profitable investments than real estate. Other taxes on property, including financial assets, have more distortionary effects on savings and capital allocation. Consumption taxes may affect incentives to work but they should not influence the inter-temporal allocation of capital if they are not expected to change over time. Personal income taxes are more damaging to growth than the taxes mentioned above because they discourage more efforts to work and do business if they are progressive, they discourage savings because they tax the return on savings (interests and dividends) on top of taxation of income that produced the savings in the first place, and they could encourage individuals to stay on social benefits rather than working. Finally, corporate income taxes are considered to have the most detrimental effects on growth because they discourage investments (including FDI) in the business sector, which is the most important sector for growth.

Evidence partially suggests that changes in taxation systems result in increased growth. Kneller et al. (1999), for example, found that distortionary taxation reduced growth. Padovano and Galli (2001) found that higher marginal income tax rates are negatively correlated with economic growth. Fölster and Henrekson (2001) indicate that larger government size in developed countries correlates with slower growth. Easterly and Rebelo (1993) and Fu et al. (2003), however, noticed that the effect of taxation on growth is difficult to isolate from other component parts of the fiscal system. Specific country cases, like the tax reform in Ireland in the late 1980s, also suggest that the reconfiguration of taxation may result in enhanced growth prospects, although the redesign of tax systems may include diverse measures like simplified tax rules, reduced tax rates and targeted distortions in the choices of individuals and firms (e.g. deductions for R&D spending) (OECD, 2015a).

Another feature of the tax system that seems to have important repercussions on economic growth is the incidence of taxes on labour, or 'tax wedge'. Figure 4.2 shows the tax wedge as the ratio between the amount of taxes paid by a single worker without children and the corresponding total labour cost for the employer for the US, Germany, the UK, France and Italy. Higher tax wedge on labour is associated with higher unemployment in developed countries, while there is no clear relationship in developing economies where the social safety net is smaller (IMF, 2014). Targeted reductions of the tax wedge could be also used to stimulate work participation of particular social groups like women or youth.

Another aim that taxation can help to attain is the stabilisation of the economy. Economies are subjected to cyclical fluctuations around long-term trends. In the long term, economies experience many fluctuations (known as Kondratiev waves) (Kondratiev, 1925), that originate from technological innovations, demographic adjustments, speculative bubbles especially on land, and debt deflation. In the short term, economies experience fluctuations or *business cycles* (Burns and Mitchell, 1946) which have been explained in many ways (e.g. as originating from technological change, demand shocks, credit cycles, political turnover, misallocation of investments or breakdowns in capital accumulation). Features of the tax system may either contribute to amplifying the fluctuations of the economy or contain the oscillations. Listokin (2012), for example, held that most present tax expenditures (i.e. tax deductions) are procyclical because they favour forms of spending that are more likely to happen in favourable

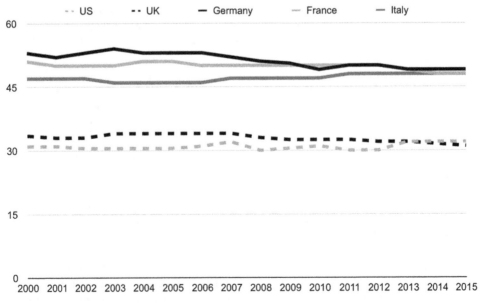

Figure 4.2 Incidence of the tax wedge in the US, Germany, the UK, France and Italy.

Source: https://data.oecd.org/tax/tax-wedge.htm

conditions, like donations to charities or purchases of houses. De Mooij et al. (2013) argued that the preferential treatment that most of the present tax codes give to debt versus equity financing (i.e. deducibility of interest) stimulates more bank leverage and results in greater chances of financial crisis.

Promoting economic development

Public financial management, and especially public sector revenue, has long been considered to play an important role in economic development (Kaldor, 1963, 1965). At present, however, most developing countries have a relatively modest capacity to levy taxes – typically less than 10% of GDP – with respect to industrialised economies (Besley and Persson, 2013). In comparison to poor countries, rich countries collect a much larger share of their income; they rely much more on income taxes rather than consumption taxes, and they typically levy taxes on a much larger tax base. Poor countries, instead, seem to lack the capacity to identify tax bases, to enforce the tax code and to collect the financial resources that would be needed to improve the delivery of public services. Yet, the improvement of tax administration is often regarded as an important means to promote economic development (Corbacho et al., 2013).

The main issues in tax revenue that developing countries face include corruption and the poor administrative capacity of tax bureaus. The administration of taxation requires the coordination of various factors, which include the selection of a skilled and motivated workforce, the provision of clear procedural rules and regulations, a system of checks and auditing, an accurate registry of properties and mechanisms for the identification of tax bases, and adequate IT systems. Conditions in developing countries may not fulfil these requirements, for reasons that include unattractive salaries for public officers, lack of investment in databases and IT infrastructure, collusion between political and business interests, and the relative importance of informal norms with respect to formal rules.

The presence of informal norms of conduct alongside formal rules, in particular, has often been considered a typical trait of so-called *neo-patrimonial* regimes. Neo-patrimonialism refers to the joint occurrence of two Weberian ideal types of control – a patrimonial rule (which originates from tradition) and a rational-legal rule (Eisenstadt, 1973; Von Soest et al., 2011; Zolberg, 1966). On the one hand, the patrimonial rule component entails that social relationships between patrons and clients are based on an exchange of gifts and protection for loyalty. On the other hand, the rational-legal rule component requires that individuals comply with formal procedures for maintaining the legitimacy of their social status and actions within contemporary systems of public institutions. The combined effects of these components result in some tolerance for practices that undermine tax administrative capacity; such as, for example, the appointment of unqualified tax officers and the interference of patrons in day-to-day operations.

One main area of taxation where developing countries lack capacity is the agriculture sector. Agriculture plays a vital role in many developing countries, both for supporting the material conditions of living for billions of people and for the contribution to GDP. The taxation of agriculture is considered, in principle, relatively easy to attain (Keen, 2013), especially when agriculture is carried out in large farms and plantation enterprises (Rajaraman, 2005). However, often agriculture is hard to tax because of the political clout that the elite provide to the sector. Political leaders, for example, can distribute favourable treatment of agriculture to selected intermediaries that help them to exert control over the countryside (Kasara, 2007).

Several works have contributed to clarifying the limits of tax systems in developing countries and indicating ways to overcome them (Bird and de Jantscher, 1992). Some highlighted the role of the large informal sector of the economy, of the relatively small size of many firms and the modest development of the financial sector in preventing the tax administration to enlarge the tax base and detect unreported tax conditions and events (Tanzi, 1987, 1992). Others showed that political institutions play an important role in tax revenue (Ricciuti et al., 2016), especially when political instability (such as, for example, the inability to control the territory) results in the poor capacity to collect taxes (Acemoglu, 2005) and when institutions originate from particular historical occurrences (Besley and Persson, 2009). Additional works took a historical perspective and looked also at the origins of the tax administrative capacity in today's industrialised countries (Dincecco, 2011, 2015; Dincecco et al., 2011).

Various efforts have been made to reform the tax systems of many countries over time. Since the 1970s, for example, several economies in the world adopted the VAT system that had been originally implemented in Europe and a few other countries. Arguments in favour of the VAT system included the possibility to effectively collect taxes on consumption and to tackle the evasion of income tax (especially because of the requirements to record invoices and the possibility to cross-check self-assessment reports). When adopting a VAT system, countries should also be attentive to avoiding the introduction of too many exemptions (e.g. for the agriculture sector or for small businesses) because they can hamper the overall effectiveness of the VAT system (Le, 2003).

A more recent instance of reform of the tax system in some developing countries consists of the creation of independent revenue authorities (IRAs). The establishment of IRAs originates from the aim to shield the tax system from the interference of politicians. Several experiences with IRAs have been carried out in the world since the 1980s (Ghana) and the 1990s (Peru, Uganda, Zambia, Kenya and Tanzania), where some evidence of improved tax efficiency and collection was gathered (Gupta and Abed, 2002). Recent research, however, casts some doubt over the effectiveness of IRAs by themselves and recommended that IRAs should be accompanied by strong political commitment and a more comprehensive modernisation of the tax system (Crandall, 2010).

The efforts to improve systems of taxation in developing countries may also build on technological innovations. In 2016, for example, Bitland Global (a NGO based in Kumana, Ghana) started offering real estate land registration services in an effort to provide records of land and real estate ownership documents and other deeds. The records of Bitland Global are stored through blockchain technology, which promises to keep data safe and impossible to falsify. For countries where most land and real estate is contested because of a lack of accurate records, such kinds of innovations promise to help enforce property and other rights. In addition, such developments may have important implications for tax administration, especially for the possibility to establish a permanent and validated registry (or cadastre).

Correcting behaviour

The distortionary effects of taxation can be used to deliberately discourage unwelcome behaviour ('sin taxes') or stimulate desired conduct. One main area of use of taxes for correcting behaviour is the environment, where 'green taxes' or 'ecotaxes' have been used in many countries of the world since 1980s. Taxes supplement other tools of environmental policy, such as regulation, by making individuals and firms internalise the cost of negative externalities that arise from polluting activities (Bovenberg and de Mooij, 1994). Apart from raising revenue, then, environmental taxes can help with reducing pollution, funding environmental monitoring and control, and reorienting the tax system to the principle of taxing the consumption of natural resources.

Environmental taxes come in many forms. In terms of the field of application, a distinction is often drawn between taxes on energy consumption, taxes on transport and taxes on pollution and non-energy natural resources. Instances of environmental taxes also include the 'feebate' (a portmanteau of 'fee' and 'rebate') where consumers of a polluting good (such as high-emission cars) pay a charge that is then passed, as a subsidy, to consumers who purchase a more environmentally friendly good (such as low-emission cars). In the EU, on average, environmental taxes amount to about 6% of total public sector revenue from taxes and social contributions (Eurostat, 2016).

Another area where taxes have been used to correct behaviour, especially since the 1980s, is the consumption of alcohol (although, for example, taxes to contain the drinking of spirits, especially gin, have been in place in the UK since the eighteenth century). Excessive drinking of spirits, wine and beer can have detrimental effects on personal and family lives, violence, work performance and income. Apart from various campaigns and policy measures to discourage consumption, levying taxes on alcoholic drinks is an effective way to influence consumer behaviour. Taxes on alcoholic can take different forms. In the UK, for example, alcoholic drinks are subjected to VAT (at the time of writing, 20%) and to excise duty (which varies depending on alcohol content and volume). Excise duties vary considerably across countries. In the EU, for example, excises are considerably higher in the UK, Ireland, Finland and Sweden with respect to other member states (London Economics, 2010).

Evidence suggests that alcohol taxes are effective to influence consumption. In a study on the UK market, Sousa (2014) showed that price elasticities of various alcoholic drinks are negative and significant (with spirits at public premises and beer and cider in shops being the most price-sensitive segments of the demand). In a review of fifty articles and 340 estimates, Wagenaar et al. (2010) found that alcohol taxation inversely correlates with alcohol-related diseases, injury outcomes, violence, traffic crash outcomes, sexually transmitted diseases, other drug use, crime and other misbehaviours in a significant way (also with suicide, but not in a statistically significant way). Carragher and Chalmers (2011), however, recommend that alcohol taxes should be combined with other policy measures, like, for example, bans on promotions and discounts, and minimum prices set.

A similar approach has been followed in the taxation of tobacco, whose consumption is estimated to kill about six million people each year (WHO, 2015). Taxation of tobacco provides a more cost-effective approach to discourage smoking than various other policy initiatives such as bans on smoking in public places and advertisements. The World Health Organization estimates that a 10% increase in the price of a pack of cigarettes is expected to reduce demand by about 4% in high-income countries and 5% in middle- and low-income countries (www.who.int/tobacco/economics/taxation/en/). Also, taxes on tobacco can take different forms. In the UK, for example, taxes on tobacco products comprise VAT and a tobacco duty (e.g. at the time of writing, for cigarettes the duty equals 16.5% of the retail price plus £3.93 on a packet of twenty).

Empirical studies provide various evidence that tobacco taxes help to reduce consumption. Chaloupka et al. (2012), for example, reviewed over 100 studies and concluded that tobacco excise taxes are a powerful tool for reducing tobacco use (for both stopping consumption and decreasing recurrent purchases) while at the same time providing a reliable source of government revenues. Other studies, however, are less conclusive. Callison and Kaestner (2014), for example, argued that the effects of tobacco taxes increases are relatively modest and that a very large tax rise (of the order of 100%) would be needed to decrease consumption by 5%. It seems, moreover, that tobacco taxes are regressive because they impact more on the income of the poor than of the rich (Gospodinov and Irvine, 2009).

More recently, 'sin taxes' also came to include forms of taxation of sugar-sweetened beverages ('soda taxes' or 'fat taxes'). Taxes on soda aim to encourage individuals to reduce the consumption of drinks that have been related to obesity, which has emerged as a main source of concern for public health in recent decades. Most of the additional calories that Americans consume nowadays, for example, originate from sugar-sweetened drinks (Ghosh and Hall, 2015). A soda tax (Soft Drinks Industry Levy) was introduced in the UK in 2016. It was designed in such a way that the tax depends on the amount of added sugar in drinks (while it does not tax natural sugars such as those found in pure fruit drinks); therefore, producers may avoid the tax if they reformulate their products by adding less sugar. There is not any nation-wide soda tax in the US yet (at the time of writing), although some city administrations have started levying it (e.g. Philadelphia in 2017).

Taxes on soda are believed to help reduce consumption (Brownell et al., 2009). Andreyeva et al. (2011), for example, estimate that soda taxes of one-penny-per-ounce of added sugar beverage tax could induce a reduction of consumption of 24% in the US. Some works, like Fletcher et al. (2010), however, suggest that a reduction of soda drink consumption may be offset by the increase of consumption of other high-calorie drinks. Also, Edwards (2011) warns that taxes on sugar beverages may induce consumers to shift attention to relatively cheaper calories, with unclear net effects on the fight against obesity. Similarly to soda, 'junk food' has also been subjected to forms of taxation in some countries (e.g. in Denmark, Japan and India).

On some occasions, taxes have also been considered to promote desired behaviour rather than discourage unwelcome behaviour. Sometimes, the use of taxes as incentives is implemented in the form of 'tax expenditures' (e.g. 'tax credits' granted to taxpayers provided that they fulfil certain conditions); that is, deductions to the tax base. The government gives up some tax revenue in order to encourage individuals and firms to carry out desired actions, such as, for example, donations to charities, participation in child-care programmes or children's sport activities, or volunteer coaching. Other forms of tax credits include, for example, the Investment Tax Credit (ITC) that individual taxpayers enjoy in the US for investments in solar power systems.

Conclusions

This chapter discussed the use of taxation for attaining policy objectives. Although the main purpose of taxation is to raise revenue for the public sector, the distortions that taxes provoke on the behaviour of individuals and firms can be exploited to make them undertake desirable actions. Levying a tax on consumption or investment can affect choice because rational actors pursue better value-for-money (or return-on-investment) decisions. In addition, decisions can be influenced by the way decision scenarios are framed and by decision-making biases. Insights from behavioural economics, for example, suggest that loss-aversion induces individuals to be more sensitive to losses than to equal amount of gains, and that individuals may internalise taxes as 'reference points' so that they are more sensitive to changes of tax rates rather than to the tax rates by themselves. Additional research is needed in order to better understand how the design of tax systems can help to correct behaviour.

Questions for discussion

- How effective is taxation for the redistribution of income and wealth?
- How can taxation increase economic growth?
- Which kind of taxation enhances the stabilisation of the economy?
- Can taxes make the economy more unstable?
- How can taxation stimulate economic development?
- What kind of unwelcome behaviour can be corrected through taxes?

5   Sub-national taxation and fiscal federalism

Fiscal decentralisation

The institutional structure of many countries in the world is arranged across multiple levels of government. In multi-layer governance systems (Hooghe and Marks, 2003), central government carries out only a part (although it could be a major one) of the functions and activities of a country's public sector, which are – to some extent – also performed by sub-national (or, occasionally, by super-national) governments. The distribution of public functions and activities across government levels poses special issues about the management of financial resources. Central government administration may retain all (or most) of the public revenue and spending functions, or it may decentralise them, in part at least, to other public authorities at different governance levels.

At one extreme, a country government retains all public revenue and spending functions. At the other extreme, sub-national governments are entitled to raise their own public revenue and decide upon public spending in their respective jurisdictions. In between these extremes, central governments and sub-national governments share public revenue and spending in various ways. For example, central governments and sub-national governments may share revenue from the same source (e.g. by sharing revenue from personal income tax or from the extraction of natural resources) or they may levy specific taxes (e.g. hotel taxes for municipalities). Also, in terms of spending, central governments may retain their decision-making power on spending in some policy domains and programmes, while sub-national governments may have exclusive competences on spending in other areas of the public sector.

Countries differ in the extent to which public sector revenue is centralised at central government level. Figure 5.1 shows the share of central government revenue with respect to the total revenue of the public sector in some major economies, namely the US, Germany, the UK, France and Italy. The UK has a relatively centralised system of revenue generation, with more than 90% of revenue raised by the central government. Relatively high centralisation is also present in France and Italy, although reforms carried out in the last decade of the twentieth century partially decentralised public revenue generation at the sub-national level. Relatively more decentralised arrangements for revenue generation are present in Germany and the US.

Fiscal decentralisation takes place for various reasons. When public finances are managed at the local level, policymakers can pay more attention to local needs. On the public spending side, sub-national governments may attend to specific policy issues that matter for local populations and direct financial resources to local public policies and programmes. On the revenue side, sub-national public authorities may pursue various forms of revenue generation, including some possibility to adjust tax rates to local circumstances. Another main argument

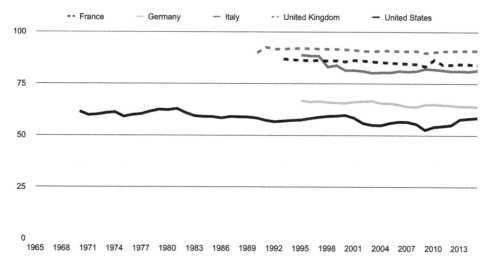

Figure 5.1 Share (%) of central government revenue with respect to total public sector revenue.

Source: OECD Fiscal Decentralisation Database, www.oecd.org/ctp/federalism/oecdfiscaldecentralisationdatabase.htm

in favour of fiscal decentralisation is the possibility to hold public officers (elected, appointed and career officers) more accountable to the public, especially because of the more tangible evidence of the quality of public services that taxpayers pay for. A related argument is that the public – either individual citizens or civil society organisations – may be more interested in following the financial management of public sector operations at the local level than at the national one, for reasons also related to the stakes that they have in local taxation and public services and the minor complexity of public financial management at the local level.

Additional reasons for fiscal decentralisation also include the possibility that public financial management at the local level may be more cost-efficient and effective than at the national level. In part, this argument builds on the assumption that the operational efficiency and effectiveness of bureaucracy may be higher on a smaller scale of operation. For example, a local administration of unemployment benefit and services (e.g. active labour market policies) could better target the needs of individuals in a flexible way than a relatively large bureaucracy which is burdened by cumbersome procedural rules and which pays less attention to personal circumstances. The argument, however, is challenged by consideration of the advantages that arise from pooling together administrative functions, especially in terms of cost-saving from economies of scale.

Another part of the argument for the cost-efficiency and effectiveness of fiscal decentralisation relates to Tiebout's (1956) theory of local expenditures, which holds that taxpayers can relocate to other jurisdictions where they receive better net benefits from taxation and public services. This argument has been criticised on the basis of the relative immobility of individuals, who typically invest in local assets and social relationships (like relatives, workplace, schools, neighbours, etc.). Some evidence, however, suggests that, indeed, individuals take taxation and quality of public services into consideration when making (re)location decisions (John et al., 1995). Others notice that empirical tests are made difficult because of the composite nature of the public services that are provided by local jurisdictions (Dowding and Mergoupis, 2003).

Fiscal decentralisation also poses some issues. When each sub-national government adopts different revenue policies (and, relatedly, possibly also different patterns of public spending), the cohesiveness of the state may be undermined. Taxpayers are subjected to different forms and levels of taxation, and citizens receive different levels and quality of public services, with the effect of threatening the unity of a country. Another issue arises from the possibility that fiscal decentralisation serves the shifting away of fiscal responsibilities from the central government to sub-national governments. The transfer of policy functions to sub-national government levels (also called 'devolution'), for example, enables central governments to avoid tackling policy issues that are controversial, unpopular or financially challenging.

Finally, it should be mentioned that the EU stands as a unique case of partial super-national fiscal centralisation. The EU raises own revenues from three main sources, namely transfers from member states (a percentage of GDP) (about 69.9% of total revenue), a share of VAT collected in each member state (about 12.3%), and most of the custom duties on imports into the EU (a small share is retained by the member states where goods arrive from outside the EU) and other revenue sources. The EU budget is spent on the common agricultural policy, common fisheries policy, rural development and environmental measures (about 42.5%), cohesion programmes (35.6%), measures for growth and employment (9%), administration (5.8%) and various other policies including foreign policy, justice, border protection, immigration, public health, consumer protection and youth. The partial super-national fiscal centralisation in the EU poses special issues, particularly in relation to the fairness of member states' contributions to the EU budget and the implementation of solidarity principles across the union.

The politics of fiscal federalism

The term 'fiscal federalism' refers to the institutional, organisational and financial arrangements where public sector financial resources are managed across different levels of government. Fiscal federalism arises when the management of public finances of a country are at least partially decentralised to the sub-national level (Oates, 1972, 1999). In addition, fiscal federalism is intertwined with arrangements of political decentralisation, where central governments partially share political functions and policy-making powers with sub-national governments. Countries differ in the extent to which powers are shared across layers of political power. Some countries, like the UK, France, China and Japan, are *unitary* in the sense that the central government is supreme and sub-national administrations may only carry out functions that are delegated from the central government authority. Other countries, like the US, India, Brazil and Germany, are *federal* in the sense that they are formed through the union of partially self-governing states, which can carry out proper functions although they may agree to have them pooled at the union level.

Studies on fiscal federalism often build on the assumption that both central governments and sub-national governments seek to maximise the social welfare of their respective constituencies (Oates, 2005). A consequence of this assumption is that the production of public goods at the sub-national level may differ from the one that central governments would make because of the particular conditions of specific sub-national jurisdictions with respect to the overall national one. In principle, each sub-national jurisdiction could produce the precise amount of public goods that are demanded by the specific population (a 'perfect mapping' or 'fiscal equivalence'; Olson, 1969). In practice, each public good may be demanded by a different population of consumers and several sub-national government jurisdictions would be needed to match taxpayers with consumers. In addition, public goods may have externalities effects on other jurisdictions. The problem of designing the geographical boundaries of sub-national jurisdictions and of determining how many layers of sub-national governments are desirable cannot be easily solved.

The most recent stream of studies on fiscal federalism (also known as 'second-generation theory'; Oates, 2005) highlights that actors (both public officers and voters alike) make fiscal decisions in order to maximise their own objective functions (e.g. probability of being re-elected or net benefits from public spending and taxation) rather than any social welfare function. Decisions, moreover, are taken in a context that includes a role for political institutions because they provide procedural rules, constraints and incentives for the choices of individuals (Weingast, 2009), and a role for information that agents possess. Under the conditions of imperfect and asymmetric information, the degree of fiscal decentralisation affects accountability on the one hand and the capacity to coordinate policies (because of internalising inter-jurisdictional interdependencies) on the other one (Besley and Coate, 2003).

Fiscal federalism poses both horizontal and vertical issues. Horizontal issues arise from imbalances between sub-national jurisdictions. One region, for example, may be richer than another one because of greater local economic activity. If public financial management is decentralised, the government of the rich region may raise relatively higher amounts of revenue and afford more public spending than the one of the poor region. Such a scenario may stimulate political tensions between the regions, and between the regions and the central government, because of the contradiction to principles of solidarity that should bind together citizens of the same nation. If public financial management is centralised, revenue that is raised in the rich region may be pooled together with others in the national budget, whose public policies and programmes may include more generous public spending in the poor regions than in the rich ones. Such a scenario may result in improved equity because of the transfer of financial resources from the rich to the poor region, although the rich region may resist contributing largely to the national budget if they perceive to receive little in return, in terms of public spending and services.

Another aspect of horizontal issues in fiscal federalism relates to the competition between sub-national governments to attract more tax base. If public financial management is decentralised, the government of a region may adopt advantageous forms of taxation (e.g. by setting relatively low tax rates) in order to induce individuals and firms to relocate from other regions where tax conditions are more adverse. A mechanism of *tax competition* could stimulate sub-national governments to make more effective and cost-efficient use of public revenue, although initial conditions (i.e. an original endowment of a large tax base) could favour rich regions because they can undertake more advantageous tax policies with relatively minor negative effects on their budget compared to poor regions. Horizontal issues may be tackled through mechanisms of 'equalisation transfers', where the central government orchestrates a system of financial compensations from the rich to the poor regions.

Vertical issues in fiscal federalism arise, first, in relation to *vertical fiscal imbalance*, which refers to a mismatch in the revenue powers and public spending responsibilities across levels of government. If a sub-national government has less power to raise revenue than responsibility for spending, then its capacity to spend on the implementation of public policies and programmes depends on transfers from the central government. In such a scenario, Eyraud and Lusinyan (2011) found that sub-national governments tend to increase their financial deficit. They recommend that the allocation of revenue powers and spending responsibility is rebalanced at the sub-national level.

Another vertical issue in fiscal federalism arises from the asymmetry of revenue generation power between the central government and the sub-national governments, or *vertical*

fiscal gap. The scholarly literature offered no conclusive argument about the optimal allocation of fiscal powers across levels of government. The attribution of more revenue powers to
the central government may be justified because of the spending on public goods that serve all
citizens and the pursuit of redistributive policies across the whole country. The distribution
of more revenue powers to sub-national governments may be explained because of greater
fiscal accountability and better targeted policy measures. The issue is also complicated by the
fact that the central government and the sub-national governments can make tax decisions
independently without taking into consideration externalities effects. For example, tax decisions made in one sub-national government may affect the tax base for both the central
government and other sub-national governments (Boadway and Keen, 1996).

The allocation of tax powers to sub-national governments changes over time. In the UK,
for example, the tax powers of Scotland have gradually increased during recent years. In the
Scotland Act 2012, Scottish Ministers were given powers to administer devolved taxes to
replace the UK Stamp Duty Land and Landfill Tax. For the first time since about three centuries ago, on 1st April, 2015, Scotland started collecting its own taxes. From 1st April, 2016,
Scotland also started levying the Scottish Rate of Income Tax (SRIT). SRIT works by deduct-
ing 10% from the UK personal income tax of Scottish taxpayers and adding the tax rate that
is decided by the Scottish Parliament (at the time of writing, the Scottish tax rate is set at
precisely 10%, so there is no material change to the personal income tax bill). Revenue from
SRIT is collected by HM Revenue & Customs and then transferred to the Scottish government. In the future, the Scottish Parliament is expected to set tax rates on income tax
(on non-savings and non-dividend income) and receive a share of VAT receipts in Scotland.

Types of sub-national government revenue

There is a variety of ways in which sub-national governments can raise revenue. In many
countries where fiscal powers have been partially decentralised, sub-national governments
receive a share of tax revenue (especially income tax and consumption taxes) that is raised by
the central government and that relates to the tax base of their respective jurisdictions. In Italy,
for example, since 1998 taxpayers pay part of their personal income tax to the government of
the region (at the time of writing, regional personal income tax rates vary across regions, and
depending on the income tax bracket, from 0.7% to 3.33%) and part to the government of the
municipality (e.g. 0.8% in Milan and 0.9% in Rome in 2016) where they are resident. Business
taxpayers pay to the regional governments a tax (*Imposta Regionale sulle Attività Produttive*
or IRAP) that is levied on the 'total production value' (gross income plus labour costs and
interest), and which is largely earmarked (i.e. designated for a particular purpose) for funding the regional health systems. More than half of VAT revenue, moreover, is assigned to the
regions where the tax revenue is generated.

In addition, in many countries sub-national governments can raise revenue through taxation. In the US, for example, most states levy sales tax (which, differently from VAT, are
charged at the retail level only) on the sale or lease of most goods and services. At the time
of writing, only Alaska, Delaware, Montana, New Hampshire and Oregon do not levy any
sales tax. Tax rates vary from one state to another, in the range between 2.9% (in Colorado)
and 7.5% (in California). In most US states, local governments are also allowed to levy local
sales taxes. In New York, for example, total sales tax comprises the state sales tax (4%) and
the local sales tax (4.5%), plus a Metropolitan Commuter Transportation District surcharge
of 0.375%. However, various items are exempted from sales tax; for example, if their value
is below a certain threshold.

Another common form of sub-national government taxation arises from tangible property (primarily land and real estate, but taxes could be levied also on mobile property like cars and boats). In the US, local governments levy a tax on land, buildings and permanent improvements, based on the market value of the property. Tax rates depend on the classification of the property (e.g. residential, commercial, industrial, vacant or blighted real property) and they vary across jurisdictions. The highest tax rates are levied in New Jersey (2.32%) and the lowest in Hawaii (0.28%). In the UK, local governments levy (since 1993) the council tax, which is a tax on property that is usually paid by the resident (e.g. the tenant) of the property. The tax is calculated on the basis of the value of the property and on the classification of the property into 'bands'.

Many countries in the world also allow local governments to levy an occupancy tax (or accommodation tax or hotel tax). The occupancy tax is paid on temporary accommodation, typically in hotels, but also even in private premises that are used for short-term lodging. Occupancy taxes are levied (at the time of writing), for example, in Berlin (a City Tax of 5% of the room rate for periods up to 21 days), in Paris (a *Taxe de Séjour* of up to €4.40 per person per night depending on the category of the accommodation) and in Rome (a *Tassa di Soggiorno* of up to €7.00 per person per night depending on the category of the accommodation).

Another form of revenue for sub-national governments originates from the privatisation of local public services. During the last decades, in many countries in the world there was a tendency among local governments to contract out local public services like water and sewage, local public transport and district central heating. In part, the privatisation was justified on the basis of higher technical efficiency and lower price under private ownership, provided that local monopoly conditions are counteracted by an appropriate contractual or regulatory regime. In part, the privatisation of local public utilities also related to the conditions of fiscal stress of local governments as well as to political and ideological orientations (Bel and Fageda, 2007).

In terms of performance, the privatisation of local public utilities has delivered uncertain results so far, which seem to depend on institutional and regulatory arrangements and context conditions (e.g. Araral, 2009a; Asquer, 2011; Megginson and Netter, 2001; Newbery, 1997; Parker, 1999). In terms of local public financial management, the contracting out of local public utilities (also referred to as a form of horizontal decentralisation) may result in various benefits for local governments. Local governments earn when local public utilities assets are sold or leased to a business entity for the provision of local public services (whose conditions and quality of service may be stipulated in franchise or concession agreements). Local governments may also avoid future liabilities when privatising loss-making local public utilities.

Inter-governmental transfers

Inter-governmental transfers provide a main source of revenue for many sub-national governments in the world (Boadway and Shah, 2007). Inter-governmental transfers consist of grants that central governments provide to fund the operations of sub-national governments. Some inter-governmental transfers are general purpose and sub-national governments can use them for funding any public policy and programme, like, for example, education or health. Other inter-governmental transfers are specifically granted for carrying out particular policies or programmes, like, for example, infrastructure development projects. Specific-purpose transfers may be attached to some conditionalities, in the form of requirements that sub-national governments have to fulfil. Some conditionalities may specify that money is spent on specific items, while other conditionalities may state that sub-national governments attain some specific result or outcome (e.g. in some form of improved conditions for target groups). Specific-purpose transfers may also have matching requirements which provide that the sub-national government contributes to jointly fund the specific policy or programme from their own resources.

Specific-purpose matching transfers can have distortionary effects on public spending decisions. The distortionary effect is illustrated in Figure 5.2, which shows how a specific-purpose matching transfer affects spending decisions. Without the transfer, a sub-national government has a budget indicated by the line between a and b, which is spent on either a good that receives a subsidy or other goods that do not receive subsidies. The sub-national government chooses to split public spending between the two types of goods at the point A in the figure (the intersection between the budget line and the highest value of indifference curves). With the transfer, the sub-national government has a new budget indicated by the line between a and c. The public good that is subsidised becomes less expensive and the sub-national government can spend more on it. The effect of the subsidy (i.e. the transfer), however, results from the combination of two effects, namely a substitution effect (i.e. because the subsidised good is cheaper, the sub-national government would purchase more of it) and an income effect (i.e. because the subsidised good is cheaper, the sub-national government is richer and then would spend more also on other public goods that are not subsidised). Although grants are provided to fund specific policies and programmes, their effect is to alter the spending decisions of sub-national governments, also impacting other policies and programmes. Generally, however, specific-purpose grants are often preferred by central governments because of the possibility to orient sub-national governments' spending decisions.

Some kinds of inter-governmental transfers are subjected to conditionality requirements to attain certain results or outcomes. Performance-oriented transfers leave to sub-national governments the discretion on the use grants. However, sub-national governments are required to be accountable for the production and delivery of public services to the local communities.

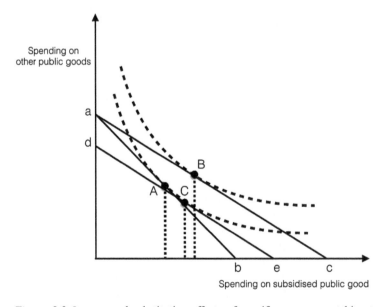

Figure 5.2 Income and substitution effects of specific-purpose matching transfers on public spending.

Public services are assessed through the measurement of indicators (key performance indicators or KPIs, which often include a reference to minimum national standards) that are believed to be illustrative of the effectiveness of public spending. In order to meet performance requirements, public officers are expected to make good use of the grants for improving efficiency and cost-effectiveness and to innovate the system of provision of public services. In principle, performance-oriented systems of inter-governmental transfers may stimulate competition between sub-national governments to meet performance requirements and, therefore, attract more grants. The system, however, may exacerbate the inequality between sub-national jurisdictions when poor-performing sub-national governments keep receiving less transfers than well-performing ones. The system, therefore, is sometimes corrected with criteria that also introduce some amount of equalisation transfers.

In principle, revenue from inter-governmental transfers enable sub-national governments to rely less on local taxation for funding their operations. In practice, it has been long noticed that inter-governmental transfers tend to stimulate more local public spending than the same amount of revenue generated from income tax. This tendency, generally known as the 'flypaper effect' (Courant et al., 1978; Hamilton, 1983), seems to originate from the behaviour of bureaucrats, who tend to expand the size of their budget (and, therefore, of public spending) in order to attain personal material advantages (e.g. higher salaries and better career prospects) (Niskanen, 1968, 1975). In addition, public officers may expand types of public spending that are partially funded by inter-governmental transfers because of a 'fiscal illusion' effect of local taxpayers, who do not correctly assess the overall burden of taxation when part of local funding takes the form of flows of grants from higher levels of government (Turnbull, 1998).

The tendency of sub-national governments to expand the size of their budget is exacerbated by opportunistic behaviour. In an effort to extract even more resources from the central government, sub-national governments may spend more than their revenue if they expect that the central government would intervene to fund their fiscal deficit. The possibility that the central government is always willing to 'pay the bill' for the sub-national governments results in a 'soft budget constraint' on sub-national administrations (Kornai, 1986; Kornai et al., 2003). Public officers of sub-national government would then pay little attention to fiscal prudence and the cost-effectiveness of public spending. Running fiscal deficits might justify claims for additional resources in future budgets.

The soft budget constraint puts the central government in a tricky position. On the one hand, the central government would like to take a firm commitment not to transfer more funds to sub-national governments than originally agreed. On the other hand, if sub-national governments run fiscal deficits then they may not be able to meet their obligations, with detrimental effects on the quality and continuity of local public service provision. If the central government cares about the preservation of local public service provision (at least at the minimum national standards), they would agree to transfer extra funds to the sub-national governments in order to maintain their capacity to operate. In doing so, however, they make the original commitment to avoid providing extra funding no more credible. The sub-national governments can anticipate that the central government would never put them in the condition to suspend or terminate the provision of local public services, and, therefore, would not take central government's commitment too seriously.

The relationship between the central government and sub-national governments has been explained through agency theory. Agency theory (Ross, 1973; Eisenhardt, 1989) aims to explain how the conduct of an entity (the agent) that is expected to carry out activities on behalf of another entity (the principal), whose objectives do not coincide, can be oriented through a system of performance-based incentives. In the context of inter-governmental transfers, the sub-national governments do not generally share the same objectives of the central government. For example, they care more about local communities than the national one, or local public officers care more about their own interests (e.g. probability of re-election) than those of other local communities that the central government cares about. The provision of grants from the central government to the sub-national governments can be understood as an incomplete contract (Hart, 1988; Hart and Moore, 1999), because sub-national governments enjoy discretion on the spending of the grants and the central government can only partially monitor how precisely money is spent and what is achieved from its spending in public policies and programmes. Sub-national governments may not fulfil what is expected from their side and rather undertake wasteful or excessive spending.

In a sense, the problem of the soft budget constraint also relates to the problem of common pool resources as applied to public sector financing. Common pool resources refer to those goods that are shared between entities (i.e. nobody can be excluded from consuming them) but whose consumption is mutually exclusive (i.e. the consumption is rivalrous between entities). The problem of common pool resources (also known as the 'tragedy of the commons'; Hardin, 2009; Ostrom, 1999) consists of the difficulty to make everyone disciplined in the use of the common pool resources: if everyone does not restrain their consumption and free rides on others' efforts to preserve the common pool resource, then the common pool resource itself would be depleted until exhaustion. In the same vein, sub-national governments may try to reap the benefit of the central government pool of public finances. If every sub-national government free rides on fiscal discipline, however, then the central government would be unable to fund the fiscal deficit of sub-national administrations without detrimental effects for central government fiscal conditions.

To some extent only can sub-national government expect that the central government would always provide extra funds for their deficits. Some sub-national governments may be 'too big to fail' because the central government prefers to avoid sharing the blame of leaving large communities without proper local public services. Sometimes, however, the central government may prefer to let individual sub-national administrations default and refuse to bail them out. In 2012, for example, the city of Detroit applied to receive financial help from the state of Michigan. In 2013, the fiscal condition of the municipal administration was so disrupted that the city filed for Chapter 9 bankruptcy protection after the federal administration made it clear that they had no plan to bail out the Detroit city government.

Fiscal decentralisation in developing and transition countries

Fiscal decentralisation has been pursued in many developing and transition countries in the last decades (Bird and Ebel, 2014; Bird and Vaillancourt, 2008). Fiscal decentralisation is expected to help in strengthening the formation of financial management institutions as well as of political ones. On the one hand, fiscal decentralisation can bring the management of public financial resources closer to the attention of local communities and more distant from remote political elites. On the other one, fiscal decentralisation can also stimulate public participation in civic affairs and help the formation of political identities and cultures at the local level.

Fiscal decentralisation in developing and transition countries poses special issues, however. A decentralised system of public financial management may serve the interests of local elites that can collude with accountants and auditors in order to misappropriate public monies. Additional issues arise from the lack of administrative and financial capacity of local bureaucracies, whose salaries may not be attractive to highly skilled professionals or may not protect the integrity of accountants and auditors from the temptation of misconduct.

Finally, many developing and transition countries have a long tradition of centralised political and fiscal systems, and the introduction of decentralised institutions may be at odds with local culture and practices.

On the other hand, decentralisation has been advocated especially by super-national organisations because of the apparent ineffectiveness of central governments to promote economic development (Litvack et al., 1998). The devolution of powers from the central government to sub-national governments is expected to result in greater political stability, public service performance, equity and macroeconomic stability. The implementation of a decentralisation policy, however, requires installing novel rules that substitute hierarchical lines between the central government and sub-national governments. The working of decentralised systems of government, moreover, requires a balance of powers between the central government and sub-national governments (e.g. representation of sub-national interests in one of the chambers in bicameral political systems).

Fiscal decentralisation in developing and transition countries has been especially pursued on the spending side. A study by Gemmell et al. (2013) suggested that spending decentralisation is associated with slower economic growth. Better growth prospects are attained if countries also decentralise their revenue function. They recommend, therefore, that the decentralisation of spending powers is reduced or accompanied by a similar decentralisation of revenue generation in order to match the fiscal competencies and responsibilities of sub-national governments.

In a review of the literature on the effects of decentralisation, Mascagni (2016) argued that developing countries generally tend to follow design prescriptions. In practice, however, the administration of decentralised fiscal systems is affected by political influences, features of the bureaucracy, electoral and non-electoral relationships of accountability at the sub-national level, capacity and leadership, and lack of strategic orientation. An important role is also played by the revenue source, where earned revenue (e.g. taxes) stimulate more political dialogue and accountability than unearned revenue (e.g. from natural resources).

The effects of fiscal decentralisation

Does fiscal decentralisation help attain public policy objectives like increased growth, stability and equity? Martinez-Vazquez et al. (2015) showed that empirical evidence on the effects of fiscal decentralisation is difficult to obtain because of issues regarding the definition and operationalisation of decentralisation and the measurement of the degree of decentralisation. Research in this area also faces the issue of endogeneity, where the presumed effects of fiscal decentralisation (e.g. economic growth) may also play the role of a cause of the very object of study (i.e. fiscal decentralisation). Martinez-Vazquez et al. (2015) highlighted that the effects of decentralisation on allocative and production efficiency are elusive, although there is some evidence that decentralisation favours spending in the social sectors and improved outcomes in education and perhaps public health. Also, the effects of decentralisation on spending on infrastructure are unclear. The perceptions of citizens, however, suggest that public services may improve with decentralisation.

Martinez-Vazquez et al. (2015) also highlighted that decentralisation has uncertain effects on economic growth. Some works, like Xie et al. (1999), Zhang and Zou (1998) and Rodríguez-Pose and Ezcurra (2011), showed that fiscal decentralisation reduced GDP growth. Others, like Feld et al. (2004), Qiao et al. (2008), Akai and Sakata (2002) and Gemmell et al. (2013), found that fiscal decentralisation has positive effects. The work of Thiessen (2003), instead, argued that fiscal decentralisation has positive effects at low levels of decentralisation but the relationship is negative beyond a certain level of decentralisation.

In terms of fiscal discipline, some studies suggest that fiscal decentralisation can improve the conduct of sub-national governments (Rodden, 2002; Neyapti, 2010; Eyraud and Lusinyan, 2013; Presbitero et al., 2014). Others, instead, find negative (de Mello, 2000) or insignificant results (Thornton, 2009). There is some evidence that fiscal decentralisation results in lower inflation (Martinez-Vazquez and McNab, 2006; Baskaran, 2012) but also that there may be no effect (Treisman, 2000; Rodden et al., 2003).

Also, the impact of fiscal decentralisation on equality seems uncertain. Some studies found that fiscal decentralisation seems to have a positive impact on equality (Von Braun et al., 2002; Lindaman and Thurmaier, 2002; Tselios et al., 2012), while others found a negative relationship (Sacchi and Salotti, 2014; Neyapti, 2006). Studies are also inconclusive about the relationship between decentralisation and poverty (Crook and Manor, 1998; Galasso and Ravallion, 2005; Bardhan and Mookherjee, 2003; Sepulveda and Martinez-Vazquez, 2011; West and Wong, 1995).

Martinez-Vazquez et al. (2015) summarised the additional findings of the literature. Fiscal decentralisation is associated with a reduction in territorial disparities (Shankar and Shah, 2003; Rodríguez-Pose and Gill, 2005; Bonet, 2006; Hill, 2008; Qiao et al., 2008), although the effect may be influenced by the level of economic development (Lessmann, 2012) and quality of governance (Kyriacou et al., 2015). Also, Blöchliger et al. (2016) argued that fiscal decentralisation can help to reduce regional disparities, especially if assigning more own-source revenue to sub-national governments and redesigning the system of inter-governmental transfers and fiscal equalisation (which may discourage lagging regions to develop their economic and fiscal bases).

Conclusions

This chapter focused on the decentralisation of the public sector revenue function. In many countries in the world, sub-national governments have some amount of discretion in raising and spending public monies, although the system of inter-governmental transfers or grants provides an important source of sub-national government revenue. Considerations for accountability, fiscal discipline and effectiveness of public spending suggest that there are benefits from decentralising fiscal functions. However, a concern for equity across a country provides a justification for having the central government coordinate fiscal equalisers between rich and poor regions.

Questions for discussion

- What are the advantages and disadvantages of fiscal decentralisation?
- Why don't central governments decentralise fiscal responsibilities to sub-national governments to the maximum extent?
- Is there an optimal design of fiscal federalism institutions?
- How can the privatisation of local public services provide a source of revenue for local governments?
- Should a central government always intervene and bail out an insolvent sub-national government?
- Is fiscal decentralisation beneficial to developing and transition countries?

6 Issues in international taxation

Taxation in the international context

Almost no government in the world can levy taxes without considering the implications of tax policies from the international perspective. The contemporary international context includes many features and tendencies that have important repercussions on the choices that individuals and businesses make. Any tax policy, therefore, does not take place in isolation but rather in combination with the tax policies of other countries (Miller and Oats, 2016).

A general feature of industrialised countries during the last century – and partially during the present one – was the increased role of the public sector in the economy, for various reasons that originate – *inter alia* – from the world wars, the measures taken to counteract the negative effects of the 1929 and the 2007–2008 crises, and the growth of the welfare state. The increased role of the public sector was accompanied by greater efforts to raise public revenues, either through the more diverse and pervasive taxation of economic conditions and events, the manipulation of tax rates or the enlargement of the tax bases.

During the last decades, various emergent, developing and (former) transition countries became more integrated into the world economy. A general tendency to reduce barriers to circulation of goods and services, capital and individuals resulted in greater mobility of people and companies across the world. Differences in tax policies started to play an important role in the decisions to locate, or to relocate, economic activity and personal interests and stakes. Those countries with lower taxations – a regime typically coupled with a relatively small public sector – became attractive destinations for affluent individuals and companies that searched for ways to cut the tax bill. In an effort to stimulate the growth of national economies, industrialised countries undertook tax policies to support business ventures and attract foreign investments.

Within such a context, countries started tackling issues related to the taxation of economic conditions and events that may be subjected to more than one jurisdiction. International taxation is an area that builds on international agreements and on customary international law (Qureshi, 1994). International agreements include the Vienna Convention on the Law of Treaties, the Treaty of Rome and several bilateral agreements on double taxation and a few multilateral ones. One main issue in international taxation is the definition of which country has the right to tax particular economic conditions or events. The issue would have relatively little importance if countries were relatively closed economic systems. In today's world, instead, the definition of the right to tax is open to controversies about which tax jurisdiction should apply to particular taxpayers or transactions.

The inclusion of economic conditions and events as part of a country's tax jurisdiction is typically based on principles of juridical location. Individual taxpayers pay income tax, for example, on the basis of their fiscal residency in a particular country. If they earn some income in another country, also the other country might claim to levy taxes on the income that has been produced within their jurisdiction. In order to avoid the same income being taxed twice, the two countries may have bilateral agreements in place that make the income earned in the country where the taxpayer is not resident immune from local taxation provided that it is reported to the tax authorities of the country where the taxpayer is resident. Alternatively, the two countries may have agreed that the income that is produced in every country is taxed, although the taxpayer is granted a tax credit to claim back (or to detract) taxes in the country where the taxpayer is resident. There are various deviations from these principles, however. The US, for example, levy income tax on the basis of residency in their territories and of citizenship, according to which US citizens pay taxes to the US government irrespective of their fiscal residency abroad. Countries like Italy and Spain do not generally tax citizens who are resident abroad, except for certain conditions where they are resident in some countries that are considered as 'tax havens'.

Business taxpayers, instead, often pay taxes on the basis of the territoriality of income generation, according to which taxes on corporate income are paid in the jurisdiction where income has been generated. There are many differences, however, in how countries treat the income that companies, which are incorporated in their jurisdictions, generate abroad: sometimes the foreign income is not taxed at all, sometimes it is subjected to taxation for the part of income tax that exceed the amount that has been paid abroad. In the US, the domestic multinational enterprises (MNEs) are subjected to US taxation, although MNEs may claim tax credits on income tax paid abroad (and they can offset high income taxes paid in countries with high tax rates with tax debt that they have for relatively low taxes paid in countries with low tax rates) and defer taxation of foreign income until income is 'repatriated' in the US. MNEs, therefore, have an incentive to reinvest income that is generated abroad rather than have it taxed at home.

Despite domestic tax legislation and international treaties, controversies about the right to tax economic conditions and events abound. On the one hand, individual taxpayers (individuals and companies alike) may try to exploit more favourable tax conditions in order to pay less taxes. On the other hand, countries have both a joint interest to prevent taxpayers to elude paying taxes through cracks in the tax codes and a conflicting interest to retain as much tax base as possible. Sometimes, tax authorities and taxpayers fight over the right to levy taxes on individual or corporate income or on the taxation of a transaction. For example, a tax authority may contest a taxpayer's claim to be resident in another country if investigations reveal that in practice the taxpayer conducted most of the personal and family life in the country that claims the right to tax the taxpayer's income (for example, on the basis of time spent in the country where family members live).

Tax competition

The tendency of countries to apply more advantageous tax conditions to the economic activity of individuals and companies results in a process of tax competition. In general terms, tax competition refers to the various policies that countries may pursue in order to enlarge the tax base at the expense of other countries. Policies include, for example, setting tax rates at relatively low levels, increasing the variety and amount of tax deductions, introducing tax breaks or holidays (e.g. no taxation for FDIs), raising barriers to the transfer of capital abroad and other administrative measures like the simplification of tax compliance.

In part, tax competition is regarded as a harmful practice because it erodes the tax bases of countries where economic activity originally took place (in a sense, it is like a 'zero-sum game' because it does not help to create new wealth but just results in the transfer of wealth from one country to another). In addition, tax competition makes it harder for a country with a relatively high level of taxation (from where taxpayers would leave) to keep raising revenue for supporting the size of the domestic public sector, which may include public spending for education, health and welfare. The country with a relatively low level of taxation (where taxpayers would move to), instead, may typically afford to raise relatively less revenue because of providing to the residents less public services. As highlighted by Bradford and Oates (1971) and Oates (1972), tax competition can result in the under-provision of public goods.

In part, tax competition is also considered as a naturally emergent – if not a positive – feature of the world economic system. Provided that any country can pursue independent economic and tax policies, it would be up to the decisions taken by the country government whether to expand the role of the public sector and to fund it through higher levels of taxation or to contain public spending and reduce the bill for taxpayers. An argument in favour of tax competition would state that the mechanism helps to keep public spending profligacy and inefficient bureaucracies under check because taxpayers would relocate to other countries where the tax bill is commensurate with the level and quality of public services that taxpayers receive ('tax arbitrage') (Wilson, 1999). In a sense, the argument for tax competition would be a variation along the lines of the 'voting by feet' of taxpayers as delineated in Tiebout (1956).

The basic model of tax competition was formulated by Zodrow and Mieszkowski (1986). The model consisted of two countries that share one mobile tax base (e.g. capital) and whose tax policies are interdependent (i.e. the revenue of one country government depends also on the tax policies of the other country government). The model explains that the two country governments engage in a 'race to the bottom' to undercut the other country government's tax policy. The outcome is a sub-optimal equilibrium where both countries end up with less financing for public goods than they would have otherwise had they coordinated their tax policies.

Extensions to this model included attention to asymmetries between countries (Genschel and Schwarz, 2011). If one country is larger than the other, the smaller country has more advantages from adopting an aggressive tax competition policy. If the difference between the two countries is large enough, the smaller country ends up in a better condition if there is tax competition than without it (an advantage of 'smallness'; Wilson, 1999). Another extension to the model was to also consider the role of domestic political pressures and institutional constraints. These factors (like, for example, budget rigidities and norms of fairness and equity) affect tax policy decisions. Countries with more 'rigidities' have less leeway to adjust tax rates than others who are less affected by domestic pressures and constraints.

During the last decades, there has been a growing tendency across countries and also sub-national jurisdictions to engage in tax competitive practices. A study on tax competition for personal income tax, for example, was the one of Feld and Kirchgässner (2001), which focused on residence decisions among cantons in Switzerland (where maximum personal income tax rates vary between 22.86% in Zug and 44.75% in Genf; KPMG, 2015). Their work showed that there is tax competition among Swiss cantons and cities, and that higher income earners choose their residency depending on the amount of personal income tax that they have to pay. The provision of local public services, instead, is significant in the decision of residence for retirees.

Evidence for tax competition has also been collected in the area of corporate income tax. A study by Slemrod (2004), for example, focused on explaining the tendency for corporate tax income rates to decline in the world from about 1985 onwards. Slemrod (2004) argued that the level of corporate tax rates was not related to the amount of revenue needed for public spending. Corporate income tax rates across several countries seemed to converge towards the mean over time, which is a possible indication of international tax competition at work. He also commented that it is possible that the US corporate income tax rate plays an important role as a 'reference point' for corporate income tax rates in other countries. The leading role of the US in setting corporate income tax rates is also contemplated in Gordon (1992), where this major economy exerts influence because of market and bargaining power.

Also, the work of Devereux and Loretz (2013) focused on evidence of corporate income tax competition. They commented that the effects of tax competition are difficult to investigate, for reasons that include the lack of a counterfactual to examine. They also summarise their literature review by concluding that there is a clear pattern of evidence of tax competition, especially in the EU where the accession of small new member states resulted in further impetus to lower corporate income tax rates. In the EU, relatively low levels of corporate income tax are found (at the time of writing), for example, in Estonia (20%), Latvia and Lithuania (15%) and Bulgaria (10%), but also in Ireland (12.5%) and the UK (20%).

There is some evidence that tax competition also takes place among developing and emergent economies, although evidence is sometimes difficult to obtain because of complicated tax codes. Various regimes of exemptions, tax holidays, temporary reduced rates and incentives for investments, in fact, make the only data on statutory corporate income tax rates inaccurate to appraise the tax burden on corporate income. A study by Abbas and Klemm (2013), however, analysed the details of the tax codes of fifty economies in 1996–2007 and found evidence of a 'race to the bottom' in corporate income tax, especially in Africa where effective tax burden on corporate income could fall close to zero.

International tax avoidance and tax evasion

The variety of tax regimes across the world opens up various opportunities for individuals and companies to bypass tax codes to pursue tax advantages. MNEs, for example, can exploit their presence in different countries to transfer income from high-level to low-level tax rate jurisdictions. If a country's tax code provides that corporate income made abroad is not taxed until it is 'repatriated', then MNEs can postpone the taxation of foreign income indefinitely. Also, individuals may take advantage of sources of income earned in different jurisdictions by not reporting part of them to the country where they are resident, provided there are no means through which the tax authorities of the home country can know about the unreported income sources.

Tax avoidance and tax evasion in the international context can take place in various ways. A common scheme to reduce the tax bill of companies is one where corporate income that is earned in one country with relatively high corporate income tax rate is shifted to another country with relatively low corporate income tax rate through *abusive* transactions (i.e. transactions that are purposely done with the precise aim to pay less taxes). An instance of such a transaction is the licensing of intellectual property (IP) between two companies, which enables the company with income earned in a relatively high corporate income tax rate country to incur costs while the other company based in a relatively low corporate income tax rate country gains some revenue. Another instance is the provision of a loan between two companies, where the one based in a relatively high corporate income tax country pays interest (which is tax deductible) to the one based in a relatively low corporate income tax rate country.

Some tax avoidance schemes take specific names depending on the contemporary country legislation that allows the advantageous schemes. The 'Double Irish with a Dutch Sandwich', for example, is a scheme that allowed companies to avoid taxation of income from IP rights. The scheme included the payment for IP to a company incorporated in Ireland, which in turn pays royalties to another company that holds the IP rights, which is as well incorporated in Ireland but fiscal resident in a zero-tax country ('tax haven', like, for example, the Cayman Islands or Bermuda). The net income that is left in the first Irish company is taxed at the relatively low rate of 12.5%. In addition, the scheme includes an intermediary role for a Dutch company in the transaction between the two Irish companies, because the payment of royalties to the Dutch company is tax deductible for the first Irish company, while the Dutch company does not need to withhold taxes on the payment made to the second Irish company for inter-EU country transactions. The scheme was used by companies like Apple and Google in the past. In 2015, however, the Irish government took action to terminate it.

Tax avoidance schemes that consist of transactions where one company supplies another with goods and services depend on the value of the agreed *transfer price*. Depending on the price, part of the corporate profits are shifted from one company to another. General international tax guidelines provide that the transfer price should be set according to the 'arm's length principle', which recommends that prices should be equal to those that would result from transactions with unrelated parties (OECD, 2010; Bartelsman and Beetsma, 2003). In practice, the arm's length principle is difficult to implement; often controversies arise between tax authorities and MNEs about whether transfer prices are appropriate or not, with each party presenting conflicting evidence about the price that would be charged in similar market transactions.

An alternative to the arm's length principle to prevent profit shifting between countries is provided by *unitary taxation* with profit apportionment. This approach consists of appraising the global (consolidated) profit that a MNE earns and dividing (apportioning) it between the jurisdictions where the business activity is carried out according to specified criteria. Criteria may include, for example, sales turnover or number of employees or value of assets. The principle of unitary taxation has not been implemented in the international arena yet, but some steps have been made in this direction. In the EU, for example, the Common Corporate Consolidated Tax Base (CCCTB) initiative that was launched in 2011 aimed to establish a single, harmonised tax base for multinational companies with operations in Europe. The initiative has been opposed by some EU member states – especially the UK, which aimed to rather pursue an aggressive (corporate income) tax competition with respect to other EU countries – but a renewed interest towards CCCTB emerged in late 2016.

Tax havens

The international tax environment is profoundly affected by the presence of jurisdictions with relatively low or zero taxation, or so-called 'tax havens'. Tax havens are important in the contemporary international tax environment because they typically facilitate the implementation of schemes for tax avoidance and tax evasion on the basis of the generous features of their country tax codes. In addition, tax havens may also provide the possibility to conduct transactions and hold assets in secrecy, especially with respect to requests for information from foreign tax authorities. The OECD defines tax havens as those countries which have no or only nominal tax rates, provide protection of personal financial information and lack transparency to acquire information on the situation of a taxpayer.

Tax havens typically consist of relatively small countries, often located on islands. Despite their apparent geographical insignificance, they play a central role in contemporary global financial system and business activity (Palan et al., 2013). Palan et al. (2013) estimate that tax havens host about two million international business companies, which were valued at about $12 trillion in 2007. About half of the world's hedge funds are based in the Cayman Islands, the British Virgin Islands, Bermuda and the Bahamas. Apart from the size of the tax haven phenomenon, Palan et al. (2013) also highlight that tax havens provide a mechanism for most profitable and wealthy individuals and companies to avoid the redistribution of the riches produced by globalisation in the last decades.

Since 1998, the OECD has highlighted the issues that tax havens pose to the international tax environment. The OECD (1998a) report, titled 'Harmful tax competition: an emerging global issue', recognised that tax havens have the potential to induce various harms to tax systems and the world economy more generally. These harms include

> distorting financial and, indirectly, real investment flows; undermining the integrity and fairness of tax structures; discouraging compliance by all taxpayers; re-shaping the desired level and mix of taxes and public spending; causing undesired shifts of part of the tax burden to less mobile tax bases, such as labour, property and consumption; and increasing the administrative costs and compliance burdens on tax authorities and taxpayers.
>
> (OECD, 1998a: 16)

Since the 2000s, the OECD has undertaken actions to define, identify and list tax havens in order to apply special tax policies for those taxpayers that carry out activities which could result in schemes of tax avoidance and tax evasion. The so-called 'List of Uncooperative Tax Havens' originally included about forty countries, which over time expressed their commitment to implement the principles of transparency that OECD required. By the end of the 2000s, no country was included in the 'List of Uncooperative Tax Havens' any more. More recently, however, the issue of tax havens regained attention, especially in the EU where a preliminary 'blacklist' was published in 2015. Various issues on the formation of the blacklist are still under discussion at the time of writing, in particular on the exclusion from the list of EU countries (e.g. the Netherlands, Cyprus and Luxembourg, whose tax codes may include provisions that enable tax avoidance or tax evasion), of Switzerland and of others like Bermuda, and on the inclusion in the list of countries that the OECD had considered as compliant with transparency requirements and that had also committed to the exchange of information.

Additional arguments on the role of tax havens in the international context were provided by Zucman (2015), who critiqued the function that they play in increasing inequality in the contemporary global economy. Tax havens host about 8% of the world financial wealth of households. They enable US companies to avoid about $130 billion taxes per year. Zucman (2015) calls for the establishment of a worldwide registry of financial wealth, by combining registries that have been developed independently so far (e.g. in the US and Luxembourg).

International tax cooperation

Since the OECD (1998b) report entitled 'Towards global tax cooperation', efforts to stimulate some cooperation among countries on international tax issues have received growing attention. In part, some results were attained with the formulation of lists of countries which called for special attention from tax authorities because of the opaque financial and business practices that they permit, and for the consequences they have on eroding the tax base of other countries. The formulation of blacklists regained some interest in 2016, after the leak of the 'Panama Papers' that disclosed the many individuals and companies (more than half in British tax havens or the UK) that the lawyer firm Mossack Fonseca had helped to evade taxes.

International cooperation to identify and take measures against tax avoidance and evasion is hampered by the specific interests of countries and differences in approaches. Some countries like France and Italy, for example, have national blacklists of foreign 'non-cooperative' countries that are relevant for taxation purposes. All countries belonging to principal international organisations or forums, like the OECD and the G20, agree that lists should be formed for identifying the countries that do not comply with transparency requirements. Divergence occurs, however, on the criteria for inclusion of countries and jurisdictions in the blacklists. For example, the UK opposed the EU criterion to consider countries with zero or low tax rates as tax havens, which would include on the blacklist some British Overseas Territories like the British Virgin Islands and Cayman Islands, Guernsey and Jersey.

Additional efforts to enhance international cooperation on tax issues coalesce around the so-called Base Erosion and Profit Shifting (BEPS) programme of the OECD. BEPS aims to support governments in the formulation of policies that aim to counteract the 'disappearance' of taxable profits through various tax avoidance and tax-evasion schemes. One main result of BEPS (which involved more than sixty countries) was the formulation of a 'package' that contained several recommendations on various tax areas, which include transfer prices, rules of controlled foreign companies, interest deductions, techniques to artificially avoid the permanent establishment status, disclosure rules and dispute resolution mechanisms (OECD, 2015b). The package of measures should be implemented through domestic legislation and international treaties. Once in place, they should prevent the many schemes that enable double non-taxation at present. Taxation would be better aligned to where business and economic activity takes place. Tax authorities would have better information to enforce rules and regulations.

The BEPS package call for a concerted effort to put the recommendations in place. If tax rules are not harmonised, it would still be possible for certain taxpayers to shop around and set up legal and accounting schemes in selected tax jurisdictions to pursue tax advantages. Part of the cooperation efforts will centre on the standardisation of country-by-country financial reporting, of monitoring mechanisms and of agreed dispute resolution procedures. Soon after releasing the BEPS package, the OECD also launched the initiative to extend its principles to other (non-OECD and non-G20) countries, which were invited to participate on an equal footing. In April 2016, the OECD opened the 'Platform for Collaboration on Tax', which aims to help countries implement BEPS recommendations together with institutions like the United Nations, the World Bank and the IMF.

Efforts to cooperate on international tax issues also clash, however, with the affirmation of the sovereignty of each specific country. As discussed by Ring (2008), the concept of sovereignty places a state at the very centre of the world, as the only entity that has rights to act in an international system. In practice, all states face some limitations to their capacity to act in the international system and also within the domestic boundaries. In part, other states may also exert a profound influence on the conduct of any other state (for various reasons that include economic relationships, political clout, military threat, etc.). In part, the emergence of international organisations (and, in some cases, of super-national ones like the EU) resulted in the voluntary compression of the sovereignty of states, at least in specific and circumscribed policy areas.

Sovereignty is deeply intertwined with taxation. The power to levy taxes within a territorial jurisdiction is a clear manifestation of the authority and legitimacy of a state government (or sub-national government). Levying taxes is typically associated with forms of accountability to hold the government responsive toward taxpayers' expectations that public monies are spend appropriately. Conservative circles, like the Centre for Freedom and Prosperity in the US, argue that cooperation on international tax issues diminishes the capacity of country governments to formulate independent tax policies, especially if high-tax countries would limit the possibility of other countries to pursue more advantageous tax policies for individuals and companies. Some scholars, however, raised some concerns that international tax cooperation results in the compression of country sovereignty (James, 2002; Littlewood, 2004). In the EU, the prospect to harmonise taxation (especially corporate income tax) was not fully shared among all member states, most notably the UK.

Taxing the digital economy

One of the main areas of contemporary economic activity that poses an issue of international taxation is the digital economy. The digital economy has deeply reconfigured the business models of many industries, from retail to travel, from advertisement to the press. Levying taxes on business activity in the digital environment is difficult because of the intangible nature of digital services, which enable companies to access foreign markets with ease, to carry out business with limited or no physical assets, and to carry out transactions in ways that can be manipulated to bypass tax codes. Also, the nature of digital goods entails that the value of assets and transactions is uncertain and contentious.

A typical scheme in the digital economy is the development of IP in a country jurisdiction, the passing of royalty rights to another country which has more advantageous taxation and the provision of digital services anywhere in the world. Country governments have an interest to tax the income that originates from IP where the IP is generated and where the digital services are provided, rather than in the (typically offshore) country where IP royalty rights are held. Collaboration on international taxation – precisely part of the BEPS package – provides guidelines for implementing these principles.

Another scheme in the digital economy is the exploitation of advantages from carrying out international business from countries where the VAT regime is more advantageous than others. Depending on where the business is registered, there may be competitive advantages from operating in jurisdictions where VAT rates are relatively low. For this reason, it has been argued that digital transactions should be taxed according to the '*destination principle*', where VAT is paid in the country where the consumer is resident. Digital transactions, however, are often anonymous, lacking a paper trial and records, and difficult to detect or monitor for tax authorities. It is hard for tax authorities, then, to levy taxes or to control that the appropriate taxes have been paid.

The application of VAT rules is also important for e-commerce transactions that involve the selling of physical goods from a distance. In the EU, the system of VAT rules provide that the residency of the customer is important because, according to the destination principle, VAT rules are those of the country where the customer is resident if the distance-selling business is above certain thresholds. When a threshold is exceeded, then distance-selling businesses have to register for VAT as non-resident sellers in the foreign country. The business, then, should follow the VAT rules of the foreign country for the transactions whose customers are based in the foreign country (e.g. VAT rates, payments, deadlines, etc.).

Conclusions

This chapter discussed the issues that arise in international taxation. The combined effect of globalisation, neoliberal policies and technological change have dramatically reshaped the business environment at the world scale during the last decades. The possibility of the greater mobility of individuals, companies, goods and capital resulted in the emergence of tendencies among countries to compete against each other to attract economic activity on the basis of more advantageous tax conditions. Individuals and companies – especially MNEs – started exploiting the possibility to cut their tax bill by relocating or through the implementation of ingenious schemes of tax avoidance and tax evasion. Tax havens played an important role in eroding the tax base of many countries, which started coordinating their efforts to counteract the loss of tax revenues. International measures include attention to the digital economy, which – because of the intangible nature of digital services and of the electronic systems of production – enables businesses to escape traditional means to detect economic conditions and events and levy taxes on them.

Questions for discussion

- Why does greater mobility of goods, labour and capital pose issues for taxation?
- Why would individuals and companies relocate on the basis of different tax conditions?
- How do tax havens help tax avoidance and tax evasion?
- What has international tax cooperation achieved so far?
- Does international tax cooperation pose a threat to state sovereignty?
- What are the challenges posed by the taxation of digital goods?

7   Revenue from foreign aid

Tendencies in foreign aid policies

Foreign aid consists of inter-governmental transfers (Official Development Assistance or ODA) between countries or between an international or super-national entity (like the World Bank, the IMF or the EU) and a recipient country. Foreign aid takes place for a number of reasons. The discourse on providing support to other countries includes a role for the solidarity between national communities, which results in inter-governmental transfers to help tackle issues of poverty, epidemics, famine, wars and other humanitarian emergencies (emergency aid). Foreign aid, instead, is also typically carried out for more pragmatic concerns. In part, donor countries may have vested interests in providing financial resources to support the economic development of other countries, which may offer market opportunities for firms of the donor country. In part, donor countries may be interested in using financial resources to exercise political influence on the foreign country, possibly for geo-strategic reasons.

A precise definition of foreign aid originates from the Development Assistance Committee (DAC) of the OECD (Tarp, 2006). Foreign aid is defined as the financial flows, technical assistance and commodities that are designed to promote economic development and welfare as the main objectives, and is provided as either grants (at least 25% of the total granted) or subsidised loans. A grant aid is fully concessional if no payment of interest or principal is required. A loan aid is concessional if the terms of repayment of the principal are mild and/ or the interest rate is lower than offered in international markets. The definition excludes, therefore, transfers that originate from non-governmental organisations (NGOs), military expenditures aid, trade aid, investment aid and cultural exchanges.

The early experiences of foreign aid originated from the financial support that the US provided for the reconstruction of post-Second World War Europe. During the following decades, foreign aid primarily took the form of targeted interventions on specific development projects. The rise of neoliberal ideas since the 1970s entailed, in the domain of foreign aid, the introduction of structural adjustment loans with the requirement that recipient countries adopt market-oriented policies. Conditionalities included privatisations, removal of trade barriers, liberalisations of industries, modernisation of public administrations and reform of the tax systems. In the following decades, foreign aid was associated with the promotion of better institutions and governance, together with measures to fight corruption and support capacity building (Easterly, 2007a). With the turn of the century, foreign aid increased in order to achieve the UN's Millennium Development Goals (established in 2000) and, later, the Post-2015 Development Agenda.

Several countries in the world currently provide ODA to various other countries. The main donor countries of the DAC (which consists of about twenty countries) include the US (about $31 billion in 2015), the UK ($18 billion), Germany ($18 billion), Japan ($9 billion), France ($9 billion), Sweden ($9 billion), the Netherlands ($6 billion), Canada ($4 billion) and Norway ($4 billion). Also, countries that are not part of the DAC, however, provide sources of foreign aid, most notably United Arab Emirates (about $4 billion), Turkey ($4 billion), Russia ($1 billion) and Israel ($0.2 billion). If we compare the amount of foreign aid to the GDP of donor countries, however, it becomes apparent that some countries devote much more resources out of public budgets than others. Countries like Sweden, Norway, Luxembourg, Denmark and the Netherlands score relatively high (the ratio of foreign aid to GDP ranging between 1.40% and 0.86%). In contrast, the amount of foreign aid provided by the US is relatively modest with respect to its GDP (about 0.17%). Most ODA is received by African, Asian and Middle Eastern countries. Main recipient countries in Africa include Egypt, Ethiopia, Tanzania, Kenya and the Democratic Republic of Congo. Main recipients in Asia are Afghanistan, Vietnam, Myanmar and Bangladesh. Other recipients include Syria, Iraq and Israel.

Every donor country tends to channel foreign aid to a particular recipient country depending on the historical and contingent circumstances. The US, for example, mainly provides foreign aid to Israel, Egypt, Afghanistan, Jordan, Pakistan and African countries like Kenya, Nigeria, Tanzania and Ethiopia. The UK especially supports Pakistan, Ethiopia, Nigeria, Sierra Leone, South Sudan, Syria, Tanzania and Afghanistan. Relatively small countries, instead, may typically focus on more specific recipients: Scotland, for example, established an International Development Fund that especially provides support to Malawi.

Kinds of foreign aid

Foreign aid can be provided in different forms. A general distinction is drawn between bilateral and multilateral aid. Bilateral agreements take place between two countries, while multilateral agreements consist of the participation of international organisations (like the World Bank or agencies of the United Nations, like UNDP, UNICEF, UNAIDS) together with donor countries and one or more recipient countries. Most of the support to recipient countries originates from public sector entities, although private organisations (charities, foundations and NGOs) may also contribute financial or material resources. Some forms of aid consist of targeted interventions in the recipient country, like the construction of infrastructure or capacity-building projects. Other forms of aid consist of programmes that support public sector spending in particular areas, like the development of particular services or industries, budget support and debt relief.

During the last decade, there has been a growing focus on programme assistance rather than targeted project support. The Paris Declaration on Aid Effectiveness (2005) built on the acknowledgement that support to targeted projects resulted in high transaction costs, short-term benefits and focus on areas that served the interests of the donors rather than of the recipients and beneficiaries. In contrast, support of programmes is expected to stimulate more ownership from the side of the recipient countries. A typical form of programme support is general budget support (GBS), which essentially consists of the transfer of funds to the treasury of the recipient country.

One issue of GBS is that funds that are transferred to the recipient country treasury are fungible, in the sense that they can be allocated to any particular budget line item. Critiques of this approach highlight that fungibility of aid reduced the possibility to monitor and control where money is spent and opens up opportunities for misallocations and misappropriations. A remedy to this problem is the so-called aid on delivery (AoD), which consists of the gradual disbursement of aid funds when the recipient country has achieved certain pre-defined goals (e.g. accomplishment of targets in areas like healthcare, education and infrastructure development). In this way, the recipient countries have discretion to administer aid funds (which should stimulate capacity to manage public finances) but they should demonstrate that they spend foreign aid funds to attain substantive results.

Sometimes, foreign aid is provided with attached conditions that the recipient country should satisfy. Aid conditionality comes in such forms as, for example, reforming parts of the public sector (like modernising technological infrastructure or conditions of employment) or privatising some public services. Generally, conditions must be satisfied after the receipt of aid funds, but in principle conditionality may also apply to certain requirements that the recipient country should fulfil before any aid is provided.

Foreign aid can come in the form of financial resources or in-kind aid. In-kind foreign aid can take the form of technical assistance, either in relation to specific projects or for supporting general policies or programmes (e.g. teachers sent to the recipient country). A related form of in-kind assistance is capacity building, where various interventions – which are especially intended to impact on the cultural and institutional conditions of the recipient country – are expected to bring about the development of skills and capabilities in the medium–long run.

In-kind foreign aid may generate various issues. Technical assistance, for example, may be expensive, especially if it comes in the form of consultants or other professionals that are hired in the donor countries. The provision of in-kind resources, moreover, may result in various impediments, including issues of delays in transport, the selection of the appropriate goods and quality of the goods. Financial resources, instead, can be transferred quickly; they can also be spent flexibly dependant upon circumstances. Sometimes, aid may be provided in the form of financial resources, but with the requirement that funds are spent on specific goods that are supplied by firms of the donor country.

Another form of financial assistance across countries is the discharge of debts that the recipient countries have with donor countries. Debt relief was especially pursued in the 1980s and 1990s, when the high level of indebtedness of developing countries seemed to place a heavy burden – in the form of debt service payments – on their capacity to grow. The policy of relieving debt is especially oriented to a list of about forty Heavily Indebted Poor Countries (defined by the IMF and the World Bank).

After debt relief, financial resources which should be used to service debt repayment become available for other forms of public spending. The 'windfall gain' of debt relief, however, should not be wasted in unnecessary or ill-targeted measures. Collier (2000) advises that, like oil or natural resources, financial resources that are liberated through debt relief should be invested for long-term benefits. Easterly (2002) also highlighted that debt relief was not effective in the past, where recipient countries that had benefited from it did not improve their growth and their level of indebtedness persisted.

The political economy of foreign aid

The provision of foreign aid results in various implications that arise from the stakes that participants have in foreign aid resources. For the recipient country, foreign aid provides a source of income to allocate or make use of for undertaking public programmes or projects and distributing benefits. It is also, however, a source of leverage in national and local political arenas. Foreign aid also provides some advantages for the donor country, such as the possibility to establish more collaborative ties with the recipient country, which may take the form of various concessions for economic or geo-political purposes.

The provision of foreign aid results in the formation of ties between the donor and recipient countries that may have various repercussions. If the aid is provided in the form of fungible funds (e.g. GBS), the government of the recipient country may spend it in ways that are not consistent with the original purposes of the inter-governmental financial support. The problem can be put in the economic terms of information asymmetry and moral hazard, where the donor does not know precisely how the money is spent. The government of the recipient country may be tempted to over-commit to pursue the policy objectives that the donor country wants. The government of the donor country may require that the recipient country agrees on policy targets and that appropriate monitoring systems are put in place. The recipient country, then, may under-commit to pursue policy objectives if additional funds are not provided, or show that previous fund allocations were not enough to attain the intended results.

Various authors (Martens et al., 2002; Araral, 2005; Radelet, 2006) highlight that foreign aid is fundamentally undermined by information asymmetry and contract incompleteness. Apart from the relationship between the government (or agencies) of the donor countries and the government (or agencies) of recipient countries, foreign aid unfolds through multiple additional relationships between elected officials, heads of aid agencies, donor agencies' employees and consultants, recipient agencies' employees and consultants, suppliers of goods, NGOs and the beneficiaries (Radelet, 2006). Problems of information asymmetry and contract incompleteness can be tackled through various instruments and transparency mechanisms, but there is generally no assurance that money spent in foreign aid delivers substantive improvements (Easterly and Pfutze, 2008; Easterly, 2007b).

The issues of information asymmetry and contract incompleteness were discussed, among others, by Araral (2009b). The analysis based on institutional rational choice theory suggests that the pursuit of self-interest and incentive structure, combined with asymmetric information and contract incompleteness, play an important role in explaining the choices of donor agencies and recipients. The donor agency can be assumed to seek the growth of its foreign aid funds portfolio, while the recipient agency is expected to seek bureaucratic survival. The model of Araral (2009b) showed that the recipient agency chooses to under-invest in development projects in order to subsidise its operational costs and to claim further foreign aid. The donor agency, instead, prefers to relax monitoring the recipient's efforts in order to avoid sanctioning the recipient if funds are misallocated and to keep foreign aid money flowing. Also, Easterly (2001) had already explained a similar tendency, which fundamentally undermines the principle of conditionality; although, in principle, the failure to meet requirements attached to foreign aid could result in penalties – in practice, both the administrative systems of the donors and of the recipients gain from maintaining or enlarging aid assistance rather than reducing it.

Another fine-grained explanation for the inefficacy of foreign aid builds on issues that arise from career motives and aid fungibility. Individuals who work in donor agencies have incentives to keep foreign aid flowing because their careers depend on the amount of money spent in cooperation programmes (Kanbur, 2000). It is not in their interest, therefore, to closely monitor and sanction the recipient agency in order to avoid the risk of halting foreign aid flow. Individuals who work in the recipient agency, instead, have incentives to divert fungible foreign aid funds from the delivery of aid services to subsidising the recipient agency's operations (Auer, 2006). The recipient agency tries to receive more fungible aid in order to expand bureaucratic spending.

Additional repercussions of foreign aid can affect the recipient country. Dependency on foreign aid may hamper the development of local administrative and financial management capacity. It may also stimulate rent-seeking behaviour in various forms where direct or indirect benefits from aid funds is preferred to undertaking entrepreneurial activities or devising alternative schemes for public sector revenue generation. More generally, the political environment of the recipient country may be influenced by the donor country, especially in relation to vital industries like energy or minerals.

The effectiveness of foreign aid

The possibility for governments of recipient countries to raise revenue from foreign aid poses the question of whether such a form of revenue is advantageous. Foreign aid is what it is – a gift (although it may come with some conditions attached). As such, issues arise about whether the recipient country is well positioned to make good use of the 'effortless' source of revenue by pursuing public programmes and projects for the advantage of the intended beneficiaries.

The effectiveness of foreign aid is controversial (Radelet, 2006). Foreign aid can play a role in reducing poverty or containing worsening living conditions, but it has often been criticised because of subsidising inefficient bureaucracies, perpetuating bad governments, enriching the elites of recipient countries and fostering corruption. Some studies have provided discouraging evidence that foreign aid is not effective. Collier (2000), for example, argued that foreign aid cooperation programmes are fundamentally undermined by a lack of credible commitments, which makes any promise of good governance and reform in the recipient countries meaningless. Kanbur (2000) showed that foreign aid provides perverse incentives not to improve the efficiency and performance of recipient government's administration because it eases their fiscal problems. Further critiques (Easterly, 2007a; Dichter, 2005; Rajan and Subramanian, 2008; Radelet, 2006) remarked that foreign aid did not help to reduce massive poverty in Africa, including illustrative cases like the Democratic Republic of Congo, Somalia, Ghana, Zambia and Tanzania. Auer (2006), Feyzioglu et al. (1998), Devarajan and Swaroop (2000), Pack and Pack (1993) and Remmer (2004) highlighted that fungible aid generates opportunities for recipients to expand governmental spending. As Easterly (2002: 226) put it, 'The tragedy is that bureaucracy captured foreign aid under conditions in which it didn't work well.'

Other works, however, provide a more positive assessment of foreign aid effectiveness. For Sachs (2005) foreign aid seems to contribute to reducing poverty and stimulating some growth; for example, in countries like Botswana, Indonesia and Mozambique. Also, Tarp (2006) acknowledged that there is positive evidence of success of foreign aid at the microeconomic and project level. Collier (2008) considered the role that foreign aid can provide to help the poorest parts of the world population.

It should be remarked that investigating the effectiveness of foreign aid meets various methodological issues. In many countries, the quality of data on the effects of foreign aid are relatively unreliable and fragmented. Various sources and forms of aid may not be separated. Some data on macroeconomic aggregates and poverty are based on rough estimates. Also, the basis for assessment is controversial. Comparing the evidence of results with targets is misleading because of the arbitrary nature of targets. Comparing *ex ante* and *ex post* conditions with respect to the interventions may be obfuscated by the joint influence of other context factors. The effects of foreign aid, moreover, may recur over medium–long periods of time rather than being immediate. In principle, a researcher should try to assess the effectiveness of foreign aid on the basis of a counterfactual scenario, where it would be possible to observe the effects of the absence of aid under conditions that are similar but independent with respect to the foreign aid intervention.

Conclusions

This chapter discussed the role of foreign aid as a source of public sector revenue. Foreign aid originates from various rationales, both idealistic (humanitarian) and pragmatic (geo-political influence and economic advantages). Apart from a transfer of financial funds, foreign aid may take other forms such as the provision of technical assistance, capacity building and debt relief. Whatever the form, it is apparent that foreign aid stimulates various repercussions on the donor and recipient countries. Issues arise from misappropriation of funds and the various interests to maintain or enlarge aid assistance irrespective of evidence of efficiency and cost-effectiveness. Evidence of effectiveness of foreign aid is mixed. Although there are indications that targeted projects can attain success, there are also concerns that aid assistance has not delivered more substantive results to raise large parts of world population out of poverty.

Questions for discussion

- Why do donor countries provide foreign aid?
- Do aid conditionalities work?
- What are the arguments in favour and against general budget support (GBS)?
- What should recipient countries do with debt relief?
- Is foreign aid effective?

8 User charges, fees and public–private partnerships

Revenue from market-like transactions

Although taxation and inter-governmental transfers provide the main source of public sector revenue for many countries, there are various alternative kinds of revenue sources. During the last decades, many countries in the world have increasingly raised revenue through various forms of commercialisation of public services (Whitfield, 1992; Easton, 1997; Needham, 2007). Commercialisation consists of the provision of public services through market-like transactions. Rather than delivering public services for free to any user who is eligible to receive them, the provision of services is accompanied by some form of payment. Commercialisation marks an important shift away from more traditional forms of delivery of public services, where taxpayers contribute to the funding of public budgets while users receive services at no charge or at a token administrative fee.

A limited repertoire of public services can be commercialised, for reasons that relate to the very non-excludability and non-rivalry features of public goods. Public sector entities would not be able to fund the production of public goods – like, for example, national defence – on the basis of transactions with individual members of a community. Every individual would find it rational to free ride on the expected monetary contributions and enjoy the public good without contributing any payment towards it. If a public service can be provided with a user paying for it, then commercialisation opportunities arise.

The reconfiguration of public services as commercial activities poses fundamental political issues. The substitution of the direct provision of public services that are funded from general taxation (or other revenue sources) with the delivery of public services through market-like transactions entails a different role for the government. In the 'traditional' model of public services funded from general taxation, the government undertakes the provision of public services on the basis of considerations that also include a role for economic growth and stabilisation, development, and equity in the opportunities to receive services that benefit both individual users and the community at large. In the commercialisation model, the government provides a more limited amount of public services that are funded from general taxation, and offers additional services whose allocation depends on individual willingness to pay.

The political issues of the reconfigured system of public service provision through commercial activities primarily arise from the asymmetries that originate from discrimination between individuals who can pay for services and those who cannot. If a service is offered through market-like transactions, then the possibility for individuals to access the service (their willingness to pay) depends on whether they can afford the price (their capacity to pay). The price to pay provides a mechanism of allocation of access to services, which selects users on the basis of their purchasing power. The market mechanism, however, is not consistent with other criteria for the allocation of access to services, such as, for example, fairness, equality and 'universal service obligations' (the requirement to provide every user with a minimum standard of service).

The pursuit of public sector revenue through commercial activities is also expected to bring various related benefits (Brown et al., 2000). If the system of delivery of the services is entirely funded from the market-like transactions, then the management of the commercial ventures is expected to pay attention to efficiency and cost-effectiveness in order to attain financial self-sufficiency. Relatedly, the commercial activity is expected to be managed according to business-like techniques, especially if it is exposed to the competition of private sector providers. The commercialisation of public services, in fact, may be accompanied by the liberalisation of industries that were previously retained under exclusive competences of public authorities. Market pressure from competitors is expected to stimulate efficiency, economy and innovativeness.

Another expected benefit of the commercialisation of public services is the role that the price plays in signalling scarcity and value. When a service is provided for free, there are no incentives for the users to self-discipline themselves and avoid wasteful consumption. If the users are required to pay a price for the service (which might even cover only a part of the full cost), instead, they limit marginal consumption depending on the marginal cost for the price to pay for additional units of service. The provision of services through market-like transactions, then, would serve the purpose of rationing the total amount of services and their distribution across the users.

Healthcare

The provision of healthcare is one of those areas of the public sector where tendencies to commercialise combine with the tax-funded provision of healthcare services. Countries vary considerably in the way healthcare services are provided. In France, for example, the government provides universal healthcare coverage (the system is called *Protection Maladie Universelle* or PUMA from 1st January, 2016). The system is largely funded by income taxation, and although individuals are required to pay for services (e.g. a visit to the general practitioner (GP) or a specialist that the patient has been referred to by the GP), the cost is refunded by the national health insurance provider. If a patient visits a specialist without the reference of the GP, then the refund only covers the standard rate, although the specialist may charge higher fees. The cost of prescriptions is only partially paid by the patient, while insurance pays for the rest. French residents, however, may also subscribe to private healthcare insurance (*mutuelle*) which may help cover the part of the costs that are not refunded by the national insurance.

In the UK – or, more precisely, in England – most funding for healthcare originates from taxation and national insurance, while about 1.2% only originates from charges to the patients (Hawe and Cockcroft, 2013). The National Health System (NHS England) provides residents with the assistance of a GP and they receive health services free at the point of need. Some specialist services like eye tests, dental care and prescriptions, however, require a contribution from the patients. Individuals can also subscribe to private health insurers, privately choose the specialists and avoid waiting lists for non-emergency procedures.

In the US, the federal government spends lot of money on the health sector (about 17.9% of GDP, the highest level in the world; WHO, 2011). Most of the cost for healthcare services, however, is paid by individuals through private insurance schemes, and doctors provide assistance under fee-for-service (FFS) terms. About 84.7% of Americans have some form of private health insurance, through their employer or the employer of their spouse or partner, purchased individually or through government programmes. There is no government health insurance company. Government programmes such as Medicare and Medicaid, however, directly cover part of the population that includes the elderly, disabled, children, veterans and some of the poor.

In other parts of the world, there has been a tendency, during the last decades, to increase forms of commercialisation of health services. In many countries, for example, patients have increasingly been asked to make out-of-pocket (OOP) payments at the point of need in addition to or as a substitution for advance payments in the form of taxation or insurance. In some countries, such as Russia, health services that were once provided for free have more recently started to have to be paid for. In some countries, such as Saudi Arabia, public hospitals started establishing 'business centres' for the provision of private health services alongside the public service part of the system of healthcare service delivery.

Higher education

Higher education is a public service that is largely provided for free at the point of delivery, but some countries deliver it upon payment of fees and others have made steps towards introducing commercial features. In Germany, for example, higher education is a public system that includes about 400 universities (serving about 2.4 million students) and it is publicly funded. After the Constitutional Court removed a ban on tuition fees in 2005 (which had been established in the 1970s), some universities started charging €1,000 per year in an effort to raise finance for service development. Following fierce protest from the students, political parties turned against the tuition fees, which were ostracised because of hampering equal opportunities. At present, university students pay administrative fees (about €150–€250 per semester) in public sector institutions, and tuition fees (up to over €10,000 per semester) in the approximately 100 private universities that are state-recognised (which enrol about 5% of total students).

In the UK, tuition fees were introduced in 1998 in anticipation of the financial needs of higher education institutions in the following decades. After devolution in 1999, the governments of Scotland and Wales started setting their own policies on fees. In England, tuition fees kept rising over time. In England, the Higher Education Act in 2004 allowed universities to charge fees of up to £3,000 per year (2006–2007). A few years later, the cap was raised up to £9,000 per year (2012–2013) and the figure is expected to rise with inflation from 2017 to 2018. About three quarters of English institutions charge the full amount. In Scotland, instead, the standard tuition fees for undergraduate students are about £1,820 per year.

In the US, higher education public institutions did not charge any fees at the time when they were founded (Thelin, 2011). Although the federal government provides some loans, grants and tax subsidies, most funding of universities in the US is based on tuition fees nowadays. The average yearly fee for private four-year institutions is about $33,000, and for public four-year college is about $9,500 (for students who are resident in the state, or 'in-state-fees') and $25,000 (for students who are resident in another state, or 'out-state-fees').

Also, in countries where the provision of higher education used to be largely a public sector affair, some forms of commercialisation have been introduced. In Italy, for example, university fees have risen over time to about €850–€1,000 per year. In Spain, university fees are approximately €680–€1,400 per year. In the Netherlands, university fees are about €2,000 per year for EU nationals. In Canada, tuition fees for nationals are about $4,500 (about $10,000 for international students) per year.

Water services

The provision of water (drinkable water supply and sewage) services in many countries used to be carried out by public sector utilities owned by sub-national governments. Although user fees were charged for the services, water utilities could not attain financial self-sufficiency and their deficit was covered by sub-national budgets. Especially in the last decades of the twentieth century, a policy orientation to improve efficiency and cost-effectiveness of water utilities led to the introduction of business-like management practices and, sometimes, to the privatisation of water services.

The privatisation of water services was carried out, for example, in England and Wales in 1989, where ten previously regional water authorities (RWAs) were transferred to private owners. The privatisation of water services resulted in increased investment, better compliance with drinking water standards and higher quality water in rivers (Van den Berg, 1997). The sector regulator, the Office of Water Services (OFWAT), also reported that the performance of the water sector improved in terms of quality and efficiency. Another effect of privatisation, however, was the increase in water tariffs, which resulted in one of the highest water bills in the world (on average, English households' water bills amount to about £400 per year).

As water utilities started pricing water services in order to make users pay for the full cost of the service (and, in some cases, also for a return on investment), water tariffs increased in many other countries as well. In Italy, for example, a reform in 1994 led to a partial privatisation of many water utilities and to the introduction of cost-recovery principles in many others that were retained in the public sector. An effect of the reform was the dramatic increase of water tariffs in many cities, although the original tariffs were often set below cost. The increase of water bills triggered a popular aversion towards the 'marketisation' of water services, which could have partially contributed to the proposal and outcome of a referendum in 2011 that abrogated the part of the legislation that provided the inclusion of a return on investment of up to 7% in the tariffs.

Only partially the pricing of water services can be related to commercial considerations, however. In the EU, for example, the Water Framework Directive in 2000 stipulated that water tariffs should be set with the aim to also stimulate a reduction of water consumption – a policy objective that is consistent with general aims to protect the environment and rationalise the use of water resources. Pricing of water in the EU, however, varies considerably across countries, as does the average consumption per capita. In those countries where water prices increased faster over time, like Hungary and Germany, water per capita consumption fell dramatically (Biswas and Kirchherr, 2012). The attitude of EU consumers has also come to acknowledge that water prices should be related to consumption volume (European Commission, 2012).

Setting user charges and fees

When public sector entities are funded through revenues raised from commercial activities, price setting for the services becomes of utmost importance. Public sector entities that receive part of their funding from general taxation may charge the users of their services, but often the price (which is typically required as an administrative fee) does not cover the full cost. Administrative fees may partially contribute to the variable part of the cost of the service (i.e. the cost that is incurred for the provision of an additional unit of the service, or 'incremental' cost). Often, they are charged for preventing the users from over-consuming public services when they are not provided for free.

As observed by Bird (2001), economic theory shows that utility firms should price their services at marginal cost. In practice, however, this prescription is hard to follow. First, company decisions are typically made on the basis of financial information rather than economics. Financial information consists of identifiable monetary expenditures (e.g. for purchases of consumables, wages and salaries, interest, etc.). Economic information, instead, consists of the opportunity costs of the inputs that are used for the production of utility services (e.g. the value of the potential benefit that was lost because of the use of the inputs, like the best alternative use of the land where the production of the services takes place). Second, economic costs are difficult to measure anyway, especially because of the many implications of production choices on other members of society (i.e. the social costs that are imposed on other individuals).

Economic theory also shows, more precisely, that prices should be set at the short-run marginal cost (SRMC). SRMC means that pricing decisions should not take into account the cost of investments (fixed costs) in the utility firm, which are assumed to be made at the most efficient scale. If prices are set at the long-run marginal cost (LRMC), then the demand for services would be lower than pricing at SLMC. If the investment in the facilities is high (a frequent scenario in utilities, which often face fluctuation of demand over time), then lower demand because of LRMC pricing would result in the under-utilisation of the facilities.

Utilities typically operate with relatively large sunk costs for infrastructure assets. Average cost tends to decline as the volume of service increases. If average cost declines, marginal cost is below the average cost. This means that the efficient pricing of the service is not sufficient to attain the break-even point. A similar argument holds for other public services – like, for example, healthcare – where up-front investments (e.g. hospital buildings, medical equipment, etc.) are needed before services are delivered.

Bird (2001) clarified that a feasible approach to pricing public services could be the average incremental cost (AIC) pricing. AIC consists of the calculation of the cost incurred for an additional user. An example is the pricing of highways: the access of an additional vehicle could be priced as a combination of a fixed charge (e.g. vehicle licensing) to help cover the fixed cost of the highway, a charge for the maintenance of the highway (e.g. a toll based on the kind of vehicle or driving record) and a charge for penalising peak time (to prevent congestion).

Another recommendation is to make use of multi-part tariffs. Multi-part tariffs consist of different price components that are charged depending on the circumstances of the users. A multi-part tariff could include a fixed charge (e.g. for connecting to the network) and a variable part (which is related to the volume of consumption). Multi-part tariffs can be also designed to discriminate between different kinds of users. As a general rule, prices should be higher the more inelastic the demand of users is. A system of discriminatory pricing would increase revenue and better allocate services, for instance by charging more at peak-time demand. High prices might discourage unnecessary consumption or induce users to search for alternative options. On the other hand, a system of discriminatory pricing is unfair because the rich have more capacity to spend and more options at their disposal.

Tariff regulation

In many industries, setting user charges and fees is subjected to regulation; that is, to the application of criteria and procedural rules that limit discretion in price setting. Price regulation is a tool of economic regulation, which consists of the institutions and activities that aim to fix market failures. Market failures arise when the market system does not result in the optimal allocation of resources. Reasons for market failure include the presence of a monopoly, of externalities in production or consumption, of asymmetry of information about the quality of goods between producers and consumers, and of lack of cooperation between producers or consumers to preserve common pool resources. Many public services fall within the category of goods that cannot be produced and allocated efficiently through the market system. Services like water supply and sanitation, for example, typically take place under monopolistic conditions. Services like healthcare and education have externalities and asymmetries between producers and consumers.

When public services are provided by public sector-owned entities, user charges and fees (or tariffs) are set according to various criteria, which may include the pursuit of financial self-sufficiency of the entity, equity and protection of the weakest consumers and the containment of wasteful consumption. In many countries in the world, however, these services are fully or partially provided by private sector entities, especially following policies of liberalisation, privatisation and re-regulation (which have especially affected infrastructure and utilities industries since the 1980s). If these services are produced by profit-seeking entities, then pricing decisions would be made with little, if any, consideration for their social effects (i.e. excluding consumers who cannot afford to pay for the services) and for the improvement of service quality (i.e. investing part of the profit for innovating).

The economic regulation of public services can take place in many forms. Gómez-Ibáñez (2009) distinguished between four models of regulation that range from the most pervasive to the least intrusive role of the government in the economy. First, regulation may take place through direct ownership and control of public service entities, such as state-owned railways or municipally owned water utilities. In this model of regulation, tariffs are set as administrative decisions of the public sector entity, typically along policy guidelines set by the government. Second, regulation may take place through franchise contracts, such as the water franchises that are applied for many water and sanitation utilities in France. In this model of regulation, tariffs (or the criteria for calculating tariffs and changing tariffs over time) are stipulated in the franchise contracts. Third, regulation may take place through the discretionary functions exercised by independent regulatory authorities (IRAs), such as the industry regulators of water in England and Wales (Water Services Regulation Authority, previously known as OFWAT), of electricity and gas (Office of Gas and Electricity Markets or OFGEM), of rails and roads (Office of Rail and Road or ORR) and of aviation and airports (Civil Aviation Authority or CAA) in the UK. In this model of regulation, tariffs are set by the IRA on a periodical basis, taking into account expected conditions (e.g. technological innovation and consumer demand) and the desired conduct of the public service entities (e.g. stimulating efficiency and innovation). Finally, the fourth model of regulation consists of letting the market system put pressure on service providers. This model of regulation is not really feasible, however, if conditions that result in market failure persist. When conditions change, however, other forms of price regulation are not necessary any more. A typical instance of such a scenario is the changed conditions in the telecommunications industry, where technological change since the 1980s opened up the market to new entrants that competed against former public sector monopolists of fixed-line telephony services.

At present, many countries in the world have adopted the model of regulation through IRAs for setting tariffs in infrastructure and utilities industries. Tariff regulation in the IRA model can take place in different ways, although the most common ones are the *rate-of-return* (ROR) and the *price cap* (PC) criteria (and their variants). In the ROR criterion, tariffs are regulated by limiting the return on investment of the regulated firm. In principle, this criterion has the advantage of letting the regulated firm decide the detailed tariff structure, provided that profit (as an indicator of the producer surplus) is capped within a given value. In practice, the ROR criterion may result in counterproductive effects because of an implicit incentive to expand the capital base (Averch and Johnson, 1962). The regulator also needs detailed and continuous information about the value of assets and costs of the regulated firms.

In the PC criterion, tariffs are regulated by setting caps on the tariffs or on the change of tariffs over a period in the future. In between the tariff reviews, regulated firms have an incentive to improve their efficiency and reduce costs because they are allowed to retain profits (Beesley and Littlechild, 1989; Littlechild, 1983). The regulation, however, may incite the temptation to rip-off the regulated firms of part of their profits by looking intrusively into their cost structures and setting more stringent price caps (or anticipating the review before the original date). The regulator also needs to assess how much the regulated firms can improve operational efficiency, possibly by setting up systems to benchmark their performance with other service providers. The regulated firms, moreover, can set detailed tariff baskets in order to cross-subsidise selected services, with effects that include allocative inefficiency and anti-competitive practices (Vickers and Yarrow, 1988; Armstrong et al., 1999).

Public–private partnerships

Public–private partnerships (PPPs) provide a financial scheme for the funding of infrastructure development that has been increasingly adopted for many public sector projects. The early adoption of PPPs dates back to the Private Finance Initiative (PFI) programme launched in the UK by John Major's government in 1992. During the following decades, projects funded through PPP schemes diffused all over Europe – with the UK being the main market, followed by Spain and Portugal. PPPs have been increasingly adopted in other regions and countries of the world, however, including Canada (Siemiatycki, 2015), India (Sahasranaman and Kapur, 2014) and China (Adams et al., 2006).

In general terms, PPPs consist of borrowing financial resources from private sector investors to invest in a public infrastructure, and of generating revenue from the use of the infrastructure for paying back the loans and providing a return on investment. The scheme is typically implemented through the creation of a special purpose vehicle (SPV) that is jointly owned by a public authority and private businesses or investors. Depending on the details of the scheme, the SPV may carry out the design of the infrastructure project, the construction and the operation and maintenance of infrastructure-related services, typically or partially for a user charge or fee (activities may be sub-contracted to other entities, however). Revenue generated from the infrastructure-related commercial activities provide the remuneration to investors.

A typical profile of the financial management of a PPP scheme is illustrated in Figure 8.1. At the beginning of the execution of the PPP scheme, financial flows are spent for the construction of the assets while the debt of the SPV increases. After the completion of the construction phase, revenue and cash flow are generated from the provision of infrastructure-related services. Part of the cash flow serves the repayment of the debt, which then gradually decreases over time.

In principle, PPPs can help governments to undertake infrastructure development programmes and to provide public services, albeit totally or partially through market-like transactions. PPPs have been used, for example, in the construction and operation of prisons, school and hospitals, in the development of transport infrastructure like highways, airport terminals, metros and parking, and in urban regeneration and development projects.

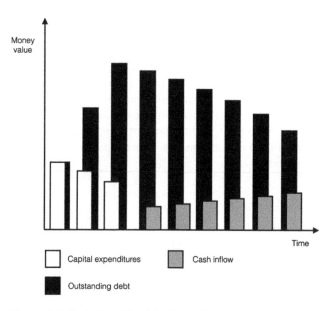

Figure 8.1 Typical profile of the financial management of a PPP scheme.

Details of the PPP projects, however, vary across industries. In highways, for example, revenue can originate from the tolls that drivers pay to transit the infrastructure. In prisons, the government would commit to pay the SPV (or a subsidiary) for detention and related services. In other projects like airport terminals, revenue may originate from a combination of charges to passengers and of rents for the commercial spaces.

Examples of PPP projects in the UK include the construction and operation of nine prisons through the PFI programme, where the management of the detention services was subjected to appraisal through various performance indicators; and the regeneration of Croydon council in London, where a partnership with the private developer John Laing was agreed in 2008 for twenty-eight years for developments that included leisure centres, residential properties and commercial areas. Examples also include, however, the negative experiences of the 'Building Schools for the Future' programme, where about £50 billion of investment in new school infrastructure took place between 2004 and 2010, but the scheme was terminated for reasons that included issues with the lack of capacity of local authorities to administer the scheme and the relatively poor quality of construction; and the PPP of the London Underground through Metronet Rail, which operated nine metro lines between 2003 and 2009, when the company collapsed and the services went back to Transport for London public authority.

An advantage of PPPs is that the scheme enables governments to fund infrastructure development by taking on more debt (the SPV is typically funded through a mix of equity and debt, such as bank loans) without disclosing it. The debt for financing infrastructure development is the SPV's. The government, however, may be required to make payments for the infrastructure-related services, or to provide safeguards or guarantees for the risks that the PPP project faces. In effect, then, the government makes financial commitments although they are not illustrated in the government's financial reports (i.e. 'off-balance sheet financing').

PPPs, however, also entail various forms of risks. The risks that PPP projects face include construction risk (whether construction is completed in time and within budget), demand risk (whether user demand – and revenue – is lower than expected), political risks (whether events like expropriation, change in laws or corruption hamper the execution of the project), financial risks (whether events like change of economic conditions, fluctuations of interest rate, inflation rate and foreign exchange rate affect the financial viability of the project), operation and maintenance risk (whether issues of cost overrun and productivity, or events of *force majeure*, hamper the provision of services), availability risk (whether services become partially or totally unavailable or fail to meet quality standards) and legal risks (whether controversies over the PPP contract or in the relationships with other entities result in legal costs or in the paralysis of the project).

Conclusions

This chapter examined the sources of public sector revenue that originate from charging users fees and tariffs. Part of what are generally conceived of as public services in the world are nowadays provided in commercial forms, where users are required to pay a price for accessing services like healthcare, higher education and water and sanitation. The use of market-like transactions for financing public services builds on various rationales, which include the need for additional sources of funding in order to attain the financial self-sufficiency of public service providers and the need for containing wasteful consumption. The tariffs that users pay should reflect their willingness to pay, although this may result in pricing policies that conflict with principles of equity of access to public services. Generating revenue from user charges and fees is a fundamental component of the PPP scheme, where governments can make use of off-balance sheet financing for supporting infrastructure development.

Questions for discussion

- Why aren't public services entirely financed by taxation revenue sources?
- Which kind of public services can be provided for a user charge or fee, and which ones cannot?
- Is it fair that those who can afford to pay for a private insurance or for private education deserve these services?
- What are the advantages and disadvantages of PPPs for governments?

9 Franchises, concessions, licences and privatisation

Franchises and concessions

Franchises and concessions provide important sources of revenue for many governments, at both the national and sub-national level. Franchises consist of contracts where a business entity is appointed to carry out the production of goods or provision of services in a regulated market, whose access is restricted on legal grounds. Franchises arise from government-granted monopolies, where public authorities provide that access and operation of certain markets are exclusively reserved to themselves. The government can decide to directly undertake the production for the government-granted monopolistic market or to allow one (or sometimes more) business entities to do it on its behalf upon payment of a fee. Instances of government-granted monopolies include public roads, water and sanitation services, radio transmission and gambling.

The boundaries of government-granted monopolies, however, change over time and depend on local institutional circumstances. The postal sector, for example, was long considered a government-granted monopoly in most countries. After postal services were liberalised in the UK on 1st January, 2006, tens of licences were issued to business operators who wanted to carry mail weighing less than 350 g and costing less than £1 to post. After the Postal Services Act in 2011, operators could provide postal services that fall outside the scope of 'universal service obligation' without the need of any licence although they are subjected to an authorisation.

Concessions consist of contracts where a business entity is granted rights over the assets of a public authority. Concessions include, for example, the use of public infrastructure like dams and aqueducts, the mining of land and the running of a catering establishment in a public leisure or sport centre. In a concession contract, the business entity pays fees for the right to exploit the asset for profit purposes. However, the public authority may require that the business entity performs certain actions; for example, taking care of maintenance of the infrastructure, restoration of the environment and compliance with health and safety regulations.

In the city of New York, for example, the Franchise and Concession Review Committee (FCRC) approves, under certain circumstances, the award of franchises and concessions. In 2014, the city had granted about sixty franchises, which resulted in more than $200 million in revenue. Concessions require FCRC approval if they are not awarded through competitive sealed bids. Concessions awarded without competitive sealed bids and which are significant (because of long duration or high value) require public hearings. In 2014, the city awarded 125 new concessions and collected about $50 million from existing concessions.

Designing franchise and concession contracts

Franchise and concession contracts pose a number of economic issues. Differently from 'spot' contracts, franchises and concessions are complex transactions which include several mutual obligations that should be fulfilled over a period of time, possibly depending on contingent conditions. Ideally, such contracts could stipulate in detail what each party should do under any possible circumstance, and provide solid methods and tools for enforcement. In practice, contracts are typically incomplete for reasons that include the impossibility to anticipate any possible future state of the world and the ambiguity of natural language (Hart, 1988; Hart and Moore, 1999; Maskin and Tirole, 1999).

Contract incompleteness opens up the possibility of opportunistic behaviour and moral hazard. Opportunistic behaviour consists of the possibility that one party of the contract does not fulfil the obligations that had been mutually agreed on between the two parties of the contract for partisan advantage, especially when taking advantage of incomplete contracts that do not specify mechanisms of enforcement in case of violation of contractual terms. Moral hazard consists of the tendency of one party to take more risk because the other party bears the cost of the risk. Moral hazard especially arises from information asymmetry, when one party of the contract does not know what the other party of the contract does.

In franchise and concession contracts, opportunistic behaviour and moral hazard arise on many fronts. The business entity, for example, may fail to comply with contractual requirements such as maintenance of assets or meeting service quality performance standards in order to save costs. The public authority that grants the franchise or concession may not know precisely how the business entity behaves. The public authority may discover only after the contact has been signed that the business entity may not have the capacity to carry out the agreed obligations. Because of these possible scenarios, designing franchise and concession contracts is extremely important.

The design of franchise and concession contracts should pay attention to some critical features. One of them is the setting up of mechanisms for 'information extraction', which are intended to encourage one party to disclose private information to the other. One main mechanism of information extraction is to select the counterpart of a franchise or concession contract through an auction (Persico, 2000; Bergemann and Pesendorfer, 2007). In auctions, bidders disclose private information about their reservation price (i.e. the highest price that they are willing to pay for the franchise or concession contract fees). Auctions can be designed in different ways, however, and some return better information advantages than others (Coppinger et al., 1980; McCabe et al., 1990).

Another important feature of franchise and concession contracts is the specification of contract termination. A main issue here is the appraisal of the value of the asset that, when the contract terminates, is returned from the business entity to the public authority. Some contracts may provide that the business party must maintain the asset and return it in good condition. Contracts, then, should provide specific criteria and mechanisms for ensuring that the business party does not shirk their responsibility to keep the asset in good condition, especially by avoiding maintenance in the terminal part of the contract period. Other contracts may provide that the public authority would reimburse the business party for any incremental value of the asset when it is returned with respect to the beginning of the contract period. Such provision, however, may induce the business party to 'gold plate' the asset in order to claim the increased value.

Revenue from licensing assets and activities

Additional forms of public sector revenue that originate from assets take the form of licences. Licences are permits to use or to own an asset, or to carry out an activity. A typical feature of licences issued by public authorities is that the use or ownership of the asset, or the carrying out of the activity, is not allowed without the licence, and mechanisms of enforcement (e.g. investigations and fines) are put into place to detect violations.

Licences vary in the kind of assets they refer to, in the length of time of the permit and in the mechanisms through which they are issued. In the UK, for example, licences are issued for burials at sea (licence cost is £175), for multiple occupation of a house (or 'house share' where the same property is rented by at least three people who are not from the same household but share facilities like the bathroom and kitchen; licence cost depends on local councils), for house collection (where money or goods are collected for charity, there is no licence cost but there are fines and penalties if the collectors are without a licence) and for road occupation for building works (licence cost depends on local councils).

Some licences are issued to permit the use of heritage. In the UK, for example, English Heritage (a charity that cares for over 400 historical buildings, monuments and sites) collaborates with partners for the production and commercialisation of licensed products. Additional kinds of licences are issued to permit the ownership and installation of durable goods, like television licences (in the UK, £145.50 per year for a colour TV), or to allow the use of durable goods, like driving licences (about £120 of statutory fees, setting aside tuition fees).

Other licences are issued to permit gambling, an activity which is considered (totally or in part) illegal in many countries. In the UK, for example, the Gambling Commission is a government agency (established under the Gambling Act of 2005) that issues licences for various kinds of gambling, including arcades, betting, bingo, casinos, gambling software, gambling machines and lotteries, also in remote (online) forms. Apart from licences, the gambling industry in the UK (totalling about £14 billion turnover) also generates revenue from a share of the National Lottery, which goes to the state and to the fund for 'good causes'. In particular circumstances, gambling may provide an important source of public revenue: for example, in Macau direct taxes on gambling (about MOP$72 billion or US$9 billion in 2016) amount to about 78% of total government revenue.

An important area where the issue of licences resulted in massive revenue for governments is the radio spectrum. The radio spectrum is the range of electromagnetic frequencies between 3 kHz and 300 GHz that can be used for wireless communication. Radio and TV stations can use part of the radio spectrum upon receiving a licence from national regulatory authorities. The surge of information and communication technology in the last decades, and especially the use of mobile phones and the growth of Internet traffic, led to high demand for third generation (3G) and fourth generation (4G) mobile services. The licensing of 3G and 4G mobile licences resulted in remarkable revenue for governments in many countries. In the UK, the Radiocommunications Agency raised about £22 billion from auctions for 3G licences in the early 2000s. In Germany, revenue from 3G licences was about €50 billion. In Italy, the government raised about €27 billion from 3G licensing.

Privatisation of public assets and state-owned enterprises

Privatisation consists of the (total or partial) transfer of assets or of public sector-owned enterprises to the private sector. Privatisation may generate considerable revenue for the public budget; like, for example, in the privatisations of British Telecom in 1984–1993 (total about £14 billion), British Gas in 1986 (about £7.7 billion) and British Rail in 1994–1997 (about £2.5 billion) (Rhodes et al., 2014). Privatisation, however, is a questionable approach to raising public money, at least because of the occasional and non-repetitive circumstances of pouring extra financial resources into the budget. Once a public asset or state-owned enterprise (SOE) is privatised, the government has no means to earn additional revenue from them, if not after buying back (re-nationalisation) of what had been sold in the first place.

Privatisation is a policy that has often occupied a pivotal position in government agendas in the last decades. Apart from occasional divestures of SOEs in earlier periods (e.g. the privatisation of Volkswagen in 1960), privatisation took off in the 1980s, especially in countries like the UK and Chile. During the 1990s and 2000s, privatisation spread throughout the world, including in the EU (where EU directives resulted in some opening of infrastructure and utilities industries to competitive pressures), Latin America (Chong and De Silanes, 2005), Africa (Bayliss, 2003), developing countries (Estrin and Pelletier, 2016) and recently in China, especially in the industries of telecommunications, finance and utilities.

The reasons for privatisation typically include motives other than raising public sector revenues (Heald, 1985). Megginson (2010) discussed that privatisations can be used for promoting economic efficiency, on the basis that business management practices make assets or enterprises perform better than when they are owned by public authorities. Another motive for privatisation is to reduce the role of the government in the economy, especially when public officers may try and influence the management of SOEs for partisan gains. Privatisation can also serve as a tool to promote wider share ownership, if citizens are assigned entitlements ('vouchers', which could be later traded and converted into shares) of the SEOs or offered the possibility to buy shares in an initial public offering (IPO). If privatisation is accompanied by measures to liberalise industries that were previously exclusively populated by SOEs, another motive for privatisation is to stimulate the entry of private investors and competition. Additional motives for privatisation originate from particular historical circumstances. For example, the privatisations in Eastern European countries in the 1990s related to the shift from a socialist regime of state ownership to one of private property and business competition.

The details of how privatisation is conducted play an important role in the generation of public sector revenue. Public assets and SOEs may be privatised through the direct sale to a private investor. On the one hand, in this way the government can select the new owner (which, for various reasons, the government may prefer to be a national actor rather than a foreign entity) and negotiate conditions for the sale. On the other hand, direct sales may not put enough pressure on the buyer to come to more advantageous terms for the selling government. The government may also collude with the buyer to arrange an advantageous sale for the buyer, which might compensate government officers with private gains.

Public assets and SOEs may also be privatised through public sales of ownership shares. In principle, this approach may result in larger revenue than through direct sales, because any prospective buyer would compete for purchasing the shares at a higher price. In practice, public sales require institutions and mechanisms for orchestrating the sale of ownership shares, as it could be conveniently done if a stock market is present in the country. With an IPO, the government may elicit the expression of interest from investors, which could include any individual if the government aims to stimulate forms of 'popular shareholding' by diffusing ownership of shares of privatised SOEs among the population.

Sometimes, the government may decide to restrict ownership of the privatised SOEs in order to pursue social or political objectives. For example, the government may reserve part of the shares of a privatised SOE for the employees, if the government believes that this scheme results in forms of employee participation that have beneficial effects in terms of motivation, productivity and concern for the long-term success of the privatised firm. Alternatively, the government may also reserve part of the shares for the management of the privatised SOEs, possibly in the form of a 'leveraged buy-out' (LBO) where financing for the purchase of shares originates from loans that are paid back out of the future cash flows of the same privatised firm. Sometimes, the government may also reserve part of the shares of the privatised SOE for itself ('golden share'), especially if they are combined with statutory provisions that enable the government to retain veto powers on the main strategic decisions of the privatised firm.

The tendency to privatise public assets and SOEs might be reinforced, in the future, if governments decide to divest themselves additional parts of their properties and ownership of firms. Christiansen (2011) estimated that the total value of SOEs that are owned by governments of OECD countries amount to about $2 trillion. OECD country governments seem to also hold the minority (but often controlling) stakes in partially privatised firms to the value of about $1 trillion. In addition, the governments possess non-financial assets – in the form of land, buildings and subsoil resources – whose total value might amount to about $35 trillion in the OECD (*The Economist*, 2014). In principle, the governments could generate massive revenue (up to about $9 trillion in OECD countries; *The Economist*, 2014) from the sale of part of these assets, many of which are often unused, unattended or abandoned. Obstacles to asset privatisation, however, arise from the poor accounting for public assets in many public sector entities (which partially originates from public sector cash-based accounting systems) and political resistance.

Part of the resistance towards privatisation arises because of ideological reasons. The privatisation of public assets and SOEs entails that the government gives up control of activities and services that can be provided through the assets and firms that are privatised. The private owners and investors of the privatised assets and firms would pursue financial and economic goals that may collide with the public interest, at least for part of society. Another reason for resistance towards privatisation is that the government may find it difficult to regain control of privatised assets or firms in the future if changed conditions make it more advantageous to pursue re-nationalisation. Some particular assets and firms, moreover, may not be privatised because they hold an important role in the pursuit of public policies (e.g. the national power grid, which is pivotal for national security, and valuable historical heritage, which is of great significance for national identity).

Conclusions

This chapter examined the generation of revenue from franchises, concessions and privatisation. Franchises and concessions are contractual arrangements where governments can earn revenue by carrying out the production of goods or the provision of services in a regulated market or from the use of public assets. The design of franchise and concession contracts is extremely important because, in the long term, parties may face unexpected circumstances and exploit contract incompleteness to their advantage. Other forms of revenue arise from the issue of licences, which regulate individual and business conduct in various areas, and from the privatisation of public assets and SOEs.

Questions for discussion

- What are the issues that arise with long-term contracts like franchises and concessions?
- Is there any way to prevent the parties of a franchise or concession contract to behave opportunistically?
- How can licences help governments to regulate behaviour?
- What are the advantages and disadvantages of privatisation?

10   Exploitation of natural resources

Revenue from natural resources

Natural resources provide a fundamental source of public sector revenue for many countries. As shown in Figure 10.1, revenue from natural resources provide about 90% of total government revenue in Saudi Arabia, Brunei and Equatorial Guinea, and the main share of total government revenue in many other African, Middle Eastern, Asian and Latin American countries. The extraction and commercialisation of natural resources (of both petroleum and minerals) should be carefully orchestrated by public authorities, therefore, in order to provide the means to exploit the natural resources in a way that is advantageous for domestic public finances.

Some countries provide illustrative examples of the effective exploitation of natural resources. Starting from initial conditions after independence in 1966, Botswana has enjoyed a long period of high growth rate since the 1960s and relatively high GDP per capita with respect to African countries, and nowadays the country largely relies on revenue from diamonds (up to about 40% of government revenue). Since the first extractions in the 1950s, the United Arab Emirates made use of hydrocarbon resources for modernising infrastructure, establishing a generous welfare system, and providing free access to education and healthcare, while also diversifying their economy into manufacturing, telecommunications, finance and tourism. After the discovery of oil and gas fields in the 1960s, Norway grew up to become the third largest petroleum exporter after Saudi Arabia and Russia. The country has been extremely successful in attaining high growth and a top-class welfare system.

Not every country that is rich in natural resources, however, seems capable of generating revenue and putting it to good use for national prosperity. Sometimes, the presence of natural resources is a source of armed conflict between governments or factions within countries. Sometimes, temptations to misappropriate the revenue from natural resources results in forms of corruption, bribery and theft. Sometimes, the governments of natural-resource-rich countries surrender part of their revenue to foreign companies which enjoy concessions to exploit natural resource fields that enable them to appropriate most of the profits. In order to avoid missing the opportunities from natural resources, governments should ponder the tools for raising revenue from natural resources and for revenue sharing.

Tools for raising revenue from natural resources

In principle, a government may be the only entity who holds the right to exploit subsoil resources (onshore and offshore) within their territorial jurisdiction and who sets up the means to extract and commercialise natural resources. The constitution of a country, for example, may provide that the government is the only legitimate claimant on subsoil resources and the

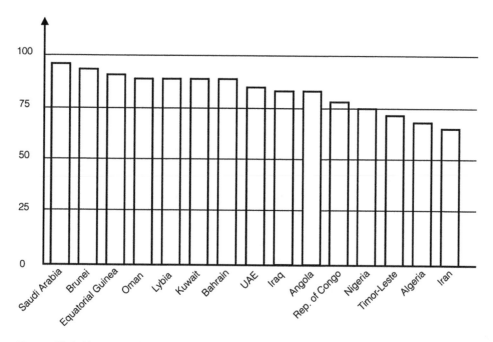

Figure 10.1 Share (%) of revenue from natural resources (petroleum and metal) with respect to total government revenue in the main resource-rich countries.

Source: Lemgruber and Shelton, 2014.

government may establish an SOE to carry out the extraction and commercialisation process. Often, however, the government does not carry out extraction and commercialisation activities; instead they are undertaken by domestic or foreign business companies, although the government may own a share of them. There are various ways for raising revenue from natural resources for the government, therefore, depending on whether the government directly undertakes or participates in the business venture, or if it employs alternative mechanisms.

A basic distinction can be drawn between concession and contractual regimes for the exploitation of natural resources (Brosio and Singh, 2015). In a concession regime, the government awards a concession to a business company, which becomes the owner of the resource once it is extracted. The business company typically pays the concession fee and taxes (e.g. corporate income tax and excises), and may possibly fulfil some requirements like providing restoration of the environment once the extraction is terminated and commercialising part of the natural resource in the domestic market at some agreed price. In a contractual regime, instead, the government retains control of some decisions, like, for example, on extraction, production and commercialisation, and contracts out with a business company to implement them. There are various contractual schemes which provide different allocations of control, risk and revenue between the government and private contractors.

The difference between concession and contractual regimes is not so sharp, however. Also, in concession regimes the government may retain the possibility to influence extraction and commercialisation decisions; in contractual regimes the government may require the payment of royalties and other taxes while the private contractor is allowed to retain part of the natural resource or a share of revenue. One main difference between the two schemes, however, is the degree of risk and control that is allocated between the government and the business companies: contractual regimes generally enable the government to retain more discretion (e.g. on setting the price of the natural resource), although it also carries more risk (e.g. revenue is dependent on price fluctuations rather than a fixed concession fee).

The tools that governments can use to raise revenue from natural resources can also be divided between *ex ante* and *ex post* instruments (Brosio and Singh, 2015). *Ex ante* instruments refer to the tools used before the extraction and commercialisation of natural resources takes place, while *ex post* instruments relate to the tools used after the resources are extracted. *Ex ante* instruments comprise auctioning exploration and exploitation rights and concession fees, signature fees and bonuses. Auctioning exploration and exploitation rights provides an immediate source of revenue to the government, if business companies do not collude to limit their offerings and retain most of the rent from the exploitation of lucrative natural resource fields. Alternatively, the government may just ask them to pay administrative fees (concession fees, signature fees and bonuses), although in this case too high fees discourage private initiative while too low fees give up opportunities for public revenue.

Ex post instruments consist of government equity in projects, production sharing and taxation. Government equity in projects enables the government to reap the fruits of the business venture, especially if they are higher than expected. On the other hand, joint ownership of the project may be a source of conflict between partners if the consequences of a decision have contrasting effects on the profitability of the business venture, society and the environment. Alternatively, a government may prefer to leave most extraction and commercialisation decisions to a business company and to gain from sharing the revenue from natural resources. In such circumstances, however, the government may retain an interest to influence business decisions. In addition, further issues arise from the asymmetry of information between the government and the business company, especially on the quantity and quality of extracted material, production costs and reliability of revenue figures.

The final *ex post* instrument – namely, taxation – can be applied in different ways (Lemgruber and Shelton, 2014). Common tax schemes include specific royalties, where a constant tax is levied per unit of output, and *ad valorem* royalties, where taxes are determined as a constant percentage of the value of the output. As any tax, royalties have distortionary effects because they increase production costs. They are advantageous for governments, however, because they can be levied as soon as extraction starts (like excises). They also pose some issues of asymmetric information, because the government needs to monitor that the volume of production is measured and reported accurately.

An alternative scheme of taxation is the levy of a higher-than-normal tax rate on corporate income (a tax surcharge). The surcharge may be directed to specific extraction and commercialisation projects. It is relatively simple to administer insofar as it is added on top of already existing corporate income tax. If the surcharge is too high, however, it will discourage investments that could have been undertaken otherwise, with negative effects on tax revenue.

A further scheme of taxation is the levy of a tax on resource rent. There are various versions of resource rent tax, but they generally consist of levying a tax on the difference between the value of production sold and all the opportunity costs that are incurred in extraction and commercialisation. Opportunity costs are calculated taking into account both capital and current expenditures. The determination of capital costs, however, is difficult because of the need to estimate depreciation, financial costs and capital losses. This would require estimates of the present value of rents, on the basis of parameters like the time horizon of the exploitation of the natural resource field and the choice of a discount rate. A cash flow tax could be applied, alternatively, in order to avoid the practical obstacles to appraise the economic value of the natural resource rent.

Many of the world's natural resource fields lay in developing or emergent countries. The selection of the instruments for raising public sector revenue largely depends on the administrative capacity of the government. Some instruments require greater capacity of public officers to interact with business partners and to navigate through complex decision scenarios. Other instruments work on the basis of knowledge and skills that public officers should possess on legal and financial matters. The business companies that operate in natural resource extraction and commercialisation, instead, typically take the form of multinationals with strong expertise in every segment of the extraction industry.

Many of the above instruments and schemes are applied in the world. In Nigeria, for example, the national oil company NNPC set up joint ventures with foreign business companies (e.g. Shell, Agip, Elf, Mobil and Chevron) for the exploration and production of oil. In the scheme, NNPC invests by borrowing from partners and paying them back in kind. The profits from the venture are then split between NNPC and the partners, which pay royalties, signature bonuses and corporate income taxes to the government. Also, in Angola, the national oil company Sonangol is a partner in extraction ventures through revenue-sharing schemes (e.g. with Eni and Total).

Revenue sharing across layers of government

In general, revenue that governments raise from the exploitation of natural resources are shared with sub-national governments of the producing area. There are various reasons for the inter-governmental sharing of natural resource revenue, including compensating local communities for the disruption of the environment because of the extractive activities. More rarely, revenue-sharing arrangements may also distribute part of the revenue to other, non-producing sub-national governments, for reasons that mainly relate to horizontal equity and income redistribution.

Centralisation of revenue from natural resources is relatively less frequent, although it is arranged in countries like Saudi Arabia, Norway and the UK. In the case of the UK, however, the revenue that originates from oil and gas in Scotland is partially compensated with grants to local governments (the so-called 'Barnett formula'). The grant transfer system has been criticised, however, on the basis of the argument that although Scotland receives more public spending than the UK average, it generates at least the same amount of taxes as the UK average.

The sharing of natural resource revenue across government layers depends on the institutional configuration of the country's system of governance. If the constitution of the country (or relevant legislation) does not provide that sub-national governments have the right to receive part of natural resource revenue, then any revenue-sharing arrangement should originate from political agreements. The central government may prefer to exert control over all revenue from natural resources and to decide upon grant transfers depending on circumstances. When revenue from natural resources are dependent on highly fluctuating market prices, for example, it could be preferable that the budget of sub-national governments is insulated from commodity price-fluctuation risks because this might result in unpredictable cuts to public spending.

Additional arguments can be formulated against the sharing of revenue between the central government and the sub-national government where the natural resource is extracted. If the sub-national government spends the natural resource revenue on better infrastructure and public services, then it would attract individuals and businesses from other sub-national areas, with the effect of distorting the spatial allocation of resources. However, the sub-national government may also spend the natural resource revenue on unnecessary projects.

If the central government and the sub-national government share the revenue from natural resources, they can arrange it in different ways. One approach is to split different kinds of revenue sources – for example, royalties are assigned to the sub-national government while corporate income tax and rent tax are paid to the central government (as, for example, in the US, Australia and Brazil). Another approach is to use the same instrument to raise revenue which is then split according to some criterion; for example, by levying a national corporate income tax and a sub-national tax surcharge that is set by the sub-national government ('concurrency' of taxes). In another approach, the split of revenue (revenue sharing) is based on the allocation of a share – decided by the central government – of revenue from national resources to the sub-national government. In one more approach, the sub-national government may receive a share of natural resource revenue in the form of investments in infrastructure and systems for public service delivery from the central government.

The resource curse

In principle, the presence of natural resources should enable a country to raise public sector revenue with beneficial effects in terms of public spending and less taxes (or other means of raising public sector revenue) on the economy. In practice, evidence has been collected that the beneficial effect of natural resources does not always materialise. Known as the 'resource curse', the presence of natural resources in a country is correlated with lower growth (and other macroeconomic indicators) in a statistically significant way (Ross, 1999; Sachs and Warner, 2001; Atkinson and Hamilton, 2003; Frankel, 2010). Apart from a few examples (e.g. Norway), many countries seem to miss the opportunity to fully exploit the potential of petroleum, mineral or other kinds of natural endowments.

The resource curse can be explained in different ways (van der Ploeg, 2011). One main explanation is that the commercialisation of natural resources abroad induces an appreciation of the national currency, with detrimental effects on any other export-oriented industry. Another explanation highlights that the profitability of the natural resource industry misallocates investments and human resources to the natural resource industry, with negative consequences on other sectors of the economy. One more explanation builds on the weaknesses of institutions in many developing and emergent countries, where natural resources stimulate corruption and misappropriation of public monies. One additional explanation is that the possibility to share revenue from natural resources discourages any other entrepreneurial venture and stimulates rent-seeking.

Among these explanations, the one related to the negative effects of natural resource abundance on the integrity of public financial management is especially relevant in developing countries. Revenue for natural resources can be used to serve partisan political purposes, such as to pacify internal dissent, loosen accountability ties and resist modernisation (Isham et al., 2005). The redistribution of part of the revenue from natural resources to the middle classes may stimulate rent-seeking and discourage entrepreneurship (Bourguignon and Verdier, 2000). For those in power, natural resource rents provide a tool for buying consensus and suppressing opposition through bribery, subsidies and profligate spending (Robinson et al., 2006). In order to maintain the status quo, those in power may also actively suppress alternative industries and technological development (Acemoglu and Robinson, 2006).

An important role, in this respect, is played by the quality of the institutions of the country. If systems and mechanisms for the control of the discretion of those in power are in place, then the misappropriation of revenue from natural resources may be contained. Systems and mechanisms include institutions of prudent and accountable public financial management, in the form of transparent planning and budgeting, accurate accounting and financial reporting, and independent auditing and assurance. In some countries with a large endowment of natural resources, however, wars, internal struggles and lack of a tradition of accountable government practices often results in 'weak' institutions that facilitate the use of natural resource revenue for personal or partisan gains.

A typical scenario of the resource curse is the so-called 'Dutch disease', which originates from the experience of the Netherlands after the discovery and exploitation of the natural gas Groningen fields in 1959. When the natural resource sector expands, it attracts labour and other resources away from other industries (a 'deindustrialisation'). In addition, the extra public sector revenue stimulates spending in public administration and public services, which (as a service sector) attract further resources away from other industries (Corden and Neary, 1982). The appreciation of the domestic currency that originates from the export of the natural resource, moreover, harms other export-oriented industries that lose part of their competitiveness abroad.

Evidence for the resource curse (and the Dutch disease in particular) has been detected on various occasions, although some countries seem better equipped to convert natural resource revenue into more public spending. A study by Caselli and Michaels (2009), for example, examined the effects of revenue from oil fields on the economy and public financial management of municipalities in Brazil. They showed that oil discoveries and exploitation resulted in an expansion of services and a contraction of non-oil industries. They also found that, in the specific country context, revenue from natural resources resulted in more public spending on housing, urban development, education, healthcare and welfare.

Revenue from woodland, forests and fisheries

Although other natural resources aside from petroleum and minerals only play a minor role as a source of revenue for public authorities, they should not be discounted. In some parts of the world, woodland and forests provide an important natural resource for the preservation of many animal species and the conduct of human lives. In part, woodland and forests can also provide a source of public sector revenue, through various forms of taxation or licensing for the acquisition of woodland and forest products (most notably, timber). Sometimes, public authorities may consider generating revenue from the selling of woodland and forests, although this option often engenders public protest (e.g. the opposition to the proposal to sell 15% of forests in England in 2013).

Other natural resources that can be exploited for generating public sector revenue include fisheries. Revenue from the exploitation of fisheries may take different forms, including access fees for other countries' vessels and licence fees for domestic vessels. For example, many Pacific islands grant access to fisheries resources (e.g. tuna) to foreign vessels (mainly from the US) and issue licences for home fishermen. In 2015, the government of Mauritania granted access to local ocean fisheries to vessels from the EU, which will pay about €59 million per year for four years in return.

The exploitation of natural resources has increasingly incorporated concerns with the measures that countries should take to contribute to environmental preservation. These measures include the establishment of 'forest carbon offsets' (or 'carbon credits'), where investment in woodland and forestry contributes to the reduction of carbon dioxide in the atmosphere by 'sequestrating' it into biomass. Once created, carbon credits can be traded in markets where buyers can acquire them in order to compensate for the polluting activities that they carry out. The European Emission Trading System (ETS) provides an instance of an institutional market for carbon credit. At the local level, during recent years there has been a growing interest in voluntary markets, where carbon credits originate from re-forestation initiatives and from avoided de-forestation actions (so-called Reduced Emissions from Deforestation and Degradation or REDD).

The generation of carbon credits provides sources of revenue for business and public sector entities alike. Projects that expand existing natural resources that absorb carbon dioxide (as computed in the Kyoto Protocol, effective from 2005) provide 'carbon sinks' which have value that can be traded in regulated markets. An instance of such an approach took place in the north-eastern regions of Italy, where the EU-funded Carbomark project assisted the creation of carbon credits and their trade (at prices between €4 and €13 per ton of carbon dioxide). The carbon credit production and market, however, requires various institutional and organisational components, such as reliable estimates of the amount of sequestrated carbon dioxide, transparent registries of transactions and the monitoring of the sustainability of the re-forestation (or the avoided de-forestation) for several years.

Spending and investing revenue from natural resources

Countries that raise revenue from natural resources face the issue of deciding what to do with the money. Revenue from natural resources originates from rents rather than any share of economic activity – production, trade, consumption or investments. As such, arguments can be made that revenue from natural resources should be used for special schemes that are not typically considered when revenue arises from taxation, foreign aid, user charges and fees, PPPs, franchises, concessions, licences and privatisation.

One such special scheme consists of distributing, at least in part, the income that originates from natural resources to the citizens. In Alaska, for example, revenue from oil resources is invested in the Permanent Fund, whose dividends are distributed annually to Alaska residents. The amount of the payment is based on a five-year average of the performance of the Permanent Fund (whose value is about $55 billion). Annual individual payments ranged between about $850 (in 2005) to about $3,300 (in 2008). Parents receive the payment on behalf of their children. The amount of money that a family can receive, then, may be substantive with respect to average household income.

The distribution of income from natural resources, however, is criticised because it rewards the present generation rather than future ones. An alternative scheme consists of investing the revenue from natural resources in physical and financial assets that improve the prospects of economic development and welfare in the years to come. In Norway, for example, revenue from oil and gas (in the form of taxes, licences and income from the partially state-owned oil company Statoil) is invested in the Government Pension Fund of Norway. The Fund, whose value is about $880 billion, largely invests in foreign stock markets (mostly equity and the rest in fixed-income securities) and, in part, in real estate. Petroleum resources have a marginal impact on the state budget, for reasons that include – apart from concern for future generations – expected inflation if massive financial resources are spent in a country whose economy relies on just about five million residents.

The use of revenue from natural resources into government-owned (or 'sovereign wealth') funds is pursued by many other resource-rich countries (such as China, United Arab Emirates,

Kuwait and Saudi Arabia), especially when revenue from natural resources generates a budget surplus and there is no stock of debt to repay. Some sovereign wealth funds consist of a form of saving of present natural resource revenue for the future. Other sovereign wealth funds, however, provide a tool for the stabilisation of the economy, especially when it is exposed to fluctuations of exchange rates that can negatively impact imports and exports. Other sovereign funds play a geo-strategic role to provide exceptional means in case of need or to expand a country's influence abroad.

For those resource-rich countries that fall into the category of 'low income' ones, however, making use of the revenue from natural resources to stimulate domestic development is a more sensible goal than investing sovereign wealth funds abroad. This is the position of the IMF (2012), which considered that the characteristics of low-income countries (scarcity of domestic capital and limited access to international capital markets) require innovative policies to stimulate development. The spending of natural resource revenue may help to build public capital in the short run, with beneficial effects on the growth of GDP from non-natural resource industries. Also, scaling-up investments can be beneficial when a country experiences a negative resource shock, and it can be coupled with a stabilisation fund to save resources in boom times to be spent in bust periods.

Conclusions

This chapter considered the sources of revenue that originate from natural resources. Natural resources provide an important source of revenue for many countries, which can extract their share of funding through various concessions and contract arrangements. Often, these arrangements also include a role for sub-national governments where the natural resources are extracted, although sometimes countries may prefer to centralise control of the natural resource revenue or, rarely, distribute part of it to non-producer sub-national governments. The natural endowment of resources, however, does not guarantee that the country flourishes. Sometimes, countries fall into the 'trap' of the resource curse, where various conditions and mechanisms contribute to hampering economic growth. Prudent use of natural resource revenue includes the investment in sovereign wealth funds, which can set revenue aside for future generations.

Questions for discussion

- What are the advantages and disadvantages of concessions and contracts for raising revenue from natural resources?
- What should resource-rich countries do to avoid the resource curse?
- What should resource-rich countries do to anticipate future scenarios where the natural resource is exhausted?
- What are the advantages and disadvantages of sharing natural resource revenue with sub-national governments?
- Should natural resource revenue be distributed to citizens?

11 Borrowing and public debt

Public sector borrowing

Borrowing has long been a method to raise money for governments. Different from other forms of public sector revenue that have been discussed so far, borrowing presents some peculiar features. Unlike taxation and inter-governmental transfers, borrowing is not based on the hierarchical relationships between a government (that can impose taxes) and the citizens, or between different layers of governments (that can transfer funds from one level of government to another, possibly under specified requirements or conditions). Similar to commercial transactions (like providing a service for a user charge or fee, or renting assets or issuing licences), borrowing is based on market exchanges – the government acquires funds in exchange for the promise to pay interest and the principal back. However, borrowing differs from commercial approaches to raising money because of its implications on the future. Borrowing entails that a government makes a commitment of part of future budgets, when part of revenue will be allocated to service the repayment of the public debt.

Borrowing has been a common method to raise money for many governments since centuries ago. In a historical analysis of the development of debt capacity of Britain in the seventeenth century, for example, Stasavage (2003) showed that institutional adjustments after the Glorious Revolution in 1688 led to increased capacity for the Crown to borrow. Partially inspired by reforms carried out in the Netherlands, the country adopted innovative institutions, like the attribution of prerogatives on public finance to Parliament and the creation of the Bank of England, which resulted in more credible commitment from the side of the Crown to pay back their debts.

The issue of creditworthiness – that is, of the credibility of the promise to pay interest and the principal back – is fundamental in public sector borrowing. If creditors of the government believe that the government may not fulfil its obligations, they may be willing to lend their money at higher interest rates, or not to lend their money at all. If, instead, creditors are willing to lend their money, the government can defer part of the cost of financing public goods. Public investments, for example, can be made without an immediate increase of taxation or other revenue sources.

The government debtor, however, may have the temptation to default on the payment of interest and principal, for example to avoid increasing taxation and alienate part of the electorate. Because of the ephemeral nature of governments in democratic regimes, elections may result in dramatic 'swings' in policy orientation. The creditors risk that a changed government (or a government coalition) may not fulfil the debt promise. Institutions such as an independent central bank and various forms of commitments (such as, for example, rules about fiscal balance written in a constitution) help to provide assurance to creditors that the government does not default on debt.

Without institutions that help to make the management of public debt immune from changed government orientations, the renegotiation of debt or default may be a permanent threat. The very issue of public debt (e.g. in the form of securities like treasury bonds or gilts) gives rise to a conflict of interest between those who own public debt (e.g. domestic banks and foreign investors) and the taxpayers, who typically bear most of the burden to provide revenue to the government. If taxpayers are a cohesive group, they may affect government policies through various means, for example by lobbying and sponsoring candidates that are supportive of renegotiating or defaulting on debt. If taxpayers are divided along various political and social dimensions, they may be more likely to carry the burden of the repayment of the debt.

The repayment of public debt also depends on the presence of various and mutually supportive interests to maintain or increase public spending. From a public choice perspective, democracies have a tendency to overspend because of the short-sightedness and selfishness of voters and opportunism of politicians (Buchanan, 1958; Buchanan and Tullock, 1962). Large public spending requires adequate sources of financing. If no part of the electorate is willing to cut public spending, politicians in government keep funding existing public policies and programmes through borrowing if other sources of revenue are not enough.

The cost of borrowing

When the government borrows money, it is not earning revenue in the same sense as when cashing in taxes or selling services. Income generated from taxation and from various forms of commercial activity is considered, in accounting terms, as the result of the recurrent operations of government. The money that is received from lenders, instead, results in the temporary transfer of financial resources to the government, which is expected to return the principal back in the agreed period of time and to pay interest on the borrowed funds.

The interest on the borrowed funds depends on the conditions of the loan. When a borrower receives funds from a bank, for example, the interest paid on the borrowed money depends on the interest rate, which is agreed on between the borrower and the lender. Since long ago, in many counties governments have borrowed money through the issue of securities (treasury bonds or gilts) in regulated financial markets. In the US, for example, the federal government used bonds ('war bonds' or 'liberty bonds') to help finance military intervention in the First World War in 1917–1918.

Treasury bonds (or sovereign bonds) are often regarded as a relatively 'safe' form of investment because public authorities can always raise revenue from taxation – or just print money – to pay back the loan. Accordingly, the interest rate of treasury bonds is often lower than the one of corporate bonds, because of the risk that businesses cannot repay their loans depending on the fortunes of their ventures. Some countries may be considered by investors to be 'risk free' if they induce strong belief that they would never default their payments. Other countries, instead, may be considered more risky by investors, depending on various circumstances like growth prospects (if the economy of a country is not expected to grow in the future, then the government would have more difficulty in raising revenue through taxation or other means) and the presence of an independent central bank (if the central bank is independent, then the government has no direct control over the printing of money).

Nowadays, treasury bonds are typically sold and traded in international financial markets. When foreign investors assess the risk of treasury bonds, then, they also take into account risk related to foreign exchange rate fluctuations. Because of this, the market-based interest rate of treasury bonds also incorporates expectations of investors about the stability of the

Table 11.1 Yields of ten-year treasury
bonds of various countries

Country	Yield (%)
Australia	2.78
France	0.92
Germany	0.42
Greece	7.21
Ireland	1.05
Italy	2.03
Japan	0.06
Portugal	3.86
Spain	1.55
Switzerland	−0.07
UK	1.43
US	2.47

Source: *Financial Times*. 22 January, 2017.

currency of the country that issues the bonds (because the government of the country would pay back the loan through taxation and other means to raise revenue in the local currency).

There is a lot of variety in the interest rates that country governments pay for their bonds. Table 11.1 shows the interest rates (which are also called yields when referring to the income earned from securities) on ten-year treasury bonds of various countries. The treasury bonds of Germany pay a relatively low yield (0.42%), which can be understood as related to the general perception of investors that the country's treasury bonds are relatively 'risk free'. The treasury bonds of Greece, instead, provide high yield (7.21%), as investors are wary that the state of public finances and growth prospects of the country pose some risk that the government defaults. A curious feature of the table is the presence of a negative yield for Switzerland (−0.07%). The negative yield can be explained by the decision of the Swiss central bank to set a negative interest rate in January 2015 in an effort to weaken demand for the Swiss franc in face of the declining value of the euro. It may be surprising that the market price for a security is negative, but this might reflect the preference of investors to pay for holding part of their wealth in what is perceived as a safe asset, or their expectation of a deflationary environment (i.e. if prices are expected to decrease more than the yield, the investor would make a gain anyway) or their intention to speculate on future fluctuations of the yield or the currency exchange. Some institutions like pension funds, moreover, may invest part of their portfolio in relatively safe assets like those denominated in Swiss francs regardless of their yield.

The yield of treasury bonds also depends on the time period of the borrowing. Table 11.2 shows the different yields of treasury bonds of the UK, the EU, the US and Japan depending on their maturity (i.e. the date of the last repayment). In the short–medium term, yields tend to be lower than in the long run. In the EU and in Japan, yields of short–medium term treasury bonds tend to be negative (for reasons which may be related to expectations of a deflationary environment).

Internal and external public debt

Government borrowing results in an increase of public debts, which poses the issue of fiscal sustainability. Fiscal sustainability refers to the capacity of the government to pay their

Table 11.2 Yields of treasury bonds depending on maturity

Maturity	UK (%)	EU (%)	US (%)	Japan (%)
1 Month	0.14	−0.85	0.46	
3 Month	0.24	−0.81	0.50	−0.31
6 Month	0.28	−0.88	0.62	−0.30
1 Year	0.10			
2 Year	0.20	−0.68	1.20	−0.23
3 Year	0.29	−0.65		−0.18
4 Year	0.48			
5 Year	0.62	−0.42	1.94	−0.12
7 Year	0.97			
8 Year	1.13			
9 Year	1.28			
10 Year	1.43	0.42	2.47	0.06
15 Year	1.80	0.64		0.32
20 Year	1.96	0.92		0.64
30 Year	2.07	1.18	3.05	0.80

Source: *Financial Times*, 22 January, 2017.

obligations, including interest and principal on government bonds. Fiscal sustainability is largely dependent on future prospects of the economy. If a country's economy grows, then the government is in a better position to raise revenue through taxation or other means. If growth is absent or negative, then the government faces the challenge to raise revenue while not harming the working of the economic system further.

Many countries in the world today have installed so-called automatic stabilisers, which consist of mechanisms for stimulating the economy in a counter-cyclical way. For example, progressive income tax rates result in higher average tax revenue when income increases (like in a boom within the economic cycle) and in lower average tax revenue when income decreases (like in a bust period). The adjustment of the tax revenue to tendencies of the income results in measures to prevent the economy from 'over-heating' in periods of boom and to ease the private sector from the tax burden in periods of bust. Relatedly, however, automatic stabilisers result in less tax revenue precisely when the economy slows down, which makes it harder for the government to meet their financial obligations on public debt.

Setting the role of automatic stabilisers aside, a government may have relatively few options to meet the obligations that arise from public debt in periods of stagnation or recession. Increasing tax rates may have further depressing effects on the private sector. Extreme measures, like the privatisation of public assets (e.g. the sale of SOEs or of tangible assets like real estate property) may not be available or desirable for their long-term consequences. Sometimes, the only feasible option for a government to raise finance to pay back existing debts is to take out more debt. This course of action may be sustainable if the economy grows in the future at rates that enable the government to meet the financial obligations of increased public debt. Sometimes, instead, increased public debt just postpones the acknowledgement that the fiscal burden of debt is not sustainable (a 'debt trap').

The question of how much public debt is sustainable has been long debated (Almuca, 2012; Collignon, 2012; Neck and Sturm, 2008; Yakita, 2008). Economic theory suggests that a primary condition to assess the sustainability of public debt relates to the nature of the creditors. If the public debt is owned by domestic investors in the domestic currency ('internal debt'), then – in a sense – the debt is 'of the citizens towards themselves'. The repayment of public debt would result, in effect, in a transfer of wealth from taxpayers to domestic bond holders. At the aggregated level, the country would keep the same amount of wealth. The public debt, in this sense, would just serve as a tool to enable the government to anticipate revenue collection in the future and to afford public spending (e.g. in infrastructure) at present.

Public debt that is held by domestic investors, however, does not have neutral effects on the economy. The levy of taxes results in a deadweight loss on the economy, and, therefore, increased levels of public debt may result in additional taxation with negative effects on the economic growth in the future. In addition, an argument has been made (by economist David Ricardo) that present taxpayers anticipate that taxes will increase when the government takes on more debt. Taxpayers would reduce consumption and save more at present in order to pay for higher tax bills in the future. In this sense, borrowing has been considered just as a form of deferred taxation ('Ricardian equivalence'; Barro, 1974). However, taxpayers are not rational actors and it is possible that public spending that is financed from borrowing may result in a positive net effect on the economy, if the positive stimulus of public spending is larger than the negative anticipation of higher taxes.

Another effect that makes internal debt not neutral for the economy is precisely the redistributional consequences of debt repayment. Taxpayers who provide the government with the financial means to repay the debt may be typically poorer than the holders of treasury bonds, who had savings to invest in the first place. Internal debt, therefore, works to the advantage of a class of rentiers who receive transfer payments from taxpayers. The redistributional effect of internal debt, however, is also dependent on the role of financial institutions. Part of the investors in internal debt, for example, may be pension funds. Internal debt, therefore, may also assist the inter-generational transfer of wealth from individuals in their working periods of life to individuals who are retired.

In their work, Reinhart and Rogoff (2009, 2013) and Reinhart et al. (2012) explore whether the amount of public debt poses issues of fiscal sustainability beyond a specific threshold of the public-debt-to-GDP ratio. Their analysis suggested that a public-debt-to-GDP ratio above 90% results in a fall of GDP growth. Their work has been subjected to some criticism (Herndon et al., 2014) and their results may be open to various interpretations (e.g. that slow growth might be the cause of high debt rather than the effect). However, high levels of public debts tend to constrain the room for action of governments, whose fiscal policies need to take into account present and future debt obligations.

If the public debt is owned by foreign investors, usually in a foreign currency ('external debt'), then the consequences of public debt on fiscal sustainability can be more severe. The repayment of external debt results in a transfer of wealth outside a country. This has negative effects in terms of domestic capital accumulation and prospects for growth. In addition, the repayment of external debt in a foreign currency brings into play currency exchange risk. If the currency exchange rate deteriorates, the value of debt obligations in terms of the debtor country currency increases, with the effect that the government will have to raise additional revenue from taxation or other means. The government would also need to earn foreign currencies though exports or sale of assets held abroad, if not through additional borrowing. If the government has control of their own currency, however, it may try to manipulate the currency exchange rate to its own advantage (e.g. by increasing interest rates in an effort to appreciate the value of their own currency). Investors, however, may anticipate the possibility of such manoeuvres and demand higher interest rates on the country's external debt in the first place.

Fiscal illusion

Measures to repay public debt require to follow the correct accounting principles and practices. If sources of revenue and public spending are not accounted for properly, then the discourse around public borrowing and debt may fail to take into consideration the proper financial condition of a government. In broad terms, 'fiscal illusion' refers to the misrepresentation of financial information. Fiscal illusion can provide the appearance that the financial condition of a government is better than it actually is, with negative consequences on financial management policy decisions.

Easterly (1999) defines fiscal illusion as a fiscal adjustment that lowers the budget deficit but leaves government net worth unchanged. Fiscal illusion, however, may take different forms. One kind of fiscal illusion arises from considering any cash flow as having an impact on budget deficit. Proper accounting would suggest, instead, that cash flow should be classified depending on the nature of the cash receipt or cash payment. Payments that are made for recurrent and ordinary public spending (such as, for example, salaries to employees and supplies of goods and services) are different from payments that are made for investment in public assets (such as hospitals, schools and roads). The second kind of payments result in the creation of durable factors that contribute to growth prospects in the long run. The pursuit of a balanced budget should include recurrent and ordinary public spending only, rather than spending on capital assets, otherwise a government may not undertake such investments.

Another kind of fiscal illusion takes place when part of the financial condition of a government is not fully disclosed in financial statements. An example is provided by PPP schemes, where debt is taken by an SPV that is typically formed as a company that is jointly owned by a public authority and private investors. As the SPV has private legal status, its debt is not typically reported in the public budget, although the SPV may undertake the development of investment projects that are ultimately in the public interest (like highways, airports, harbours or various forms of real estate). In addition, sometimes PPP schemes provide that the public partner offers some guarantees (e.g. in the form of top-up fees or insurance) to the SPV. If exposure to risk is not disclosed, the public may not appraise correctly the amount of (contingent) liabilities that the government may be required to pay in the future.

Another example of fiscal illusion originates from the tendency of many countries to decentralise, or devolve, part of public policy functions to sub-national governments. When sub-national governments are entrusted to carry out public policies and programmes at the local level, they may be also granted the discretion to fund their operations by taking more debts (e.g. sub-national government bonds). Although the sub-national government is expected to repay its debt, in the case of default the central government could be expected to bail out the defaulting sub-national government for reasons of public interest (e.g. for ensuring the continuation of fundamental services at the local level). Financial reports of the central government, however, may include no information about the sub-national government debt and about the risk that the central government might be required to subsidise it in the case of default.

The government may undertake forms of fiscal illusion for various reasons. For example, public officers may try to take advantage of the misrepresentation of financial information for electoral purposes, when they omit reporting the correct amount of public deficit and debt made during their office. As another example, public officers may find it advantageous to misrepresent the financial condition of the government in front of investors, foreign aid donors and international organisations to show compliance with expected financial performance or avoid stricter requirements to fulfil.

In part, fiscal illusion may be contained when the government adopts international accounting standards – like, for example, International Public Sector Accounting Standards (IPSAS). IPSAS (like other accounting standards at the international and national level) recommend that public sector entities follow principles of accrual accounting for providing the representation of the financial conditions of public entities. Accrual accounting principles draw a clear distinction between revenue and expenditures related to recurrent and ordinary sources on the one hand, and those that relate to capital transactions on the other (like, for example, borrowing and investing in public assets). IPSAS also provide detailed guidance on the provision of information on actual or potential (contingent) liabilities, on stakes in other entities and business ventures and on the consolidation of accounts and financial statements.

Another way to counteract fiscal illusion is to extend the attention to the financial condition of a government from the short term (i.e. yearly budget) to the medium–long term. The inter-temporal budget constraint is a financial management model where financial appraisals take into account future conditions as well as immediate ones. In the inter-temporal budget constraint model, the value of assets and liabilities depends on the present value of their future revenue and costs. For example, a pension liability is accounted for by taking into consideration the present value of the future flow of payments. When adopting the inter-temporal budget constraint model, a government should make policy decisions on the basis of the principle that the present value of all future government revenue must be sufficient to cover the present value of all future government spending and the present stock of debt. This would require a considerable effort to anticipate projections of future financial flows, but fiscal policy decisions would be taken on a sounder accounting and financial basis.

Rules for fiscal sustainability

Many countries in the world have established systems of rules and regulations for ensuring fiscal sustainability, or at least to signal to investors that they are committed to ensure that public debts are sustainable. A general principle of fiscal sustainability is that countries should avoid funding debt repayment with additional borrowing, otherwise they would face a spiral of increasing debt over time (a debt trap). A related general principle is that governments should pursue a surplus in the primary balance – that is, the balance before interest payments – otherwise additional debt will be needed to finance public spending for the implementation of public policies and programmes.

Another general principle of fiscal sustainability is that countries should pay attention to containing the interest rate (yield) on treasury bonds. High yields are related to perceptions of high risk to invest in treasury bonds, like in the case of Greece in recent years. High interest rates on treasury bonds have various negative repercussions on the economy, especially in the form of diverting investments away from the private sector to the more lucrative treasury bonds, with negative consequences on economic growth. This effect – also known as 'crowding out' (Buiter, 1977) – results in discouraging firms from making investments that they would have made otherwise if interest rates were lower. The effect of public borrowing on interest rates, however, also depends on whether the economy is at full potential output. If this is the case, then public borrowing can trigger an increase in interest rates. If the economy is not at full potential, then public borrowing should not have an effect on interest rates and there may be no crowding out effect.

If high interest rates are paid for external debt, there may be also negative repercussions on exchange rates because the government would need to acquire higher amounts of foreign currencies. If investors perceive the debt of the country as extremely risky, moreover, they may even stop purchasing government bonds at all. This scenario may be catastrophic for countries that rely on borrowing for sustaining existing levels of public debt and funding public spending.

Rules and regulations for fiscal sustainability can take different forms. Some countries may self-impose limits on public spending. Others may establish the requirement to attain a primary budget surplus or a budget balance, and to allow borrowing only for capital investment (a so-called 'golden rule', like the UK from the 1990s to 2008). Other kinds of rules and regulations consist of applying some limits to the size of budget deficit and/or to the size of public debt, like in the EU. Sometimes, rules and regulations for fiscal sustainability are not self-imposed but required by external entities; like, for example, international donors as a conditionality attached to foreign aid.

A common, albeit approximate, indicator of fiscal sustainability is provided by the ratio between public debt and GDP (which is understood as an indirect indication of tax revenue prospects). If the ratio is high, then investors anticipate that the government may find it harder to raise enough tax revenue from the economy to meet debt obligations. A related indicator is offered by the difference between the (expected) growth of GDP and the (expected) interest rate or yield on government bonds. If the economy of the country is expected to grow at a higher rate than the interest rate, then investors may be reassured that tax revenue prospects enable the government to repay debts. Other indicators to take into consideration are the amount of public debt which is held by overseas creditors and the country's export-to-GDP ratio. The more public debt is held by foreign investors, the more the issue of currency exchange risk is important. A higher export-to-GDP ratio, in this case, can provide an indication of the ability of a country to acquire foreign currencies through sales overseas.

The issue of fiscal sustainability has become increasingly important in the last decade, especially when the public debt of many countries increased in relation to efforts from governments to stimulate the economy after the 2007–2008 financial crisis and to salvage parts of the banking sector. 'Austerity' measures, in the form of public spending cuts and increased taxation, were adopted to adjust public budgets to stricter requirements that were intended to contain – or start reducing – public borrowing and debt. In part, the effort to attain a balanced budget was also pursued under the favourable conditions of relatively low interest rates, which originated from the massive monetary expansionary policies of central banks.

The tendency towards austerity measures was especially evident in the EU. Various interventions by EU institutions (Council of the European Union, EU Commission and European Central Bank) and the IMF, in collaboration with EU member states, resulted in increasingly tight constraints on fiscal policy (lastly, through the 2012 European Fiscal Compact). In large parts of Europe – especially in southern countries – austerity measures contributed to stifling economic growth and worsening public services, especially healthcare. Poor economic performance exacerbated the problem of non-performing bank assets (such as business loans), with the effect of calling for additional forms of financial support for the banking sector.

Conclusions

This chapter paid attention to another form of financing public policies and programmes, namely the borrowing of money. Different from other forms of public sector revenue like taxation and commercial activities, borrowing entails that the government should be more sensitive to medium–long-term consequences. Borrowing increases public debt, which requires future governments to fund the payment of interest and principal. The cost of borrowing depends on the interest rate, although if debt is also held by foreign investors the currency exchange rate plays an important role. It is generally believed that a high level of public debt results in negative effects on economic growth and, relatedly, on the capacity of the government to pay back the loans. How precisely high public debt affects the economy, and how much public debt a government can stand, are controversial issues. It is important, however, that governments follow the correct accounting principles in order to avoid fiscal illusion and manage public finances prudently.

Questions for discussion

- Why do governments borrow to finance public spending?
- What is the role of interest rates in public sector borrowing?
- What is the role of currency exchange rates in public sector borrowing?
- Why does it matter if public debt is held by internal or external creditors?
- Why should a government avoid fiscal illusion?
- What are the benefits of austerity policies?

12 Seignorage

The right of the lord

Seignorage provides an additional way for governments to raise revenue from the economy. Seignorage is often discussed in critical tones in public discourse, for reasons that may relate to the somehow obscure mechanisms that permit the appropriation of wealth through control of the creation of money ('mint') and to the undemocratic nature of financial institutions (such as central banks and various financial intermediaries) whose decisions impact on the value of the currency (and, relatedly, on the purchasing power of income and savings) for the many. Seignorage, however, has been long used as a means to finance the operation of governments, and it still provides a component of public sector revenue in many countries.

The very origin of the term seignorage signals the hierarchical nature of this tool of public sector revenue. Seignorage derives from the French *seignorage*, which, in turn, relates to the Italian '*aggio del signore*' that means the 'right (or "premium") of the lord' to gain from the issue of money. Historically, seignorage could be levied when precious metals were minted into coins, whose value was socially and legally sanctioned by stamping official signs on them. The very origin of seignorage, in this sense, is related to an excise or fee for the production of money. As the levy could be paid as a share of the metal that was converted into coins, seignorage resulted in the divergence between the intrinsic value of the metal (what the coins were made of) and the nominal value of the coin (which carried a value expressed in the local currency).

During the course of the twentieth century, modern economic systems gradually abandoned the use of metals as the economic basis for the value of currencies. In the contemporary economic system, the very use of money has been largely de-materialised with the diffusion of electronic methods of storage and transfer of financial wealth. The amount of seignorage that can be levied from the issue of tangible money (that is, coins and banknotes) is relatively modest with respect to the total value of fiat money in circulation. Nowadays, central banks also issue fiat money in intangible form. The seignorage, in this case, arises from the difference between the interest earned on securities that central banks purchase when issuing new money and the cost of issuing, distributing and replacing the amount of physical money in circulation.

In contemporary financial and fiscal systems in many countries, central banks administer the issue of money and earn the seignorage revenue. Central banks typically pass seignorage revenue to their country governments, net of operating expenditures. In the UK, for example, the Bank of England keeps a separate accounting entity, the Issue Department, for computing seignorage income that is then paid to the UK Treasury on a regular basis (Bholat and Darbyshire, 2016). In 2015–2016, the Issue Department of the Bank of England generated

£462 million net income from the management of about £67.8 billion of securities and other assets. The income of the Issue Department is paid to the UK National Loans Fund, which provides financial support for infrastructure development and other public sector projects. In other countries, instead, the revenue from seignorage may be confounded with other sources of revenue and there is no specific appraisal of the seignorage income transferred to the government.

Seignorage and inflation tax

Revenue from seignorage is deeply intertwined with inflation. If a government who controls the issue of money aims to raise seignorage revenue by expanding the monetary base, then the increased amount of money in the economy can stimulate inflation, depending on conditions of economic growth. If the economy does not operate at full potential, the injection of additional money (and, relatedly, the public spending that is financed from seignorage) may produce a stimulus in the economy without triggering inflation. If this is not the case, however, the economy may 'over-heat' with inflationary pressures on the general level of prices.

Sometimes, a government may deliberately accept to introduce some amount of inflation in the economy for the sake of raising some revenue from seignorage. Inflation, however, reduces the purchasing power of income and savings (which may especially harm fixed-salary employees and poor–middle classes). In effect, stimulating inflation while collecting revenue for seignorage results in an 'inflation tax' on every individual whose purchasing power is reduced over time because of the loss of value of the currency.

It is apparent that the 'inflation tax' contradicts the principles of good taxation. As a way of transferring wealth from individuals to the government, the inflation tax is not transparent and harms individuals regardless of their economic condition. The inflation tax, however, can be collected at relatively low cost and it has been argued to provide the only means to tax economic activity in the informal economy (Mankiw, 1987).

If the economy does not grow fast enough with respect to the high pace of introduction of additional money in the economy system, it is possible to stimulate hyper-inflation. Hyper-inflation is a scenario where the general level of prices increases at exceptionally high rates. Hyper-inflation has long been documented in history since ancient Greece and Rome. In modern times, exceptionally high levels of inflation were experienced in Germany after the First World War, when a massive production of paper money was accompanied by a dramatic loss of value of the currency. Under the Republic of Weimar, the German economy experienced inflation rates of up to more than 600% per year and banknotes were issued with nominal values of up to mark 100 billion. Additional cases of hyper-inflation took place in Italy and Greece (1940s), Latin American countries (1970s–1990s), Russia (1990s), former Yugoslavia (1990s) and Zimbabwe (2000s).

In order to prevent governments from arbitrarily manoeuvring the monetary base to earn seignorage revenue, central banks have been generally removed from the direct influence of governments in many countries. Central bank independence is important to enable the institution that issues money to regulate the economy through monetary policies that are intended to pursue statutory mandates only. The European Central Bank (ECB), for example, has the primary objective to maintain price stability in the Eurozone. It is without prejudice to the objective of price stability that the ECB can also support the general economic policies of the EU by helping to achieve objectives like full employment and balanced economic growth. The mandate of the US Federal Reserve is to pursue maximum employment, stable prices and moderate long-term interest rates.

Seignorage from the internationalisation of currencies

Sometimes, the local domestic currency may be substituted – or circulated alongside with – a foreign currency as a means for storing value and clearing transactions (legal tender). This scenario may take place, for example, when local residents expect that the domestic currency may lose value because of inflation and, therefore, they convert their savings into a foreign currency that they believe could preserve purchasing power over time. The expectation of inflation, in turn, may originate from residents' beliefs that the government could pursue monetary policies that expand money supply.

When a foreign currency circulates within an economic system alongside or as a substitution for the local domestic currency, the government loses its grip on seignorage revenue. Residents seek to sell the domestic currency to buy the foreign one, with the effect that part of the domestic currency monetary basis is subtracted from the economy. Residents may be also less willing to accept the domestic currency in payment, and new issues of domestic money may be promptly exchanged for the foreign one. When a foreign currency is primarily used for storing value abroad, individuals typically seek banknotes of the largest nominal value such as, for example, $100, €500 and Swiss franc 1,000.

For the foreign country, the use of their own currency for storing value and clearing transactions in another country is an additional source of seignorage revenue. For example, the US government benefits from the issue of dollars that are used as a reserve currency and means of payment in many other countries. It is possible that a country whose currency is used in the economy of another country shares part of the seignorage revenue. For example, within the framework of the Common Monetary Area (CMA), South Africa shares part of the seignorage revenue with Lesotho, Namibia and Swaziland, which use the South African Rand as legal tender in their domestic economies. In Europe, seignorage collected by the ECB is distributed among central banks of the Eurozone.

Conclusions

This final chapter looked at another tool for raising public sector revenue, seignorage. The practice of earning money while issuing money has long been practiced in history in various ways, depending on the principles and techniques of money creation (from coinage to banknote printing to the electronic generation of fiat money). Nowadays, seignorage is collected by central banks which typically pass it over to their countries' governments. The independence of central banks is important to prevent the abuse of monetary policies by governments, which may be imputed to be part of the responsibilities for periods of hyper-inflation in the past. A strong currency may be beneficial in this respect, because a country may generate additional seignorage revenue when their currency is used as legal tender abroad.

Questions for discussion

- How is seignorage possible with the issue of electronic fiat money?
- Does seignorage provoke inflation?
- Does seignorage provoke hyper-inflation?
- Should countries share their seignorage revenue with other countries that use their currency as legal tender?

Glossary

Abusive transactions   Abusive transaction are transactions that are purposely done with the precise aim to pay less taxes. Abusive transactions are relevant in the context of tax avoidance and tax evasion. They consist of schemes that are devised to reduce the tax bill of companies, such as, for example, the transfer of income that is earned in a country with a relatively high corporate income tax rate to another country with a relatively low corporate income tax rate. Abusive transactions may be justified by the provision of services like the use of another company's intellectual property or by the lending of financial resources for which one company pays interest to another company.

Accommodation tax   Accommodation tax (or occupancy tax or hotel tax) is levied by local governments on temporary accommodations, such as, for example, the presence of guests in hotels or in private premises that are used for short-term lodging.

Accountability   Accountability is a central concept in public financial management. In broad terms, accountability refers to holding the government (and civil officers more specifically) responsible for taxpayers' expectations that public monies are spent appropriately. More precisely, accountability consists of institutions, systems and mechanisms that make it possible to scrutinise the conduct of public officers and to ask for justification for their behaviour. Accountability is assisted, for example, by transparent planning and budgeting, accurate accounting and financial reporting, and independent auditing and assurance.

Auction   An auction is a mechanism that is used to select a contractual counterpart. In the context of public sector revenue, auctions are used in the award of franchise or concession contracts. Auctions are used to make bidders disclose private information about their reservation price (i.e. the highest price that they are willing to pay for the franchise or concession contract fees). Auctions can be also used for the assignment of licences for exploration and exploitation rights of natural resources.

Austerity policies   Austerity policies are measures that aim to attain better fiscal sustainability by implementing public spending cuts and increased taxation. Austerity policies have been pursued in many countries in the world since the 2007–2008 financial crisis, when – after expansionary monetary policies and other interventions to salvage the banking sector and stimulate the economy – governments turned to greater fiscal discipline.

Automatic stabilisers   Automatic stabilisers consist of mechanisms for stimulating the economy in a counter-cyclical way. Examples of automatic stabilisers include progressive income tax rates, which result in higher average tax revenue when income increases during a boom within the economic cycle and in lower average tax revenue when income decreases in a bust period. Automatic stabilisers play an important role to provide stimuli to the economy in an economic downturn and to prevent 'over-heating' the economy in periods of high growth.

Average cost   Average cost is the ratio between total cost and the volume of output of a firm. Average cost is highly dependent on the cost structure of a firm. When a firm has relatively high fixed costs, the average cost is lower when the firm produces higher levels of output (because fixed costs are divided across a larger volume of output).

Average incremental cost (AIC)   Average incremental cost is the cost that is incurred for an additional user. The average incremental cost can be used for pricing public services, because it includes in the price various components of the tariff to help cover fixed and variable costs.

Average tax rate   Average tax rate is the ratio between the total tax paid by a taxpayer and the total base of taxation for the taxpayer. For example, the average personal income tax rate is obtained by dividing the income tax by the income of the taxpayer.

Base erosion and profit shifting (BEPS)   Base erosion and profit shifting (BEPS) consists of a concerted set of policies that OECD countries undertake to fight tax avoidance and tax evasion at the international level. Base erosion refers to the reduction of the taxable base of countries when part of the base (e.g. corporate income) is transferred abroad. Profit shifting refers to the practices that enable taxpayers to carry out transfers across jurisdictions.

BEPS programme   The Base Erosion and Profit Shifting (BEPS) programme refers to recommendations that have been formulated by the OECD BEPS initiative for various tax areas, including transfer prices, rules of controlled foreign companies, interest deductions, techniques to artificially avoid the permanent establishment status, disclosure rules and dispute resolution mechanisms.

Benefit taxation   Benefit taxation is a criterion for the design of tax systems. Benefit taxation posits that taxpayers should contribute to public finance according to the benefits that they receive from public expenditures. The application of the principle of benefit taxation is limited, however, because taxpayers may free ride on tax obligations and it is difficult to make taxpayers reveal their preferences for alternative public goods.

Blacklist   A blacklist is a list of countries that are considered 'non-cooperative' for taxation purposes. Blacklists have been formulated in many countries where transactions are treated under special provisions for tax purposes. Internationally, blacklists may be contested between countries, which may have different views about the criteria for inclusion of foreign countries into the blacklist.

Borrowing   Borrowing is a common and long-standing method for raising money for governments. It differs from other forms of public sector revenue generation – like taxation and various forms of commercial activities – because of its implications for the future. When borrowing, a government makes a commitment in future budgets, when revenues are needed to pay the interest and principal of the loan.

Budget   The budget is a fundamental tool of public financial management. The budget is used to help the government plan in advance the forms and amount of revenue and public spending that accompany the execution of public policies and programmes. The format of the budget does vary considerably across countries, but generally it consists of a document that illustrates the financial implications of policy decisions. The budget is then used for executing revenue collection and public spending, and for monitoring that public monies are administered as planned.

Budget deficit   The budget deficit is the net negative difference between revenue and expenditures. A budget deficit means that a government expects that public spending is larger than revenue. The difference between public spending and revenue, therefore, must be covered through other means, like drawing from cash resources of the Treasury or borrowing money from banks and investors.

Budget surplus   The budget surplus is the net positive difference between revenue and expenditures. A budget surplus means that a government expects that revenue is larger than public spending. The difference between revenue and public spending can be used to increase cash resources of the Treasury or to invest into assets or loans.

Budgeting   Budgeting is the process of managing the budget. As a process, the budget includes the stages of budget formation (when budget decisions are negotiated), budget approval (when the budget is approved by a public authority like a king or an elected representative body) and budget execution (when revenue is collected and money is spent as planned). At the end of a fiscal year (or accounting year), it is possible to compare the budget with actual results.

Business cycle   The business cycle is the natural tendency of economic activity to fluctuate over time along the long-run trend. Business cycles have implications for public sector revenue because they influence the tax base. In a period of boom, for example, the government can collect more revenue from income tax and indirect taxes. In a period of bust, instead, revenue collection declines as economic activity is reduced and individuals and companies earn less income.

Club goods   Club goods (or toll goods) consist of goods that are non-rivalrous but excludable (such as, for example, transit on highways and listening to concerts). Club goods can be jointly consumed by multiple individuals and it is possible to charge a fee for accessing the consumption.

Commercialisation   Commercialisation consists of the introduction of market-like features into the delivery of public services. Commercialisation takes place, for example, when part of public services are offered to users for a fee or charge as if in a market transaction. The fee or charge may cover the full cost or not, however, depending on policies that may protect the most vulnerable users.

Common Corporate Consolidated Tax Base (CCCTB)   The Common Corporate Consolidated Tax Base (CCCTB) is an initiative that was launched in the EU in 2011 which aimed to establish a single, harmonised tax base for multinational companies with operations in Europe. A renewed interest towards CCCTB emerged in 2016. The initiative aims to simplify tax management for multinational companies and to ensure that taxes from the corporate income of multinationals are allocated in a fair way among countries where the business activity takes place.

Common goods   Common goods consist of goods that are non-excludable but rivalrous (such as, for example, clean air and water). Common goods can be jointly consumed by multiple individuals and none of them can be precluded access to the common good.

Common pool resources   Common pool resources are goods that are shared between entities (i.e. nobody can be excluded from consuming them) but whose consumption is mutually exclusive (i.e. the consumption is rivalrous between entities). Common pool resources require some form of coordination and rationing, otherwise intensive use may result in the exhaustion of the common pool resource. Coordination and rationing can be provided by public authorities (or, alternatively, through systems of community self-regulation).

Concurrency of taxes   Concurrency of taxes takes place when multiple layers of government levy taxes on the same tax base. For example, the central government may levy income tax on a taxpayer and a sub-national government may levy a surcharge to the income tax on the same taxpayer. Concurrency of taxes may also take place when both the central government and the local government levy taxes on the use of the natural resources that are extracted in the jurisdiction of the local government.

Conditionality   A conditionality is a requirement that the recipient of funds should fulfil. In inter-governmental transfers, for example, a conditionality is what the recipient sub-national government should do in order to receive a grant from the central government. In foreign aid, a conditionality is the condition that the recipient country should satisfy in order to receive aid from the donor.

Contingent liability   A contingent liability is a potential liability that may occur, depending on the outcome of a future uncertain event. International Public Sector Accounting Standards (IPSAS) provide guidance on the provision of information about contingent liabilities in financial statements.

Corporate income tax   Corporate income tax is the tax that is levied on the income that a corporation makes in an accounting period. The tax base is the taxable income, which is determined on the basis of the net difference between corporate income and deductible expenses.

Council tax (UK)   In the UK, the council tax has been levied by local governments on property since 1993. The tax is usually paid by the resident (e.g. the tenant) of the property. The tax is calculated on the basis of the value of the property and on the classification of the property into 'bands'.

Crowding out   Crowding out is the negative effect that high interest rate paid on government borrowing has on private sector investments. Investors prefer to invest their money on high-yield government bonds than on private investments that do not deliver a commensurate return, taking into account differences in risk. With crowding out, some private sector investments do not take place but might be reconsidered if the interest rate on government borrowing decreases.

Cyclical deficit   A cyclical deficit is the (estimated, negative) difference between the budget surplus (or deficit) and the structural surplus (or deficit). The cyclical deficit signals a contingent state of public finances where expenditures exceed revenues in a particular condition of the business cycle.

Cyclical surplus   A cyclical surplus is the (estimated, positive) difference between the budget surplus (or deficit) and the structural surplus (or deficit). The cyclical surplus signals a contingent state of public finances where revenue exceeds expenditures in a particular condition of the business cycle.

Custom duties   Custom duties are taxes that are levied on international trade. The tax is typically levied when a good crosses a national border and the tax base refers to the market value of the traded good.

Deadweight loss   A deadweight loss is the net loss in the economy that results from the levy of a tax. In economic theory, deadweight loss arises because the value of tax revenue for the government is less than the total value of the consumer surplus and of the producer surplus that are lost because of the tax. Indirect taxes, for example, result in a deadweight loss because the tax incidence or wedge increases the price that consumers pay for the goods and decreases the profit that producers make when selling the goods.

Debt relief   Debt relief is the discharge of debts that recipient countries have with donor countries. Debt relief is a form of foreign aid because it results in 'windfall gains' for the recipient countries. Issues arise whether debt relief is effective and how the recipient country should make use of the financial resources that arise from debt relief.

Debt-to-GDP   Debt-to-GDP is a ratio that helps to indicate the capacity of a government to attain fiscal sustainability. GDP is considered an indication of the tax revenue that a government can raise to fulfil the financial obligations (interest and principal) for public debt.

Debt trap   The debt trap is when a government borrows additional funds in order to fulfil the financial obligations (interest and principal) for public debt. The debt trap arises when the primary balance of a government is insufficient to pay for the interest on public debt.

Defined benefit plans   Defined benefit plans consist of social security schemes where employees receive retirement benefits (pensions) that are commensurate with the economic conditions when they give up work (e.g. salary, seniority, etc.).

Defined contribution plans   Defined contribution plans consist of social security schemes where employees receive retirement benefits that arise from the return on investment of the contributions made during their working life.

Destination principle   The destination principle is a criterion for charging VAT on international transactions. The principle posits that VAT on international transactions should be paid in the country where the consumer is resident.

Devolution   Devolution is the process of transferring policy competences from central government to sub-national governments. It may be accompanied by some degree of fiscal decentralisation, including authority for local taxation.

Direct taxation   Direct taxation consists of taxes that are paid directly from taxpayers to imposing entities. Examples of direct taxation include personal income tax, corporate income tax and inheritance tax.

Double dividend   The double dividend is the argument that taxes on pollution ('green taxes') result in two advantages: on the one hand, taxes reduce the polluting activities; on the other one, they provide a source of revenue that can be used to decrease taxation in other areas.

Double Irish with a Dutch sandwich   The Double Irish with a Dutch sandwich is a tax avoidance scheme that allowed companies to avoid taxation of income from intellectual property (IP) rights. The scheme was used by companies like Apple and Google in the past. In 2015, however, the Irish government took action to terminate it.

Earmark   A tax is earmarked when the revenue from the tax is reserved for a specific policy purpose or programme.

Ecotaxes   Ecotaxes (or 'green taxes') are taxes that are levied on polluting activities. They provide a tool of environmental policy that aims to make individuals and firms internalise the cost of negative externalities that arise from polluting activities.

Equalisation transfers   Equalisation transfers are mechanisms where the central government orchestrates a system of financial compensations (transfers) from the rich to the poor regions. Mechanisms of equalisation are intended to reduce the gap between rich and poor regions in a country.

Excise   An excise is a tax that is levied on the production of goods. It is an instance of indirect taxation because the taxpayer (the producer) can totally or partially shift the burden of the tax to the consumers.

Export-to-GDP   The export-to-GDP ratio is an indication of the capacity of a government to sustain external debt. The value of export is considered an indication of the capacity of the government to acquire foreign currencies through the export of goods and services.

External debt   External debt (or foreign debt) is the amount of public debt that is owned by foreign investors. External debt is important because repayment of the debt (interest and principal) results in a loss of net wealth in the economy.

Externalities   Externalities refer to the repercussions that acts of production or consumption have on other individuals. Examples of externalities include vaccinations (a positive externality) and pollution (a negative externality).

Fat taxes   Fat taxes are a kind of 'sin taxes' that aim to discourage the consumption of fat food (or junk food) by levying taxes on its consumption.

Feebate   A feebate is a tax whose revenue is used as a subsidy for an activity that the government wants to encourage. For example, a tax on a polluting good can be used to subsidise the purchase of a welcome good.

Fiat money   Fiat money is money that is rendered as such (a legal tender) by government decree. Fiat money is different from commodity money (like coins with a metallic content) and representative money (like banknotes with a certified nominal value).

Fiscal decentralisation   Fiscal decentralisation is the process of transferring part of the competences on fiscal policies to sub-national governments. Fiscal decentralisation can bring the management of public financial resources closer to the attention of local communities and more distant from remote political elites. Fiscal decentralisation can also stimulate public participation in civic affairs and help the formation of political identities and cultures at the local level.

Fiscal equivalence   Fiscal equivalence or 'perfect mapping' is the principle that each sub-national jurisdiction could produce the precise amount of public goods that are demanded by the specific local population.

Fiscal federalism   Fiscal federalism refers to the institutional, organisational and financial arrangements where public sector financial resources are managed across different levels of government. In fiscal federalism, the management of public finances of a country are at least partially decentralised to the sub-national level. Fiscal federalism is also intertwined with arrangements of political decentralisation, where central governments partially share political and policy-making powers with sub-national governments.

Fiscal illusion   Fiscal illusion refers to the misrepresentation of financial information. It may result in the appearance that the financial condition of a government is better than it actually is, with negative consequences on financial management policy decisions. It is also understood as a fiscal adjustment that lowers the budget deficit but leaves government net worth unchanged.

Fiscal stability   Fiscal stability refers to the general principle that public sector finances should be managed in a sustainable way, that is, by sustaining current spending on public policies and programmes while avoiding conditions of insolvency or default.

Fiscal sustainability   Fiscal sustainability refers to the principles and criteria that should orient sound public financial management policies. Fiscal sustainability takes the form of principles such as that countries should avoid funding debt repayment with additional borrowing, otherwise they would face a spiral of increasing debt over time (a 'debt trap'). A related general principle is that governments should pursue a surplus in the primary balance – that is, the balance before interest payments – otherwise additional debt is needed to finance public spending for the implementation of public policies and programmes. Another general principle of fiscal sustainability is that countries should pay attention to containing the interest rate (yield) on government bonds.

Flat income tax   Flat income tax consists of the charge of a constant tax rate irrespective of the level of income.

Flypaper effect   The flypaper effect refers to the tendency for inter-governmental transfers to stimulate more local public spending than the same amount of revenue generated from income tax. The flypaper effect seems to originate from the behaviour of bureaucrats, who tend to expand the size of their budget (and, therefore, of public spending) in order to attain personal material advantages. In addition, public officers may expand public spending that are partially funded by inter-governmental transfers because of a 'fiscal illusion' effect on local taxpayers, who do not correctly assess the overall burden of taxation when part of local funding takes the form of flows of grants from higher levels of government.

Foreign aid   Foreign aid consists of inter-governmental transfers (Official Development Assistance or ODA) between countries or between an inter-national or super-national entity (like the World Bank, the IMF or the EU) and a recipient country. Foreign aid takes place for a number of reasons.

Franchise   Franchises consist of contracts where a business entity is appointed to carry out the production of a good or the provision of services in a regulated market, whose access is restricted on legal grounds.

General budget support (GBS)   General budget support (GBS) consists of the transfer of funds to the treasury of the recipient country. The funds are fungible, in the sense that they can be allocated to any particular budget line item.

Gini coefficient   The Gini coefficient is an indicator of the level of inequality in the distribution of income in a population.

Golden share   The golden share is a part of the shares of a privatised state-owned enterprise (SOE) that is retained by the government. Golden shares may be combined with statutory provisions that enable the government to retain veto powers on the main strategic decisions of the privatised firm.

Good taxation   Good taxation are criteria that assist the assessment of a tax or a tax system. For example, Adam Smith (1776) formulated as criteria of good taxation those of fairness, certainty, convenience and efficiency.

Goods and service tax (GST)   The goods and service tax (GST) is a tax that is levied on sales to final consumers (retail sales). It is an instance of indirect taxation.

Green taxes   Green taxes (or 'ecotaxes') are taxes that are levied on polluting activities. They provide a tool of environmental policy that aims to make individuals and firms internalise the cost of negative externalities that arise from polluting activities.

Horizontal equity   Horizontal equity means that taxpayers under similar economic conditions should pay the same amount of taxes. Horizontal equity forms the basis for arguments about fighting tax avoidance and tax evasion.

Hotel tax   Hotel tax (or occupancy tax or accommodation tax) is levied by local governments on temporary accommodations, such as, for example, the presence of guests in hotels or in private premises that are used for short-term lodging.

Hyper-inflation   Hyper-inflation refers to the conditions of an economy when the inflation rate is extremely high. An instance was the hyper-inflation in the Republic of Weimar in 1920s, when the German economy experienced inflation rates of up to more than 600% per year and banknotes were issued with a nominal value of up to mark 100 billion.

Income tax   Income tax is the tax that is levied on the income that individuals or companies make in an accounting (or fiscal) period. Income tax is an instance of direct taxation.

Independent regulatory authorities   Independent regulatory authorities consist of technical agencies that are entrusted by the government to regulate infrastructure or utilities industries and firms. The independence of the agency is expected to remove regulatory decisions from the influence of the government.

Independent revenue authorities   Independent revenue authorities consist of technical agencies that are entrusted by the government to administer the taxation process. The independence of the agency is expected to remove tax administrative decisions from the influence of the government.

Indirect taxation   Indirect taxation consists of taxes that are paid indirectly from the bearer of the ultimate tax burden to imposing entities through an intermediary. Examples of indirect taxation include sales tax, VAT, excises and custom duties.

Inflation tax   Inflation tax refers to the reduction of purchasing power of individuals because of inflation that originates from the issue of money by the government for the sake of collecting seignorage revenue.

Information asymmetry   Information asymmetry refers to the gap in information that exists between two parties. Information asymmetry is important in many circumstances, such as the negotiation of contracts, the regulation of tariffs and the enforcement of conditionalities attached to inter-governmental transfers or foreign aid.

Information extraction   Information extraction refers to the mechanisms that are intended to make one party disclose private information to another party. Auctions are an example of mechanisms that are intended to make a party (bidding company) reveal the reservation price on a contract.

Inheritance tax   Inheritance tax is the tax that is levied on the estate (property, money and possessions) of an individual who has died. Inheritance tax is an instance of direct taxation.

Initial public offering (IPO)   An initial public offering (IPO) is the first sale of the stocks of a company to the public. Initial public offerings are relevant to public sector revenue because it is a method to privatise state-owned enterprises.

Inter-governmental grants   Inter-governmental grants (or inter-governmental transfers) consist of the transfer of financial resources between levels of government.

Inter-governmental transfers   Inter-governmental transfers (or inter-governmental grants) consist of the transfer of financial resources between levels of government.

Internal debt   Internal debt is the amount of public debt that is owned by domestic investors. Internal debt results in transfers of wealth from taxpayers to the holders of public debt; therefore, it does not affect the net wealth of a country's economy.

Kondratiev waves   Kondratiev waves are long-term fluctuations of the economy that originate from technological innovations, demographic adjustments, speculative bubbles, especially on land, and debt deflation.

Laffer curve   The Laffer curve is a graphical representation of the argument that too high a level of corporate taxation results in detrimental effects on income generation and growth. The Laffer curve posits an inverse-U-shaped relationship between tax rates and tax revenue.

Leveraged buy-out (LBO)   Leveraged buy-out (LBO) is a form of privatisation where a state-owned enterprise is sold to investors who finance the purchase of shares through loans that are paid back out of the future cash flows of the same privatised firm.

Licence   Licences are permits to use or to own an asset, or to carry out an activity. A typical feature of licences issued by public authorities is that use or ownership of the asset, or the carrying out of the activity, is not allowed without the licence, and mechanisms of enforcement (e.g. investigations and fines) are put into place to detect violations.

Long-run marginal cost (LRMC)   Long-run marginal cost (LRMC) is the marginal cost of an additional unit of output in the long run, when all factors of production are considered variable.

Marginal cost   The marginal cost is the change in total cost when the production is increased by one unit.

Marginal tax rate   The marginal tax rate is the tax rate that is levied on an additional unit of income. The marginal tax rate is important if individuals and firms make decisions at the margin, that is, taking into account the marginal improvement of their condition.

Matching requirement   A matching requirement refers to the conditionality attached to a grant transfer, where the recipient government must allocate its own financial resources to a programme or project for which a grant is received from the donor government.

Merit goods   Merit goods are those goods that are supplied by public authorities purely because they are considered worthy of social benefit, such as, for example, concerts.

Moral hazard   Moral hazard occurs when a person takes on more risk because someone else will bear the cost of the risk. It is a type of information asymmetry where one party (that bears the consequences of risk) does not know what the other party (that makes the decision to bear risk) does, or where the party that makes the decision to bear risk does not know the consequences of risk on another party.

Multi-part tariff   Multi-part tariffs consist of different price components that are charged depending on the circumstances of the users. A multi-part tariff could include a fixed charge (e.g. for connecting to the network) and a variable part (which is related to the volume of consumption). Multi-part tariffs can be also designed to discriminate between different kinds of users.

Occupancy tax   Occupancy tax (or hotel tax or accommodation tax) is levied by local governments on temporary accommodations, such as, for example, the presence of guests in hotels or in private premises that are used for short-term lodging.

Optimal tax theory   Optimal tax theory is an area of economics that is concerned with the design of tax systems that maximise a social welfare function. The issue is posed in terms of a social planner that takes the wellness of individuals under consideration (in the analytic form of utility functions) when choosing which taxes should be levied and at what rates.

Personal income tax   Personal income tax is the tax that is levied on personal (individual) income. Personal income tax is an instance of direct taxation.

Pigouvian taxes   Pigouvian taxes are taxes that are levied on taxpayers in order to make them take into account the negative effect of externalities of the activity that is taxed. An example of Pigouvian taxes is the environmental taxes that are intended to discourage polluting activities.

Price regulation   Price regulation consists of institutions, systems and mechanisms for influencing the price that firms of regulated industries can charge. Price regulation is usually carried out in monopolistic industries (like water and sewage) or in industries where barriers to entry limit competition (like energy, gas and public transport).

Primary budget deficit   The primary budget deficit indicates the (negative) difference between revenue and expenditures but without counting interest payments.

Primary budget surplus   The primary budget deficit indicates the (positive) difference between revenue and expenditures but without counting interest payments.

Private goods   Private goods (such as, for example, a pair of shoes) are typically produced by the private, or business, sector. They are excludable goods; therefore, access to private goods can be granted upon payment of a price. They are rivalrous goods; therefore, access to private goods can be allocated on the basis of individuals' willingness to pay for privileged access.

Privatisation Privatisation consists of the sale of public assets or state-owned enterprises to private investors.

Progressive taxation Progressive taxation is a feature of tax systems where the tax rate increases with the income of the taxpayer. Progressive tax systems contribute to redistributing wealth and income because the rich are taxed at higher rates than the poor, who may also typically consume more public goods.

Public goods Public goods are those goods that exhibit properties of non-excludability and non-rivalry. A good is defined as excludable when it is possible to prevent an individual from consuming it. A good is defined as rivalrous if its consumption by an individual diminishes the consumption of another individual.

Public–private partnership (PPP) A public–private partnership is a scheme for the financing of infrastructure and other public projects. It consists of the agreement between a public authority and a private investor to jointly finance a project which generates revenue to pay back the loans and provide a return on investment.

Public services Public services are those services that are provided by the government. The boundaries of public services change over time and across countries, depending on what society expects to fall within the competencies of public authorities.

Public spending Public spending is the amount of money that the government spends on implementing public policies and programmes.

Race to the bottom The race to the bottom is the tendency of countries to progressively lower tax rates in order to make the domestic environment more attractive to foreign individuals and businesses. The race to the bottom may be a consequential effect of tax competition between countries.

Regressive taxation Regressive taxation is a feature of tax systems where the tax rate decreases with the income of the taxpayer. Regressive tax systems contribute to increasing the differences in wealth and income because the rich are taxed at lower rates than the poor.

Repatriation Repatriation takes place when income that is earned abroad by individuals or companies is brought into the country where the taxpayer is resident.

Resource curse The resource curse is the empirical tendency of natural-resource-rich countries to attain lower economic growth than natural-resource-poor countries. Various explanations for the resource curse have been offered, from the role of appreciation of the currency of the natural-resource-rich country to the role of corruption and misappropriation of the country's natural resources.

Sales tax Sales tax is a tax that is levied on sales to final consumers (retail sales). It is an instance of indirect taxation.

Seignorage Seignorage is the money earned by a government when new money is issued. Seignorage may take different forms, depending on the principles and techniques of money creation (from coinage to banknote printing to the electronic generation of fiat money).

Short-run marginal cost (SRMC) Short-run marginal cost (SRMC) is the marginal cost of an additional unit of output in the short run, when some factors of production are variable, while others are fixed.

Sin taxes Sin taxes are those takes that are intended to correct unwelcome behaviour. Examples of sin taxes are taxes on alcohol, tobacco, fatty foods and added-sugar drinks.

Social security   Social security is the system of social protection of individuals because of unwelcome occurrences during their life, like unemployment or illness, and because of retirement.

Soda taxes   Soda taxes are a kind of 'sin taxes' that aim to discourage the consumption of added-sugar drinks by levying taxes on their consumption.

Soft budget constraint   The soft budget constraint refers to the impossibility for a funding entity to keep the recipient disciplined to a fixed budget. The soft budget constraint results in the recipient spending more money than provided in the budget and in the funding entity paying for the budget deficit.

Structural deficit   The term structural deficit indicates the (estimated, negative) difference between revenue and expenditures when an economy is at full employment.

Structural surplus   The term structural surplus indicates the (estimated, positive) difference between revenue and expenditures when an economy is at full employment.

Tax arbitrage   Tax arbitrage refers to the tendency of taxpayers to relocate to countries where the tax bill is commensurate with the level and quality of public services that taxpayers receive. Tax arbitrage arises from the tax competition between countries.

Tax avoidance   Tax avoidance is the reduction of the tax bill by legal means. Tax avoidance can happen in many ways depending on the tax regime of specific countries. An example is when a small business owner hires their spouse as an employee, with the effect that the income of the business is split between two individuals who may both benefit from tax-free allowances or whose marginal income tax rate is lower than the tax rate that the business owner would pay if the income is not split.

Tax base   The tax base is what is subjected to taxation. Examples of tax bases include income, sales, property and inheritance.

Tax bracket   A tax bracket is a tranche of income where marginal income above a certain threshold is taxed at a different tax rate from other tax brackets. For example, in many countries personal income tax rate increases when the total income surpasses certain thresholds.

Tax competition   Tax competition is the conduct of countries to lower their tax rates in order to make the domestic environment more attractive to foreign individuals and businesses.

Tax credits   Tax credits (or tax detractions) are expenditures that are subtracted from the tax bill.

Tax deductions   Tax deductions are expenditures that are subtracted from the taxable income.

Tax detractions   Tax detractions (or tax credits) are expenditures that are subtracted from the tax bill.

Tax evasion   Tax evasion is the reduction of the tax bill by illegal means. Tax evasion happens when taxpayers pay less taxes than they should by infringing tax rules. An example is when a small business under-reports income (like when invoices are not issued for the sale of goods and services) or inflates expenses (like when fake invoices are registered).

Tax expenditures   Tax expenditures are tax deductions or tax credits that are granted to taxpayers in order to carry out welcome expenditures. With tax expenditures, the government subsidises certain expenditures because it gives up the opportunity to collect part of the income tax revenue.

Tax havens   Tax havens are jurisdictions with relatively low or zero taxation. Tax havens are important in the contemporary international tax environment because they typically facilitate the implementation of schemes for tax avoidance and tax evasion because of generous features of their country's tax codes.

Tax incidence Tax incidence (or tax wedge) is the distortion that taxation provokes in the economy. A deadweight loss is the quantification of the net loss in the economy that results from the levy of a tax.

Tax rate The tax rate is the percentage of the value of the taxed economic condition or event that forms the basis for calculating the tax bill.

Tax wedge Tax wedge (or tax incidence) is the distortion that taxation provokes in the economy. A deadweight loss is the quantification of the net loss in the economy that results from the levy of a tax.

Taxation Taxation is the main method for raising public sector revenue. It consists of administrative institutions, systems and mechanisms for levying taxes on the economy.

Toll goods Toll goods (or club goods) consist of goods that are non-rivalrous but excludable (such as, for example, transit on highways and listening to concerts). Toll goods can be jointly consumed by multiple individuals and it is possible to charge a fee for accessing the consumption.

Too big to fail Too big to fail is a phrase that refers to the condition when an entity is not allowed to fail because failure would bring about a systemic crisis with catastrophic conditions. In the context of public sector revenue, it may refer to the conduct of subnational governments who undertake excessive public spending because they consider themselves covered by the central government if anything goes wrong.

Tragedy of the commons The tragedy of the commons is the problem of the management of common pool resources. It is difficult to make everyone disciplined in the use of the common pool resources: if everyone does not restrain their consumption and free rides on others' efforts to preserve the common pool resource, then the common pool resource itself would be depleted until exhaustion.

Transfer price The transfer price is the price that two companies agreed on in the exchange of goods and services in the international market. Transfer prices enable companies to shift profits from one country's jurisdiction to another. As such, transfer prices are often subjected to close scrutiny by tax authorities in order to counteract tax avoidance schemes.

Triple dividend Triple dividend is the argument that taxes on pollution ('green taxes') result in an additional advantage apart from the 'double dividend'. The third advantage is that green taxes result in an improved environment that can induce more economic growth.

Unitary taxation Unitary taxation is a tax approach that consists of consolidating the profits of multinational enterprises and then dividing (apportioning) it between the jurisdictions where the business activity is carried out according to specified criteria.

Universal service obligation Universal service obligation is the basic or essential amount and quality of public service that the government should commit to provide at an affordable price through state-owned enterprises or regulated firms.

Value-added tax (VAT) Value-added tax (VAT) is levied on business transactions. VAT that is collected on the value of the transaction is a VAT debt for the collector (the seller) and a VAT credit for the taxpayer (the buyer). The VAT system works by having VAT-registered entities periodically paying to the tax authority the net difference between VAT debt and VAT credit. The ultimate bearer of taxation is the final consumer. VAT is an instance of indirect taxation.

Vertical equity Vertical equity means that taxpayers under better economic conditions should pay more taxes than those in worse economic conditions. Vertical equity forms the basis for arguments about fairness of progressive taxation, where taxpayers with higher income pay higher income tax rates than those with lower income.

Vertical fiscal gap   The vertical fiscal gap is the asymmetry of revenue generation power between the central government and the sub-national governments.

Vertical fiscal imbalance   The vertical fiscal imbalance is the mismatch in the revenue powers and public spending responsibilities across levels of government.

Voting by feet   Voting by feet is a mechanism of competition between governments, where mobile citizens and taxpayers move from one jurisdiction to another depending on the quality of public services and taxation.

Bibliography

Abbas, S.A. and Klemm, A., 2013. A partial race to the bottom: Corporate tax developments in emerging and developing economies. *International Tax and Public Finance*, 20(4), pp. 596–617.

Acemoglu, D., 2005. Politics and economics in weak and strong states. *Journal of Monetary Economics*, 52(7), pp. 1199–1226.

Acemoglu, D. and Robinson, J.A., 2006. Economic backwardness in political perspective. *American Political Science Review*, 100(1), pp. 115–131.

Acemoglu, D., Golosov, M. and Tsyvinski, A., 2011. Political economy of Ramsey taxation. *Journal of Public Economics*, 95(7), pp. 467–475.

Adams, J., Young, A. and Zhihong, W., 2006. Public private partnerships in China: System, constraints and future prospects. *International Journal of Public Sector Management*, 19(4), pp. 384–396.

Akai, N. and Sakata, M., 2002. Fiscal decentralization contributes to economic growth: Evidence from state-level cross-section data for the United States. *Journal of Urban Economics*, 52(1), pp. 93–108.

Akerlof, G.A., 1978. The economics of 'tagging' as applied to the optimal income tax, welfare programs, and manpower planning. *The American Economic Review*, 68(1), pp. 8–19.

Al-Darwish, M.A., Alghaith, N., Behar, M.A., Callen, M.T., Deb, M.P., Hegazy, M.A., Khandelwal, P., Pant, M.M. and Qu, M.H., 2015. *Saudi Arabia: Tackling Emerging Economic Challenges to Sustain Growth*. Washington, DC: International Monetary Fund.

Alesina, A. and Passalacqua, A., 2015. The political economy of government debt (No. w21821). National Bureau of Economic Research.

Alesina, A. and Tabellini, G., 1990. A positive theory of fiscal deficits and government debt. *The Review of Economic Studies*, 57(3), pp. 403–414.

Almuca, A., 2012. Sustainability of public debt. *Journal of US-China Public Administration*, 9(6), pp. 718–722.

Andreyeva, T., Chaloupka, F.J. and Brownell, K.D., 2011. Estimating the potential of taxes on sugar-sweetened beverages to reduce consumption and generate revenue. *Preventive Medicine*, 52(6), pp. 413–416.

Araral, E., Jr., 2005. Bureaucratic incentives, path dependence, and foreign aid: An empirical institutional analysis of irrigation in the Philippines. *Policy Sciences*, 38(2–3), pp. 131–157.

Araral, E., 2009a. The failure of water utilities privatization: Synthesis of evidence, analysis and implications. *Policy and Society*, 27(3), pp. 221–228.

Araral, E., 2009b. The strategic games that donors and bureaucrats play: An institutional rational choice analysis. *Journal of Public Administration Research and Theory*, 19(4), pp. 853–871.

Armstrong M., Cowan, S. and Vickers, J., 1999. *Regulatory Reform: Economic Analysis and British Experience*. Cambridge, MA: MIT Press.

Arnold, J., 2008. Do tax structures affect aggregate economic growth?: Empirical evidence from a panel of OECD countries (No. 643). OECD Publishing.

Arnold, J.M., Brys, B., Heady, C., Johansson, Å., Schwellnus, C. and Vartia, L., 2011. Tax policy for economic recovery and growth. *The Economic Journal*, 121(550), pp. F59–F80.

Asquer, A., 2011. Liberalization and regulatory reform of network industries: A comparative analysis of Italian public utilities. *Utilities Policy*, 19(3), pp. 172–184.

Atkeson, A., Chari, V.V. and Kehoe, P.J., 1999. Taxing capital income: A bad idea. *Federal Reserve Bank of Minneapolis Quarterly Review*, 23(3), p. 3.

Atkinson, A.B., 1977. Optimal taxation and the direct versus indirect tax controversy. *Canadian Journal of Economics*, 10(4), pp. 590–606.

Atkinson, A.B. and Stiglitz, J.E., 1976. The design of tax structure: Direct versus indirect taxation. *Journal of Public Economics*, 6(1), pp. 55–75.

Atkinson, G. and Hamilton, K., 2003. Savings, growth and the resource curse hypothesis. *World Development*, 31(11), pp. 1793–1807.

Auer, M.R., 2006. Foreign aid to promote energy efficiency in Mexico: An institutional analysis. *Journal of Energy and Development*, 31(1), p. 85.

Auerbach, A.J., 1985. The theory of excess burden and optimal taxation. *Handbook of Public Economics*, 1, pp. 61–127.

Auerbach, A.J., Devereux, M.P. and Simpson, H., 2008. Taxing corporate income (No. w14494). National Bureau of Economic Research.

Averch, H. and Johnson, L.L., 1962. Behavior of the firm under regulatory constraint. *The American Economic Review*, 52(5), pp. 1052–1069.

Backhaus, J., 2002. Fiscal sociology: What for? *The American Journal of Economics and Sociology*, 61(1), pp. 55–77.

Bardhan, P. and Mookherjee, D., 2003. Political economy of land reform in West Bengal. *Journal of Political Economy*, 110(2), pp. 239–289.

Bardhan, P. and Mookherjee, D., 2006. Decentralisation and accountability in infrastructure delivery in developing countries. *The Economic Journal*, 116(508), pp. 101–127.

Bardi, U., 2009. Peak oil: The four stages of a new idea. *Energy*, 34(3), pp. 323–326.

Barro, R.J., 1974. Are government bonds net wealth? *Journal of Political Economy*, 82(6), pp. 1095–1117.

Barro, R.J., 1989. The Ricardian approach to budget deficits. *The Journal of Economic Perspectives*, 3(2), pp. 37–54.

Bartelsman, E.J. and Beetsma, R.M., 2003. Why pay more? Corporate tax avoidance through transfer pricing in OECD countries. *Journal of Public Economics*, 87(9), pp. 2225–2252.

Baskaran, T., 2012. Revenue decentralization and inflation: A re-evaluation. *Economics Letters*, 116(3), pp. 298–300.

Bayliss, K., 2003. Utility privatisation in Sub-Saharan Africa: A case study of water. *The Journal of Modern African Studies*, 41(4), pp. 507–531.

Beblawi, H. and Luciani, G. (eds), 2015. *The Rentier State*. London: Routledge.

Beesley, M.E. and Littlechild, S.C., 1989. The regulation of privatized monopolies in the United Kingdom. *The RAND Journal of Economics*, 20(3), pp. 454–472.

Bel, G. and Fageda, X., 2007. Why do local governments privatise public services? A survey of empirical studies. *Local Government Studies*, 33(4), pp. 517–534.

Bergemann, D. and Pesendorfer, M., 2007. Information structures in optimal auctions. *Journal of Economic Theory*, 137(1), pp. 580–609.

Besley, T. and Coate, S., 2003. Centralized versus decentralized provision of local public goods: A political economy approach. *Journal of Public Economics*, 87(12), pp. 2611–2637.

Besley, T. and Persson, T., 2009. The origins of state capacity: Property rights, taxation, and politics. *The American Economic Review*, 99(4), pp. 1218–1244.

Besley, T. and Persson, T., 2013. Taxation and development. In A.J. Auerbach, R. Chetty, M. Feldstein and E. Saez (eds), *Handbook of Public Economics* (Vol. 5). Oxford: Newnes, p. 51.

Bholat, D. and Darbyshire, R., 2016. Accounting in central banks. Bank of England Staff Working Paper (No. 604). London: Bank of England.

Bird, R.M., 1971. Wagner's 'Law' of expanding state activity. *Public Finance*, 26(1), pp. 1–26.

Bird, R.M., 2001. User charges in local government finance. In M. Freire and R.E. Stren (eds), *The Challenge of Urban Government: Policies and Practices*. Washington, DC: World Bank, pp. 171–182.

Bird, R.M. and de Jantscher, M.C. (eds), 1992. *Improving Tax Administration in Developing Countries* (Vol. 19). Washington, DC: International Monetary Fund.

Bird, R.M. and Ebel, R.D. (eds), 2014. *Fiscal Fragmentation in Decentralized Countries*. Edward Elgar Publishing.

Bird, R.M. and Vaillancourt, F., 2008. *Fiscal Decentralization in Developing Countries*. Cambridge: Cambridge University Press.

Bird, R.M. and Zolt, E.M., 2004. Redistribution via taxation: The limited role of the personal income tax in developing countries. *UCLA Law Review*, 52(6), p. 1627.

Biswas, A. and Kirchherr, J., 2012. Water prices in Europe need to rise substantially to encourage more sustainable water consumption. LSE European Politics and Policy Blog entry, 31st October (http://blogs.lse.ac.uk/europpblog/2012/10/31/europe-water-prices/) (accessed 24 January 2017).

Blais, A., Blake, D. and Dion, S., 1993. Do parties make a difference? Parties and the size of government in liberal democracies. *American Journal of Political Science*, 37(1), pp. 40–62.

Blöchliger, H., Bartolini, D. and Stossberg, S., 2016. Does fiscal decentralisation foster regional convergence? OECD Economic Policy Papers (doi: 10.1787/2226583X).

Boadway, R. and Keen, M., 1996. Efficiency and the optimal direction of federal-state transfers. *International Tax and Public Finance*, 3(2), pp. 137–155.

Boadway, R.W. and Shah, A. (eds), 2007. *Intergovernmental Fiscal Transfers: Principles and Practices*. Washington, DC: World Bank Publications.

Boadway, R., Bruce, N. and Mintz, J., 1983. On the neutrality of flow-of-funds corporate taxation. *Economica*, 50(197), pp. 49–61.

Bonet, J., 2006. Fiscal decentralization and regional income disparities: Evidence from the Colombian experience. *The Annals of Regional Science*, 40(3), pp. 661–676.

Bourguignon, F. and Verdier, T., 2000. Oligarchy, democracy, inequality and growth. *Journal of Development Economics*, 62(2), pp. 285–313.

Bovenberg, A.L. and de Mooij, R.A., 1994. Environmental levies and distortionary taxation. *The American Economic Review*, 84(4), pp. 1085–1089.

Bovenberg, A.L. and van der Ploeg, F., 1996. Optimal taxation, public goods and environmental policy with involuntary unemployment. *Journal of Public Economics*, 62(1), pp. 59–83.

Bowen, W.G., Davis, R.G. and Kopf, D.H., 1960. The public debt: A burden on future generations?. *The American Economic Review*, 50(4), pp. 701–706.

Bradford, D.F. and Oates, W.E., 1971. The analysis of revenue sharing in a new approach to collective fiscal decisions. *The Quarterly Journal of Economics*, 85(3), pp. 416–439.

Brosio, G. and Singh, R.J., 2015. Raising and sharing revenues from natural resources: A review of country practices. Discussion Paper MFM Global Practice (No. 5). Washington, DC: The World Bank.

Brown, K., Ryan, N. and Parker, R., 2000. New modes of service delivery in the public sector: Commercialising government services. *International Journal of Public Sector Management*, 13(3), pp. 206–221.

Brownell, K.D., Farley, T., Willett, W.C., Popkin, B.M., Chaloupka, F.J., Thompson, J.W. and Ludwig, D.S., 2009. The public health and economic benefits of taxing sugar-sweetened beverages. *New England Journal of Medicine*, 361(16), pp. 1599–1605.

Brueckner, J.K., 1986. A modern analysis of the effects of site value taxation. *National Tax Journal*, 39(1), pp. 49–58.

Buchanan, J.M., 1958. *Public Principles of Public Debt*. Homewood, IL: Richard D. Irwin.

Buchanan, J.M., 1976. Barro on the Ricardian equivalence theorem. *Journal of Political Economy*, 84(2), pp. 337–342.

Buchanan, J.M. and Tullock, G., 1962. *The Calculus of Consent* (Vol. 3). Ann Arbor, MI: University of Michigan Press.

Buiter, W.H., 1977. 'Crowding out' and the effectiveness of fiscal policy. *Journal of Public Economics*, 7(3), pp. 309–328.

Burns, A.F. and Mitchell, W.C., 1946. *Measuring Business Cycles*. NBER Books.

Cagan, P., 1956. Monetary dynamics in hyperinflation. In M. Friedman (ed.), *Studies in the Quantity Theory of Money*. Chicago, IL: University of Chicago Press, pp. 25–117.

Callison, K. and Kaestner, R., 2014. Do higher tobacco taxes reduce adult smoking? New evidence of the effect of recent cigarette tax increases on adult smoking. *Economic Inquiry*, 52(1), pp. 155–172.

Calvo, G.A., 1988. Servicing the public debt: The role of expectations. *The American Economic Review*, 78(4), pp. 647–661.

Carragher, N. and Chalmers, J., 2011. *What are the Options?: Pricing and Taxation Policy Reforms to Redress Excessive Alcohol Consumption and Related Harms in Australia*. Sydney, NSW: NSW Bureau of Crime Statistics and Research.

Caselli, F. and Michaels, G., 2009. Resource abundance, development, and living standards: Evidence from oil discoveries in Brazil. NBER Working Paper (No. 15550). New York: National Bureau of Economic Research.

Chaloupka, F.J., Yurekli, A. and Fong, G.T., 2012. Tobacco taxes as a tobacco control strategy. *Tobacco Control*, 21(2), pp. 172–180.

Chamley, C., 1986. Optimal taxation of capital income in general equilibrium with infinite lives. *Econometrica: Journal of the Econometric Society*, 54(3), pp. 607–622.

Chari, V.V. and Kehoe, P., 1999. Optimal fiscal and monetary policy. In J. Taylor and M. Woodford (eds), *Handbook of Macroeconomics*, Vol. 1. Elsevier.

Chaudhry, K.A., 1994. Economic liberalization and the lineages of the rentier state. *Comparative Politics*, 27(1), pp. 1–25.

Chong, A. and De Silanes, F.L. (eds), 2005. *Privatization in Latin America: Myths and Reality*. World Bank Publications.

Christiansen, H., 2011. The size and composition of the SOE sector in OECD countries. OECD Corporate Governance Working Paper (No. 5). Paris: OECD.

Cole, A., 2015. Estate and inheritance taxes around the world. Fiscal Fact No. 458. The Tax Foundation (http://taxfoundation.org) (accessed 24 January 2017).

Collier, P., 2000. Conditionality, dependence and coordination: Three current debates in aid policy. In C.L. Gilbert and D. Vines (eds), *The World Bank: Structure and Policies*. Cambridge: Cambridge University Press, pp. 299–324.

Collier, P., 2008. *The Bottom Billion: Why the Poorest Countries are Failing and What Can Be Done About It*. New York: Oxford University Press.

Collignon, S., 2012. Fiscal policy rules and the sustainability of public debt in Europe. *International Economic Review*, 53(2), pp. 539–567.

Conesa, J.C., Kitao, S. and Krueger, D., 2009. Taxing capital? Not a bad idea after all! *The American Economic Review*, 99(1), pp. 25–48.

Coppinger, V.M., Smith, V.L. and Titus, J.A., 1980. Incentives and behavior in English, Dutch and sealed-bid auctions. *Economic Inquiry*, 18(1), pp. 1–22.

Corbacho, A., Cibils, V. and Lora, E. (eds), 2013. *More than Revenue: Taxation as a Development Tool*. Springer.

Corden, W.M. and Neary, J.P., 1982. Booming sector and de-industrialisation in a small open economy. *The Economic Journal*, 92(368), pp. 825–848.

Cornes, R. and Sandler, T., 1996. *The Theory of Externalities, Public Goods, and Club Goods*. Cambridge: Cambridge University Press.

Courant, P.N., Gramlich, E.M. and Rubinfeld, D.L., 1978. The stimulative effects of intergovernmental grants: Or why money sticks where it hits. In P. Mieszkowski and W.H. Oakland (eds), *Fiscal Federalism and Grant-in-Aid*. Washington, DC: Urban Institute, pp. 5–21.

Crandall, W.J., 2010. Revenue administration: Autonomy in tax administration and the revenue authority model (No. 2010-2012). International Monetary Fund.

Cremer, H. and Gahvari, F., 1995. Uncertainty, optimal taxation and the direct versus indirect tax controversy. *The Economic Journal*, 105(432), pp. 1165–1179.

Cremer, H., Pestieau, P. and Rochet, J.C., 2001. Direct versus indirect taxation: The design of the tax structure revisited. *International Economic Review*, 42(3), pp. 781–800.

Crivelli, E. and Gupta, S., 2014. Revenue substitution in resource-rich economies: Evidence from a new dataset. VoxEU (http://voxeu.org/article/tax-policies-resource-rich-economies) (accessed 24 January 2017).

Crivelli, E., De Mooij, R.A. and Keen, M.M., 2015. Base erosion, profit shifting and developing countries (No. 15-118). International Monetary Fund.

Crook, R.C. and Manor, J., 1998. *Democracy and Decentralisation in South Asia and West Africa: Participation, Accountability and Performance.* Cambridge: Cambridge University Press.

Cui, W., 2015. A critical review of proposals for destination-based cash-flow corporate taxation as an international tax reform option (No. 1521). Oxford University Centre for Business Taxation.

Cusack, T.R., 1997. Partisan politics and public finance: Changes in public spending in the industrialized democracies, 1955–1989. *Public Choice*, 91(3–4), pp. 375–395.

De Mello, L.R., 2000. Fiscal decentralization and intergovernmental fiscal relations: A cross-country analysis. *World Development*, 28(2), pp. 365–380.

De Mooij, R.A., Keen, M. and Orihara, M., 2013. Taxation, bank leverage, and financial crises (No. 13-48). Washington, DC: International Monetary Fund.

Devarajan, S. and Swaroop, V., 2000. The implications of foreign aid fungibility for development assistance. In C.L. Gilbert and D. Vines (eds), *The World Bank: Structure and Policies.* Cambridge: Cambridge University Press, pp. 196–209.

Devereux, M. and Freeman, H., 1991. A general neutral profits tax. *Fiscal Studies*, 12(3), pp. 1–15.

Devereux, M.P. and Loretz, S., 2013. What do we know about corporate tax competition?. *National Tax Journal*, 66(3), pp. 745–774.

Diamond, P.A. and Mirrlees, J.A., 1971. Optimal taxation and public production II: Tax rules. *The American Economic Review*, 61(3), pp. 261–278.

Dichter, T., 2005. Time to stop fooling ourselves about foreign aid – a practitioner's view. Foreign Policy Briefing (No. 86). Washington, DC: Cato Institute.

Dincecco, M., 2011. *Political Transformations and Public Finances: Europe, 1650–1913.* Cambridge: Cambridge University Press.

Dincecco, M., 2015. The rise of effective states in Europe. *The Journal of Economic History*, 75(3), pp. 901–918.

Dincecco, M., Federico, G. and Vindigni, A., 2011. Warfare, taxation, and political change: Evidence from the Italian Risorgimento. *The Journal of Economic History*, 71(4), pp. 887–914.

Dowding, K. and Mergoupis, T., 2003. Fragmentation, fiscal mobility, and efficiency. *Journal of Politics*, 65(4), pp. 1190–1207.

Easterly, W., 1999. When is fiscal adjustment an illusion? *Economic Policy*, 14(28), pp. 56–86.

Easterly, W., 2001. *The Elusive Quest for Growth: Economists' Adventures and Misadventures in the Tropics.* Cambridge, MA: MIT Press.

Easterly, W., 2002. The cartel of good intentions: The problem of bureaucracy in foreign aid. *The Journal of Policy Reform*, 5(4), pp. 223–250.

Easterly, W., 2007a. *The White Man's Burden: Why the West's Efforts to Aid the Rest Have Done So Much Ill And So Little Good.* Oxford: Oxford University Press.

Easterly, W., 2007b. Was development assistance a mistake?. *The American Economic Review*, 97(2), pp. 328–332.

Easterly, W. and Pfutze, T., 2008. Where does the money go? Best and worst practices in foreign aid. *The Journal of Economic Perspectives*, 22(2), p. 29.

Easterly, W. and Rebelo, S., 1993. Fiscal policy and economic growth. *Journal of Monetary Economics*, 32(3), pp. 417–458.

Easton, B.H., 1997. *The Commercialisation of New Zealand.* Auckland University Press.

Edwards, R.D., 2011. Commentary: Soda taxes, obesity, and the shifty behavior of consumers. *Preventive Medicine*, 52(6), pp. 417–418.

Eisenhardt, K.M., 1989. Agency theory: An assessment and review. *Academy of Management Review*, 14(1), pp. 57–74.

Eisenstadt, S.N., 1973. *Traditional Patrimonialism and Modern Neopatrimonialism* (Vol. 1). Thousand Oaks, CA: SAGE Publications.

Engen, E.M. and Skinner, J., 1996. Taxation and economic growth (No. w5826). National Bureau of Economic Research.

Ernst & Young, 2015. Experiences with cash flow taxation and prospects. Final report. EU Commission Taxation Papers (No. 55). Luxembourg: Office for Official Publication of the European Communities.

Estrin, S. and Pelletier, A., 2016. Privatisation in developing countries: What are the lessons of recent experience? Forschungsinstitut zur Zukunft der Arbeit (Institute for the Study of Labor) Discussion Paper Series (No. 10297). Bonn, Germany: IZA.

European Commission, 2012. Attitudes of Europeans towards water-related issues. Flash Eurobarometer 344 (http://ec.europa.eu/public_opinion/flash/fl_344_sum_en.pdf) (accessed 24 January 2017).

Eurostat, 2016. Environmental tax statistics (http://ec.europa.eu/eurostat/statistics-explained/index.php/Environmental_tax_statistics) (accessed 24 January 2017).

Eyraud, L. and Lusinyan, L., 2011. Decentralizing spending more than revenue: Does it hurt fiscal performance?. IMF Working Papers, pp. 1–33.

Eyraud, L. and Lusinyan, L., 2013. Vertical fiscal imbalances and fiscal performance in advanced economies. *Journal of Monetary Economics*, 60(5), pp. 571–587.

Farrington, J. and Slater, R., 2006. Introduction: Cash transfers: Panacea for poverty reduction or money down the drain? *Development Policy Review*, 24(5), pp. 499–511.

Feld, L.P. and Kirchgässner, G., 2001. Income tax competition at the state and local level in Switzerland. *Regional Science and Urban Economics*, 31(2), pp. 181–213.

Feld, L.P., Zimmermann, H. and Döring, T., 2004. Federalism, decentralization, and economic growth (No. 200430). Philipps-Universität Marburg, Faculty of Business Administration and Economics, Department of Economics (Volkswirtschaftliche Abteilung).

Feldstein, M. and Vaillant, M., 1994. Does federal tax deductibility explain state tax progressivity? NBER Working Paper (No. 4785). New York: National Bureau of Economic Research.

Feldstein, M. and Wrobel, M.V., 1998. Can state taxes redistribute income? *Journal of Public Economics*, 68(3), pp. 369–396.

Feyzioglu, T., Swaroop, V. and Zhu, M., 1998. A panel data analysis of the fungibility of foreign aid. *The World Bank Economic Review*, 12(1), pp. 29–58.

Fischer, S., 1982. Seigniorage and the case for a national money. *Journal of Political Economy*, 90(2), pp. 295–313.

Fiszbein, A., Schady, N.R. and Ferreira, F.H., 2009. *Conditional Cash Transfers: Reducing Present and Future Poverty*. World Bank Publications.

Fletcher, J.M., Frisvold, D.E. and Tefft, N., 2010. The effects of soft drink taxes on child and adolescent consumption and weight outcomes. *Journal of Public Economics*, 94(11), pp. 967–974.

Fölster, S. and Henrekson, M., 2001. Growth effects of government expenditure and taxation in rich countries. *European Economic Review*, 45(8), pp. 1501–1520.

Frankel, J.A., 2010. The natural resource curse: A survey (No. w15836). New York: National Bureau of Economic Research.

Fu, D., Taylor, L.L., Yücel, M.K. and Dallas, F.R.B.O., 2003. *Fiscal Policy and Growth* (Vol. 3, No. 1). Dallas, TX: Federal Reserve Bank of Dallas.

Fullerton, D. and Metcalf, G.E., 1997. Environmental taxes and the double-dividend hypothesis: Did you really expect something for nothing? (No. w6199). National Bureau of Economic Research.

Galasso, E. and Ravallion, M., 2005. Decentralized targeting of an antipoverty program. *Journal of Public Economics*, 89(4), pp. 705–727.

Galbraith, J.K., 1998. *The Affluent Society*. Boston, MA: Houghton Mifflin Harcourt.

Gemmell, N., Kneller, R. and Sanz, I., 2013. Fiscal decentralization and economic growth: Spending versus revenue decentralization. *Economic Inquiry*, 51(4), pp. 1915–1931.

Genschel, P. and Schwarz, P., 2011. Tax competition: A literature review. *Socio-Economic Review*, 9(2), pp. 339–370.

George, H., 1879. *Progress and Poverty: An Enquiry into the Cause of Industrial Depressions, and of Increase of Want with Increase of Wealth. The Remedy.* London: K. Paul, Trench & Company.

Ghosh, S. and Hall, J., 2015. The political economy of soda taxation (No. 15-50). Department of Economics, West Virginia University.

Gini, C., 1909. Concentration and dependency ratios (in Italian). English translation in *Rivista di Politica Economica*, 87(1997), pp. 769–789.

Golosov, M., Kocherlakota, N. and Tsyvinski, A., 2003. Optimal indirect and capital taxation. *The Review of Economic Studies*, 70(3), pp. 569–587.

Gómez-Ibáñez, J.A., 2009. *Regulating Infrastructure: Monopoly, Contracts, and Discretion.* Harvard University Press.

Goodstein, E., 2003. The death of the Pigovian tax? Policy implications from the double-dividend debate. *Land Economics*, 79(3), pp. 402–414.

Gordon, R.H., 1992. Can capital income taxes survive in open economies?. *The Journal of Finance*, 47(3), pp. 1159–1180.

Gospodinov, N. and Irvine, I., 2009. Tobacco taxes and regressivity. *Journal of Health Economics*, 28(2), pp. 375–384.

Gupta, M.S. and Abed, M.G.T., 2002. *Governance, Corruption, and Economic Performance.* Washington, DC: International Monetary Fund.

Hager, S.B., 2016. *Public Debt, Inequality, and Power: The Making of a Modern Debt State.* Oakland, CA: University of California Press.

Hall, R.E. and Rabushka, A., 1983. *Low Tax, Simple Tax, Flat Tax.* New York: McGraw-Hill.

Hamilton, B.W., 1983. The flypaper effect and other anomalies. *Journal of Public Economics*, 22(3), pp. 347–361.

Harberger, A.C., 1964. The measurement of waste. *The American Economic Review*, 54(3), pp. 58–76.

Hardin, G., 2009. The tragedy of the commons. *Journal of Natural Resources Policy Research*, 1(3), pp. 243–253.

Hart, O., 1988. Incomplete contracts and the theory of the firm. *Journal of Law, Economics, & Organization*, 4(1), pp. 119–139.

Hart, O. and Moore, J., 1999. Foundations of incomplete contracts. *The Review of Economic Studies*, 66(1), pp. 115–138.

Hawe, E. and Cockcroft, L., 2013. *OHE Guide to UK Health and Health Care Statistics*, 2nd edition. London: Office of Health Economics.

Heald, D., 1985. Will the privatization of public enterprises solve the problem of control?. *Public Administration*, 63(1), pp. 7–22.

Herndon, T., Ash, M. and Pollin, R., 2014. Does high public debt consistently stifle economic growth? A critique of Reinhart and Rogoff. *Cambridge Journal of Economics*, 38(2), pp. 257–279.

Hill, H., 2008. Globalization, inequality, and local-level dynamics: Indonesia and the Philippines. *Asian Economic Policy Review*, 3(1), pp. 42–61.

HM Revenue & Customs, 2014. Official statistics rates of income tax. London: HM Revenue & Customs.

HM Revenue & Customs, 2016. A disaggregation of HMRC tax receipts between England, Wales, Scotland and Northern Ireland. Annual historical record. An Official Statistics release. London: HM Revenue & Customs.

Hood, C., 2007. Intellectual obsolescence and intellectual makeovers: Reflections on the tools of government after two decades. *Governance*, 20(1), pp. 127–144.

Hooghe, L. and Marks, G.W., 2003. Unraveling the central state, but how? Types of multi-level governance. *American Political Science Review*, 97(2), pp. 233–243.

IMF, 2012. Macroeconomic policy frameworks for resource-rich developing countries. Washington, DC: International Monetary Fund.

IMF, 2014. Fiscal monitor: Back to work, how fiscal policy can help. Washington, DC: International Monetary Fund.

Isham, J., Woolcock, M., Pritchett, L. and Busby, G., 2005. The varieties of resource experience: Natural resource export structures and the political economy of economic growth. *The World Bank Economic Review*, 19(2), pp. 141–174.

Jackson, R.H. and Rosberg, C.G., 1982. Why Africa's weak states persist: The empirical and the juridical in statehood. *World Politics*, 35(1), pp. 1–24.

Jaimovich, N. and Rebelo, S., 2012. Non-linear effects of taxation on growth (No. w18473). National Bureau of Economic Research.

James, V.E., 2002. Twenty-first century pirates of the Caribbean: How the Organization for Economic Cooperation and Development robbed fourteen CARICOM countries of their tax and economic policy sovereignty. *The University of Miami Inter-American Law Review*, 34(1), pp. 1–50.

Johansson, Å., Heady, C., Arnold, J., Brys, B. and Vartia, L., 2008. Taxation and economic growth (No. 620). Paris: OECD Publishing.

John, P., Dowding, K. and Biggs, S., 1995. Residential mobility in London: A micro-level test of the behavioural assumptions of the Tiebout model. *British Journal of Political Science*, 25(3), pp. 379–397.

Johnson, M., 2006. The Wicksellian unanimity rule: The competing interpretations of Buchanan and Musgrave. *Journal of the History of Economic Thought*, 28(1), pp. 57–79.

Johnson, P., 2014. Tax without design: Recent developments in UK tax policy. *Fiscal Studies*, 35(3), pp. 243–273.

Judd, K.L., 1985. Redistributive taxation in a simple perfect foresight model. *Journal of Public Economics*, 28(1), pp. 59–83.

Kaldor, N., 1963. Taxation for economic development. *The Journal of Modern African Studies*, 1(1), pp. 7–23.

Kaldor, N., 1965. The role of taxation in economic development. In E.A.G. Robinson (ed.), *Problems in Economic Development*. London: Palgrave Macmillan UK, pp. 170–195.

Kanbur, R., 2000. Aid, conditionality and debt in Africa. In F. Tarp (ed.), *Foreign Aid and Development: Lessons Learnt and Directions for the Future*. New York: Routledge, pp. 409–422.

Kasara, K., 2007. Tax me if you can: Ethnic geography, democracy, and the taxation of agriculture in Africa. *American Political Science Review*, 101(1), pp. 159–172.

Keen, M., 2013. Taxation and development—again. In C. Fuest and G.R. Zodrow (eds), *Critical Issues in Taxation and Development*. MIT Press, p. 13.

King, M.A., 1987. The cash flow corporate income tax. In M. Feldstein (ed.), *The Effects of Taxation on Capital Accumulation*. Chicago, IL: University of Chicago Press, pp. 377–400.

King, R.G. and Rebelo, S., 1990. Public policy and economic growth: Developing neoclassical implications (No. w3338). National Bureau of Economic Research.

Kneller, R., Bleaney, M.F. and Gemmell, N., 1999. Fiscal policy and growth: Evidence from OECD countries. *Journal of Public Economics*, 74(2), pp. 171–190.

Kocherlakota, N.R., 2005. Zero expected wealth taxes: A Mirrlees approach to dynamic optimal taxation. *Econometrica*, 73(5), pp. 1587–1621.

Koester, R.B. and Kormendi, R.C., 1989. Taxation, aggregate activity and economic growth: Cross-country evidence on some supply-side hypotheses. *Economic Inquiry*, 27(3), pp. 367–386.

Kondratiev, N.D., 1925. The major economic cycles. *Voprosy Konjunktury*, 1(1), pp. 28–79.

Kornai, J., 1986. The soft budget constraint. *Kyklos*, 39(1), pp. 3–30.

Kornai, J., Maskin, E. and Roland, G., 2003. Understanding the soft budget constraint. *Journal of Economic Literature*, 41(4), pp. 1095–1136.

KPMG, 2015. Individual taxation in comparison. KPMG Switzerland (https://home.kpmg.com/ch/en/home/services/tax/swiss-individual-tax-rates.html) (accessed 24 January 2017).

Krugman, P. and Wells, R., 2009. *Microeconomics*. New York: Worth Publishers.

Kyriacou, A.P., Muinelo-Gallo, L. and Roca-Sagalés, O., 2015. Fiscal decentralization and regional disparities: The importance of good governance. *Papers in Regional Science*, 94(1), pp. 89–107.

Laffer, A.B., 2004. The Laffer curve: Past, present and future. *Backgrounder*, 1765(1), pp. 1–16.

Le, T.M., 2003. Value added taxation: Mechanism. design, and policy issues. Paper prepared for the course on Practical Issues of Tax Policy in Developing Countries, 28 April–1 May, World Bank, Washington, DC.

Lemgruber, M.A. and Shelton, S., 2014. *Revenue Administration: Administering Revenues from Natural Resources: A Short Primer*. Washington, DC: International Monetary Fund.

Lessmann, C., 2012. Regional inequality and decentralization: An empirical analysis. *Environment and Planning A*, 44(6), pp. 1363–1388.

Lindahl, E., 1958. Just taxation—a positive solution. In R.A. Musgrave and A.T. Peacock (eds), *Classics in the Theory of Public Finance*. London: Palgrave Macmillan UK, pp. 168–176.

Lindaman, K. and Thurmaier, K., 2002. Beyond efficiency and economy: An examination of basic needs and fiscal decentralization. *Economic Development and Cultural Change*, 50(4), pp. 915–934.

Listokin, Y., 2012. Equity, efficiency, and stability: The importance of macroeconomics for evaluating income tax policy. *Yale Journal on Regulation*, 29(1), p. 45.

Littlechild, S., 1983. *Regulation of British Telecommunications' Profitability*. London: Department of Trade and Industry, HMSO.

Littlewood, M., 2004. Tax competition: Harmful to whom? *Michigan Journal of International Law*, 26(1), p. 411.

Litvack, J.I., Ahmad, J. and Bird, R.M., 1998. Rethinking decentralization in developing countries. World Bank Sector Studies Series. Washington, DC: World Bank Publications.

London Economics, 2010. Study analysing possible changes in the minimum rates and structures of excise duties on alcoholic beverages. Final report to EC DG Taxation and Customs Union. London: London Economics.

McCabe, K.A., Rassenti, S.J. and Smith, V.L., 1990. Auction institutional design: Theory and behavior of simultaneous multiple-unit generalizations of the Dutch and English auctions. *The American Economic Review*, 80(5), pp. 1276–1283.

McGrattan, E.R., 1994. The macroeconomic effects of distortionary taxation. *Journal of Monetary Economics*, 33(3), pp. 573–601.

Mankiw, N.G., 1987. The optimal collection of seigniorage: Theory and evidence. *Journal of Monetary Economics*, 20(2), pp. 327–341.

Mankiw, N.G. and Weinzierl, M., 2010. The optimal taxation of height: A case study of utilitarian income redistribution. *American Economic Journal: Economic Policy*, 2(1), pp. 155–176.

Mankiw, N.G., Weinzierl, M. and Yagan, D., 2009. Optimal taxation in theory and practice. *The Journal of Economic Perspectives*, 23(4), pp. 147–174.

Martens, B., Mummert, U., Murrell, P. and Seabright, P., 2002. *The Institutional Economics of Foreign Aid*. Cambridge: Cambridge University Press.

Martinez-Vazquez, J. and McNab, R., 2006. The interaction of fiscal decentralization and democratic governance. In E. Gomez, G. Peterson and P. Smoke (eds), *Decentralization in Asia and Latin America: Towards a Comparative Interdisciplinary Perspective*. London: Edward Elgar Publishing, pp. 15–40.

Martinez-Vazquez, J., Lago-Peñas, S. and Sacchi, A., 2015. The impact of fiscal decentralization: A survey. International Center for Public Policy Working Paper (No. 1502).

Martinez-Vazquez, J., Vulovic, V. and Liu, Y., 2011. Direct versus indirect taxation: Trends, theory and economic significance. In E. Albi and J. Martinez-Vazquez (eds), *The Elgar Guide to Tax Systems*. Edward Elgar Publishing, pp. 37–92.

Mascagni, G., 2016. Is fiscal decentralisation delivering on its promises? A review of the theory and practice in developing countries. Institute of Development Studies Working Paper (No. 466).

Maskin, E. and Tirole, J., 1999. Unforeseen contingencies and incomplete contracts. *The Review of Economic Studies*, 66(1), pp. 83–114.

Megginson, W.L., 2010. Privatization and finance. *Annual Review of Financial Economics*, 2, pp. 145–174.

Megginson, W.L. and Netter, J.M., 2001. From state to market: A survey of empirical studies on privatization. *Journal of Economic Literature*, 39(2), pp. 321–389.

Migdal, J.S., 1988. *Strong Societies and Weak States: State-Society Relations and State Capabilities in the Third World*. Princeton, NJ: Princeton University Press.

Miller, A. and Oats, L., 2016. *Principles of International Taxation*. Bloomsbury Publishing.

Mirrlees, J.A., 1971. An exploration in the theory of optimum income taxation. *The Review of Economic Studies*, 38(2), pp. 175–208.

Mirrlees, J.A. and Adam, S., 2010. *Dimensions of Tax Design: The Mirrlees Review*. Oxford University Press.

Mirrlees, J.A. and Adam, S., 2011. *Tax by Design: The Mirrlees Review* (Vol. 2). Oxford University Press.

Mitchell, B.R., 2011. *British Historical Statistics*. Cambridge, MA: Cambridge University Press.

Musgrave, R.A., 1959. *Theory of Public Finance; A Study in Public Economy*. New York: McGraw-Hill.

Musgrave, R.A., 1990. Horizontal equity, once more. *National Tax Journal*, 43(2), pp. 113–122.

Myles, G.D., 2009. Economic growth and the role of taxation-aggregate data (No. 714). Paris: OECD.

Neck, R. and Sturm, J.E., 2008. *Sustainability of Public Debt*. Cambridge, MA: MIT Press.

Needham, C., 2007. *The Reform of Public Services under New Labour: Narratives of Consumerism*. Springer.

Nellen, A.M., 2002. The AICPA's 10 guiding principles. *The Tax Adviser*, 33(2), pp. 100–107.

Netzer, D. (ed.), 1998. *Land Value Taxation: Can It and Will It Work Today?*. Lincoln Institute of Land Policy.

Newbery, D.M., 1997. Privatisation and liberalisation of network utilities. *European Economic Review*, 41(3), pp. 357–383.

Neyapti, B., 2006. Revenue decentralization and income distribution. *Economics Letters*, 92(3), pp. 409–416.

Neyapti, B., 2010. Fiscal decentralization and deficits: International evidence. *European Journal of Political Economy*, 26(2), pp. 155–166.

Niskanen, W.A., 1968. The peculiar economics of bureaucracy. *The American Economic Review*, 58(2), pp. 293–305.

Niskanen, W.A., 1975. Bureaucrats and politicians. *The Journal of Law & Economics*, 18(3), pp. 617–643.

Oates, W.E., 1972 (reprint 2011). *Fiscal Federalism*. Edward Elgar Publishing.

Oates, W.E., 1999. An essay on fiscal federalism. *Journal of Economic Literature*, 37(3), pp. 1120–1149.

Oates, W.E., 2005. Toward a second-generation theory of fiscal federalism. *International Tax and Public Finance*, 12(4), pp. 349–373.

OECD, 1996. Definition of taxes. Expert Group No. 3 on Treatment of Tax Issues in the MAI (Multilateral Agreement on Investment). Paris: OECD.

OECD, 1998a. Harmful tax competition: An emerging global issue. Paris: OECD.

OECD, 1998b. Towards global tax cooperation. Report to the 2000 Ministerial Council Meeting and Recommendations by the Committee on Fiscal Affairs. Paris: OECD.

OECD, 2010. Transfer pricing guidelines for multinational enterprises and tax administrations. Paris: OECD.

OECD, 2011a. Restoring public finances. *OECD Journal on Budgeting*, Vol. 2011/2. Paris: OECD.

OECD, 2011b. Divided we stand: Why inequality keeps rising. Paris: OECD.

OECD, 2014. Consumption tax trends 2014. VAT/GST and excise rates, trends and policy issues. Paris, OECD.

OECD, 2015a. Fiscal policy and growth: Why, what, and how? G20 Ankara paper. Paris: OECD.

OECD, 2015b. OECD/G20 Base Erosion and Project Shifting Project. Final report. Paris: OECD.

OECD, 2016a. Revenue statistics 2016. Paris: OECD.

OECD, 2016b. OECD Income Distribution Database (IDD): Gini, poverty, income, methods and concepts. Paris: OECD.

Olson, M., 1969. The principle of 'fiscal equivalence': The division of responsibilities among different levels of government. *The American Economic Review*, 59(2), pp. 479–487.

Orenstein, M.A., 2013. Pension privatization: Evolution of a paradigm. *Governance*, 26(2), pp. 259–281.

Ostrom, E., 1999. Coping with tragedies of the commons. *Annual Review of Political Science*, 2(1), pp. 493–535.

Ostrom, E., Gardner, R. and Walker, J., 1994. *Rules, Games, and Common-Pool Resources*. Ann Arbor, MI: University of Michigan Press.

Otaki, M., 2015. Public debt as a burden on the future generation: A Keynesian approach. *Theoretical Economics Letters*, 5(5), p. 651.

Pack, H. and Pack, J.R., 1993. Foreign aid and the question of fungibility. *The Review of Economics and Statistics*, 75(2), pp. 258–265.

Padovano, F. and Galli, E., 2001. Tax rates and economic growth in the OECD countries. *Economic Inquiry*, 39(1), pp. 44–57.

Palan, R., Murphy, R. and Chavagneux, C., 2013. *Tax Havens: How Globalization Really Works*. Cornell University Press.

Parker, D., 1999. Regulation of privatised public utilities in the UK: Performance and governance. *International Journal of Public Sector Management*, 12(3), pp. 213–236.

Persico, N., 2000. Information acquisition in auctions. *Econometrica*, 68(1), pp. 135–148.

Pezzey, J.C. and Park, A., 1998. Reflections on the double dividend debate. *Environmental and Resource Economics*, 11(3–4), pp. 539–555.

Pigou, A.C., 1912. *Wealth and Welfare*. London: Macmillan.

Pigou, A.C., 1920. *The Economics of Welfare*. London: McMillan.

Piketty, T. and Saez, E., 2012. A theory of optimal capital taxation (No. w17989). National Bureau of Economic Research.

Piketty, T. and Saez, E., 2013. A theory of optimal inheritance taxation. *Econometrica*, 81(5), pp. 1851–1886.

Pomerleau, K. and Cole, A., 2015. International Tax Competitiveness Index 2015. The Tax Foundation (http://taxfoundation.org) (accessed 24 January 2017).

Presbitero, A.F., Sacchi, A. and Zazzaro, A., 2014. Property tax and fiscal discipline in OECD countries. *Economics Letters*, 124(3), pp. 428–433.

Qiao, B., Martinez-Vazquez, J. and Xu, Y., 2008. The tradeoff between growth and equity in decentralization policy: China's experience. *Journal of Development Economics*, 86(1), pp. 112–128.

Qureshi, A.H., 1994. *The Public International Law of Taxation: Text, Cases and Materials*. Graham & Trotman.

Radelet, S., 2006. A primer on foreign aid. Center for Global Development Working Paper (No. 92).

Rajan, R.G. and Subramanian, A., 2008. Aid and growth: What does the cross-country evidence really show? *The Review of Economics and Statistics*, 90(4), pp. 643–665.

Rajaraman, I., 2005. Taxing agriculture in a developing country: A possible approach. In J.R. Alm, J. Martinez-Vazquez and S. Wallace (eds), *Taxing the Hard-to-tax: Lessons from Theory and Practice* (*Contributions to Economic Analysis*, Vol. 268). Emerald Group Publishing Limited, pp. 245–268.

Ramsey, F.P., 1927. A contribution to the theory of taxation. *The Economic Journal*, 37(145), pp. 47–61.

Rawlings, L.B. and Rubio, G.M., 2005. Evaluating the impact of conditional cash transfer programs. *The World Bank Research Observer*, 20(1), pp. 29–55.

Reich, J., 2011. Seigniorage–where does it come from and who gets it? An institutional perspective on currency creation. In *15th FMM Conference*, Berlin, 28–29 October.

Reinhart, C.M. and Rogoff, K.S., 2009. *This Time is Different: Eight Centuries of Financial Folly*. Princeton, NJ: Princeton University Press.

Reinhart, C.M. and Rogoff, K.S., 2013. Financial and sovereign debt crises: Some lessons learned and those forgotten (No. 13-266). International Monetary Fund.

Reinhart, C.M., Reinhart, V.R. and Rogoff, K.S., 2012. Public debt overhangs: Advanced-economy episodes since 1800. *The Journal of Economic Perspectives*, 26(3), pp. 69–86.

Remmer, K.L., 2004. Does foreign aid promote the expansion of government? *American Journal of Political Science*, 48(1), pp. 77–92.

Rhodes, C., Hough, D. and Butcher, L., 2014. Privatisation. Research paper 14/61. UK House of Commons Library. London: UK Parliament.

Ricciuti, R., Savoia, A. and Sen, K., 2016. How do political institutions affect fiscal capacity? Explaining taxation in developing economies (https://ssrn.com/abstract=2835498 or http://dx.doi.org/10.2139/ssrn.2835498) (accessed 24 January 2017).

Richter, B.K., Samphantharak, K. and Timmons, J.F., 2009. Lobbying and taxes. *American Journal of Political Science*, 53(4), pp. 893–909.

Riley, J. and Chote, R., 2014. Crisis and consolidation in the public finances. Office for Budget Responsibility (OBR) Working Paper (No. 7).

Ring, D.M., 2008. What's at stake in the sovereignty debate: International tax and the nation-state. *Virginia Journal of International Law*, 49(1), pp. 155–233.

Robinson, J.A., Torvik, R. and Verdier, T., 2006. Political foundations of the resource curse. *Journal of Development Economics*, 79(2), pp. 447–468.

Rodden, J., 2002. The dilemma of fiscal federalism: Grants and fiscal performance around the world. *American Journal of Political Science*, 46(3), pp. 670–687.

Rodden, J., Eskeland, G. and Litvack, J., 2003. *Fiscal Decentralization and the Challenge of Hard Budget Constraints*. Cambridge, MA and London: MIT Press.

Rodríguez-Pose, A. and Ezcurra, R., 2011. Is fiscal decentralization harmful for economic growth? Evidence from the OECD countries. *Journal of Economic Geography*, 11(4), pp. 619–643.

Rodríguez-Pose, A. and Gill, N., 2005. On the 'economic dividend' of devolution. *Regional Studies*, 39(4), pp. 405–420.

Ross, M.L., 1999. The political economy of the resource curse. *World Politics*, 51(2), pp. 297–322.

Ross, S.A., 1973. The economic theory of agency: The principal's problem. *The American Economic Review*, 63(2), pp. 134–139.

Sacchi, A. and Salotti, S., 2014. The effects of fiscal decentralization on household income inequality: Some empirical evidence. *Spatial Economic Analysis*, 9(2), pp. 202–222.

Sachs, J., 2005. *The End of Poverty: Economic Possibilities for Our Time*. New York: Penguin.

Sachs, J.D. and Warner, A.M., 2001. The curse of natural resources. *European Economic Review*, 45(4), pp. 827–838.

Saez, E., 2001. Using elasticities to derive optimal income tax rates. *The Review of Economic Studies*, 68(1), pp. 205–229.

Sahasranaman, A. and Kapur, V., 2014. *The Practice of PPP in Urban Infrastructure. Urbanisation in India: Challenges, Opportunities and the Way Forward*. SAGE Publishing, p. 176.

Salamon, L.M. and Elliott, O.V., 2002. *The Tools of Government: A Guide to the New Governance*. Oxford University Press.

Samuelson, P.A., 1954. The pure theory of public expenditure. *The Review of Economics and Statistics*, 36(4), pp. 387–389.

Samuelson, P.A., 1995. Diagrammatic exposition of a theory of public expenditure. In S. Estrin and A. Marin (eds), *Essential Readings in Economics*. Macmillan Education UK, pp. 159–171.

Sand, E. and Razin, A., 2006. Immigration and the survival of social security: A political economy model (No. w12800). National Bureau of Economic Research.

Sandmo, A., 1976. Optimal taxation: An introduction to the literature. *Journal of Public Economics*, 6(1), pp. 37–54.

Seater, J.J., 1993. Ricardian equivalence. *Journal of Economic Literature*, 31(1), pp. 142–190.

Sepulveda, C.F. and Martinez-Vazquez, J., 2011. The consequences of fiscal decentralization on poverty and income equality. *Environment and Planning C: Government and Policy*, 29(2), pp. 321–343.

Shankar, R. and Shah, A., 2003. Bridging the economic divide within countries: A scorecard on the performance of regional policies in reducing regional income disparities. *World Development*, 31(8), pp. 1421–1441.

Siemiatycki, M., 2015. 4 Public Private Partnerships in Canada. In A. Akintoye, M. Beck and M. Kumaraswamy (eds), *Public Private Partnerships: A Global Review*. Routledge, p. 59.

Slemrod, J., 2004. Are corporate tax rates, or countries, converging? *Journal of Public Economics*, 88(6), pp. 1169–1186.

Smith, A., 1776. *The Wealth of Nations*. New York: The Modern Library.

Sousa, J., 2014. Estimation of price elasticities of demand for alcohol in the United Kingdom. HMRC Working Paper (No. 16). London: HM Revenue & Customs.

Stasavage, D., 2003. *Public Debt and the Birth of the Democratic State: France and Great Britain 1688–1789*. Cambridge: Cambridge University Press.

Stiglitz, J.E., 2014. *Reforming Taxation to Promote Growth and Equity*. New York: Roosevelt Institute.

Straub, L. and Werning, I., 2014. Positive long run capital taxation: Chamley-Judd revisited (No. w20441). National Bureau of Economic Research.

Tanzi, V., 1987. The response of other industrial countries to the US Tax Reform Act. *National Tax Journal*, 40(3), pp. 339–355.

Tanzi, V., 1992. 12 structural factors and tax revenue in developing countries: A decade of evidence. In I. Goldin and L.A. Winters (eds), *Open Economies: Structural Adjustment and Agriculture*. Cambridge: Cambridge University Press, p. 267.

Tanzi, V. and Schuknecht, L., 2000. *Public Spending in the 20th Century: A Global Perspective*. Cambridge: Cambridge University Press.

Tarp, F., 2006. Aid and development. *Swedish Economic Policy Review*, 13(2), pp. 9–61.

Tarschys, D., 1975. The growth of public expenditures: Nine modes of explanation. *Scandinavian Political Studies*, 10(A10), pp. 9–31.

Tax Foundation, 2013. U.S. federal individual income tax rates history, 1862–2013 (nominal and inflation-adjusted brackets) (http://taxfoundation.org/article/us-federal-individual-income-tax-rates-history-1913-2013-nominal-and-inflation-adjusted-brackets) (accessed 24 January 2017).

The Economist, 2014. The $9 trillion sale (11th January). London: *The Economist*.

Thelin, J.R., 2011. *A History of American Higher Education*. JHU Press.

Thiessen, U., 2003. Fiscal decentralisation and economic growth in high-income OECD countries. *Fiscal Studies*, 24(3), pp. 237–274.

Thornton, J., 2009. The (non) impact of revenue decentralization on fiscal deficits: Some evidence from OECD countries. *Applied Economics Letters*, 16(14), pp. 1461–1466.

Tiebout, C.M., 1956. A pure theory of local expenditures. *Journal of Political Economy*, 64(5), pp. 416–424.

Tobin, J., 1996. A currency transactions tax, why and how. *Open Economies Review*, 7(1), pp. 493–499.

Treisman, D., 2000. Decentralization and inflation: Commitment, collective action, or continuity?. *American Political Science Review*, 94(4), pp. 837–857.

Tselios, V., Rodríguez-Pose, A., Pike, A., Tomaney, J. and Torrisi, G., 2012. Income inequality, decentralisation, and regional development in Western Europe. *Environment and Planning A*, 44(6), pp. 1278–1301.

Tsujiyama, H. and Heathcote, J., 2014. Optimal income taxation: Mirrlees meets Ramsey. 2014 Meeting Papers (No. 260). Society for Economic Dynamics.

Tuomala, M., 1990. *Optimal Income Tax and Redistribution*. Oxford: Oxford University Press.

Turnbull, G.K., 1998. The overspending and flypaper effects of fiscal illusion: Theory and empirical evidence. *Journal of Urban Economics*, 44(1), pp. 1–26.

US GPO (Government Publishing Office), 2015. Budget of the United States Government. Washington, DC: Government Publishing Office.

Van den Berg, C., 1997. Water privatization and regulation in England and Wales (No. 11585). The World Bank.

Van der Ploeg, F., 2011. Natural resources: Curse or blessing? *Journal of Economic Literature*, 49(2), pp. 366–420.

Vickers, J. and Yarrow, G., 1988. *Privatization: An Economic Analysis*. Cambridge, MA: MIT Press.

Von Braun, J., Grote, U., Ahmad, E. and Tanzi, V., 2002. *Managing Fiscal Decentralization*. London: Routledge.

Von Soest, C., Bechle, K. and Korte, N., 2011. How neopatrimonialism affects tax administration: A comparative study of three world regions. *Third World Quarterly*, 32(7), pp. 1307–1329.

Wagenaar, A.C., Tobler, A.L. and Komro, K.A., 2010. Effects of alcohol tax and price policies on morbidity and mortality: A systematic review. *American Journal of Public Health*, 100(11), pp. 2270–2278.

Wanniski, J., 1978. Taxes, revenues, and the Laffer curve. *The Public Interest*, 50, p. 3.

Weingast, B.R., 2009. Second generation fiscal federalism: The implications of fiscal incentives. *Journal of Urban Economics*, 65(3), pp. 279–293.

West, L.A. and Wong, C.P., 1995. Fiscal decentralization and growing regional disparities in rural China: Some evidence in the provision of social services. *Oxford Review of Economic Policy*, 11(4), pp. 70–84.

Whitfield, D., 1992. *Welfare State: Privatisation, Deregulation, Commercialisation of the Private Sector: Alternative Strategies for the 1990s*. London: Pluto Press.

WHO, 2011. World health statistics. Geneva: World Health Organization.

WHO, 2015. The economic and health benefits of tobacco taxation. Geneva: World Health Organization.

Wicksell, K., 1958. A new principle of just taxation. In R.A. Musgrave and A.T. Peacock (eds), *Classics in the Theory of Public Finance*. London: Palgrave Macmillan UK, pp. 72–118.

Wilson, J.D., 1999. Theories of tax competition. *National Tax Journal*, 52(2), pp. 269–304.

Xie, D., Zou, H.F. and Davoodi, H., 1999. Fiscal decentralization and economic growth in the United States. *Journal of Urban Economics*, 45(2), pp. 228–239.

Yakita, A., 2008. Sustainability of public debt, public capital formation, and endogenous growth in an overlapping generations setting. *Journal of Public Economics*, 92(3), pp. 897–914.

Zhang, T. and Zou, H.F., 1998. Fiscal decentralization, public spending, and economic growth in China. *Journal of Public Economics*, 67(2), pp. 221–240.

Zodrow, G.R. and Mieszkowski, P., 1986. Pigou, Tiebout, property taxation, and the underprovision of local public goods. *Journal of Urban Economics*, 19(3), pp. 356–370.

Zolberg, A.R., 1966. *Creating Political Order: The Party-States of West Africa*. Chicago, IL: Rand McNally, p. 6.

Zucman, G., 2015. *The Hidden Wealth of Nations: The Scourge of Tax Havens*. Chicago, IL: University of Chicago Press.

Index